GREAT
Southern
MYSTERIES

GREAT Southern MYSTERIES

TWO VOLUMES IN ONE

E. RANDALL FLOYD

BARNES
&NOBLE
BOOKS
NEW YORK

This book is for Uncle Curt, who taught me the magic of words;
for my mother, who waited so long;
for Selma, who wouldn't let me give up;
and for Anne, who stayed by my side.

SGREAT
Southern
MYSTERIES

BIGFOOT, WATER WITCHES, THE CAROLINA BAYS,
THE BILOXI MERMAID, AND OTHER ENDURING
MYSTERIES OF THE DEEP SOUTH

E. RANDALL FLOYD

Contents

Fabled Lands And
Vanished Peoples

Blue-Eyed Savages and Talking Books

EUROPEAN SETTLERS PUSHING inland along the rugged Lumber River in the eighteenth century were surprised to discover a tribe of English-speaking Indians who dressed like white frontiersmen and lived in remarkably comfortable houses. Even more astounding was the way many of these strange "savages" looked. Although most had dark skins, a few were fair-complexioned and had blond hair and blue eyes. Some could even read, claiming white gods had long ago taught their ancestors how to "talk in books," which, the explorers understood, meant to read and write.

Today the descendants of that mysterious group of people are known as the Lumbees, and they still inhabit the same harsh region of North Carolina where they were discovered more than two centuries ago. Since they were one of the largest groups of Indians in the United States, it is ironic that few people outside the states of North Carolina and Virginia have ever heard of them. The reason, according to scholars, is that at some time in the remote past the Lumbees apparently lost their own language and cultural identity. While cultural and linguistic traditions continued to flourish among better known southeastern tribes, such as the Cherokees, Choctaws, and Creeks, the heritage of the Lumbees became obscure.

Who were these blue-eyed Indians, and how did their ancestors learn to "talk in books"? One intriguing theory is that the estimated forty thousand modern Lumbees are descended from the survivors of Sir Walter Raleigh's lost colony of Roanoke, which vanished without a trace in 1589 along with more than a hundred men, women, and children. The settlement was the brainchild of Sir Walter Raleigh, a dashing, daring, and somewhat reckless consort of Queen Elizabeth who, along with his older brother—Sir Humphrey Gilbert, a famed explorer and soldier of fortune—sought adventure and wealth in the newly discovered lands beyond the great sea. In 1584 Raleigh asked for and received a charter to explore the southern coast of the New World, with the intention of setting up a buffer colony in the path of advancing Spanish settlers. Raleigh's reconnoitering force made landfall two thousand miles south of New Foundland and spent the next month exploring the dark, unfriendly coast south of Chesapeake Bay.

One year later Raleigh outfitted an expedition to settle Roanoke Island, a remote wooded isle near the present boundary between Virginia and North Carolina. The settlement failed, however, mainly because of the colonists' preoccupation with finding gold rather than tending fields. Unfriendly natives also influenced their decision to abandon the colony that summer and to return to England by hitching a ride with Sir Francis Drake, fresh from piratical raids in the West Indies.

In spite of tremendous personal financial losses with the first expedition, Raleigh was determined to send another group of colonists, this time about 130 persons under the command of John White, who in time would become famous for his early drawings of colonial life in North America. White spent about a month getting the new settlement started, then returned to England for fresh supplies. Among the settlers he left behind were his daughter, her husband, and their newborn daughter, Virginia Dare (believed to be the first child of European parents born in the New World). Before departing, he left strict instructions that should the remaining colonists be forced to leave the settlement in his absence, they were to inscribe their destination in a "conspicuous place."

As fate would have it, war broke out with Spain later that year and White was unable to return to the colony on schedule. The entire Spanish fleet had attacked England, forcing every available ship into military service. Not until 1590—two

11

years later—was the war-weary governor able to return to his settlement, three thousand miles away from the bloody battlefields and bays of Europe.

It was a grim sight that awaited White upon his arrival at Roanoke. Not only had the settlement been ransacked and destroyed, but the entire population had vanished—every man, woman, and child, including his daughter and baby granddaughter. In vain the grief-stricken governor searched the island for signs of their fate. The only clue to the whereabouts of the settlers was a single word carved into a wooden post—"Croatan." White finally decided that the colonists must have abandoned Roanoke when supplies ran out and made their way to nearby Hatteras. Although he conducted a limited search for the settlers, bad weather and pressing royal obligations back in England forced him to leave fairly soon. Why he never returned or at least ordered a full-scale investigation into the colonists' disappearance has never been fully explained.

Historians still argue over the meaning of "Croatan." That was the name of an island south of Roanoke, known to have been inhabited by the friendly Hatteras tribe. Nevertheless, some researchers believe it was the name of an Indian tribe that attacked the settlement and killed the colonists. They say that after the massacre the settlers may have been cannibalized, since no trace of their bones or belongings has been found. Other experts theorize that most of the settlers probably starved to death or died of unknown diseases. Hostile Indians could have done away with any survivors, or simply carried off some of the women and children into slavery. Charles Hudson, a University of Georgia anthropologist and author of *The Southeastern Indians*, suggests that Roanoke's settlers simply joined up with a local Indian tribe in order to survive. Still others speculate they were hauled off by pirates—even though there were no known pirates operating in those waters at the time—while at least one researcher believes the colonists were kidnapped by extraterrestrials.

A number of scholars believe it is possible that the survivors of Roanoke reached the Croatan island and intermarried with the Hatteras. This is the most reasonable explanation for the sudden disappearance of the Roanoke settlers, the one most widely accepted by historians of that period, and the one held by Governor White at the time. Researchers studying the modern Lumbees point to that group's blue eyes, blond hair, and fair complexions as lingering proof of their ancestral contact with the Europeans at Roanoke. The Lumbees themselves insist they are descended from the Roanoke colony, and there is additional evidence to indicate their claim might be justified. Of the 95 surnames of the lost colonists of Roanoke—names such as Sampson, Cooper, and Dare—no fewer than forty-one can be found among the Lumbees.

Starting in about 1650 many Hatteras Indians migrated to the mainland, settling in the Lumber River Valley. And when the first whites reached the wild hinterland of the Lumber River swamps in the late eighteenth century, the Indians they encountered wore handsome, European-style clothing, lived in multi-room dwellings, and were familiar with the English language. They were also familiar with whiskey and displayed drinking habits hauntingly reminiscent of sixteenth-century Europeans. When asked to identify themselves, these Indians said they were "Croatans"—the same name Governor White had found carved on the wooden palisade in 1590.

The Mystifying Melungeons

WHEN EUROPEANS FIRST settled the southern United States, Indians were considered savages, little better than animals. Some explorers were not even convinced that Indians were human at all. If God had created a place for them in his great cosmic scheme, then why hadn't he bothered to mention them in the Bible, his own Holy Word?

Later, as more and more whites poured into the once remote valleys and plains of the southern Appalachian wilderness, conflict with the original inhabitants became inevitable. The "subhuman" status of the Indians was reason enough for gold-hungry settlers to justify gobbling up lands, ransacking forests, and massacring any natives who got in the way.

Then came the nineteenth century, when some conscience-smitten Europeans and Americans began looking upon the "Red Man" as a kind of "noble savage," descended, certainly, from proud European or Near Eastern stock. How else could they account for the dazzling stone pyramids in the jungles of Central America and the enormous earthen monuments scattered throughout the southeastern United States and Mississippi Valley? Where else could native Americans have learned the technology required to erect such striking structures? How could their intricate cultures, no matter how paganized and vulgar, have developed without assistance and cultural influences from advanced civilizations beyond the sea?

These and other troubling questions were on the minds of many eighteenth- and nineteenth-century historians, archaeologists, and clergymen as they roamed the southern frontier. The birth of archaeology in the nineteenth century, and particularly discoveries made in Egypt and other areas of the Middle East, only enlarged rather than resolved these questions. For a time it was thought that the American Indians were descended from—or at least related to—the Romans, Carthaginians, Libyans, Chinese, Basques, Iberians, and even the Irish. The nineteenth century saw the rise of theories that survivors from the lost continent of Atlantis had reached the New World, mingling with local Indians along the southern coast and eventually masterminding construction of the pyramids on both sides of the Atlantic. Thus they supposedly imported the advanced technologies that enabled the savage Indians to rise from their Stone Age culture.

Today, despite increasingly accurate means of analyzing evidence, the origins of native Americans still inspire elaborate theorizing—from Gladwyn's belief that part of the fleet of Alexander the Great brought civilization to southern waters, to Erich von Daniken's proposition that beings from outer space engendered the human race. However, in spite of more than four centuries of speculation and research, no conclusive evidence supports any theory linking prehistoric America with trans-Atlantic, extraterrestrial, or Atlantean contacts.

In Hancock County, Tennessee, along the rugged Virginia border high in the southern Appalachian mountains, there lives a group whose uncertain origins are a prime example of the controversy. Intelligent and quiet, they are known locally as the Melungeons—perhaps because of their curious mixture of ethnic traits, or *mélange*, which includes reddish-copper skin, straight, fair hair, thin lips, and narrow faces.

Some scholars think the Melungeons are the grandchildren of shipwrecked Portuguese sailors who intermarried with their coastal ancestors. Others believe they may be descended in part from Spanish soldiers who deserted Hernando De Soto's army in the sixteenth century. Yet another explanation is that the Melungeons might be descended from the so-called

Ten Lost Tribes of Israel. That theory has also been used to account for the bewildering accomplishments of other native American civilizations, most notably the Aztecs of Mexico, the Mayans of Central America, and even the Incas of Peru. Some scholars see physical and cultural links between these Old and New World societies, pointing to architectural, religious, artistic, and linguistic similarities. It has also been posited that the Melungeons' ancestors were Mayans, Moors (thought to have sailed to America during the American Revolution), or Phoenicians, an ancient race of seafarers. Or perhaps the clan is descended from one or two Indians or blacks who intermarried locally. Thus they would be of very recent origin, perhaps late colonial or even antebellum times.

And who do the Melungeons themselves say they are? They claim to be descended from survivors of Sir Walter Raleigh's ill-fated colony on Roanoke Island in North Carolina. They are a reclusive people, mostly farmers, preferring the lonely hills and simple village life to the razzle-dazzle of modern society. They have a rich store of folktales and excel in the telling of tall tales. Their ancestors, they say, migrated to the mountains from a "land at the edge of the great sea," bringing with them unusual customs and traditions that resembled those of Europeans at the time of the North American conquest.

The Riddle of the Mounds

WHEN THE FIRST Spanish explorers reached North America, they were surprised to find tens of thousands of huge, pyramid-shaped mounds of earth dotting the landscape from Louisiana to Virginia. At first they were intrigued by these strange artificial hills, many of which towered above the dark virgin forests and mosquito-infested river valleys. As they probed deeper into the wilderness, they couldn't help but wonder who had built—and apparently abandoned—the massive earthenworks. Certainly not the primitive natives. It had to be somebody else—some powerful, long-vanished race of people. But the Spanish, lured on by prospects of finding gold and silver, never really bothered to ponder the mysteries of the mounds. That challenge was left up to a new wave of Europeans arriving on the scene—the English.

During the 1600s and 1700s, numerous reports trickled back to the British colonies about earthen structures dominating the landscape of several southern states. It is now thought that over 100,000 American mounds existed at the time of the Europeans' arrival. They came in all shapes and sizes, from low heaps of earth sculpted into the shapes of giant birds, people, and real or mythological animals, to great geometrically shaped pyramids with steep, well-graded slopes and flat tops accessible by ramps. There were so many mounds in some areas that they could only be appreciated from the air—an odd distinction in the era before airplanes.

In some ways these hillocks rival anything built by the

ancient Egyptians or the Meso-American cultures of Central and South America. At one mound site called Poverty Point in northern Louisiana, it has been determined that some 530,000 cubic yards of earth were used in erecting a single mound. Over three million man-hours of labor were expended during the project, according to James A. Ford and C.H. Webb, two archaeologists who have studied the site thoroughly.

Another important mound complex was located along the banks of the Ocmulgee River near Macon, Georgia. Ocmulgee's origins date back several thousand years and probably preceded another powerful southeastern group that developed an equally dazzling culture on the banks of the Etowah River near Cartersville, Georgia. Like mound complexes located elsewhere in the Southeast, the Georgia sites were dominated by a group of major mounds surrounded by several smaller hills and underground ceremonial chambers.

A third mound site, located on a plateau by the Black Warrior River near Tuscaloosa, Alabama, consisted of a palisaded area covering about three hundred acres with twenty platform mounds (the largest of which rises almost sixty feet) and a 7.5-acre plaza. This settlement, known as Moundville, was believed to have been built more than a thousand years ago. In time it became one of the most powerful city-states in the Southeast, controlling a territory of more than 250 square miles.

Small wonder that pioneers coming upon the grand monuments were hard-pressed for explanations. But their curiosity was only piqued further when they tried to inquire. Although a few of the mounds were still in use when the Europeans arrived, not even the native Americans themselves knew the origins of the older mounds. When questioned by advancing colonists about the earthenworks, the customary explanation was that they had been built long ago, in the dim past, ages before the present era.

These explanations were all that was needed for the overactive imagination of most European-Americans to link the mounds with some legendary ancient race, some enormously superior civilization that had flowered and vanished in remote antiquity. Like their Spanish predecessors, European and American travelers thought it impossible that the primitive tribes they encountered were capable of such engineering and technological marvels.

For years the controversy raged, pitting one school of experts against another. Cotton Mather, the fiery preacher and witch-hunter from Boston, had a simple answer. In 1702 he asserted that the devil had brought the "Red Men" to America and that they were not the architects of the mounds. That credit had to go to some other group of people, perhaps ancient Europeans who had settled the wild American shores at some time in the distant past.

Thomas Jefferson may have been the first American seriously to ponder the meaning of the enigmatic mounds. He did so while conducting the world's first scientific "dig" on his farm in Virginia. Using his own methodology for tunneling through a large mound on his property, Jefferson carefully recorded the recovery of bones and artifacts by layer—a system that would in time be adopted by archaeologists the world over. Jefferson wrote about his excavation in a small book entitled *Notes on Virginia*. The book proved immensely popular, both among scholars and lay people, and served to ignite considerable interest in American antiquities.

Others responded to the mounds in different ways. They theorized that the builders of the mounds might have come from Atlantis, the mythological continent that supposedly sank beneath the sea during a cataclysmic upheaval between ten and fifty thousand years ago. Survivors of that disaster could have reached North America, intermingled with natives there, and helped them advance culturally.

The ancient Egyptians also figure prominently in early trans-oceanic theories. Stories began circulating in the late 1700s and throughout the 1800s that Egyptian, Phoenician, and Libyan traders crossed the Atlantic regularly on international trading expeditions. Naturally they could have lent a technological hand to the New World "savages."

In time even wilder theories emerged. Colonel James Churchward in 1931 announced that he had finally solved the riddle of the mounds. According to Churchward, who believed mankind originated on a legendary land mass located in the Pacific Ocean called Mu, "The oldest records of man are not to be found in Egypt or the Valley of the Euphrates, but right here in North America and in the Orient where Mu planted her first colonies!"

Modern archaeologists cringe at the word "mound-builder," since in their view there was not just one people responsible for the earthen structures. Instead, numerous groups of Indians contributed to the mound-building tradition through the centuries—a tradition which probably had already ended before the arrival of the first Europeans. The people who built the mounds in Mississippi, Louisiana, Virginia, Georgia, Tennessee, Alabama, Florida, and the Carolinas were the ancestors of modern Indians.

In spite of the large number of mounds scattered throughout the Southeast, surprisingly few Americans know they exist. Their ignorance is probably due to the fact that until a few years ago native American history was conspicuously absent from school textbooks. Nowadays, interest in America's pre-colonial past continues to grow. Hundreds of new books and films about ancient America attest to the country's new love affair with pre-Columbian times. Perhaps it will be only a matter of time before we can satisfactorily close the book on the mystery of the great earthen mounds.

The World Within

TENS OF THOUSANDS of years ago, our ancestors moved into caves to protect themselves from the elements and other dangers of the outside world. Not only did caves serve as homes, but also they took on importance as ceremonial and religious chambers, places where people could go to communicate quietly and directly with their gods. Most of these sacred realms were probably hidden away from the rest of the cave—dank recesses where silence and flickering shadows helped worshippers get closer to the spirit world.

Over time, such subterranean worlds began to seize the human imagination, and tortured fantasies were constructed to help account for boiling lakes of fire found in volcanoes and vast, beast-filled hollows and caverns beneath mountains and hills. During the age of exploration and discovery, adventurers began descending into formerly forbidden realms to poke, probe, and ponder the mysteries within. Invariably these were places said to be haunted by giants, devils, evil dwarfs, prehistoric monsters, and a nightmarish array of other unholy horrors. Occasionally stories were published in newspapers about the discovery of lost worlds far below the earth, or of lost civilizations inhabited by advanced peoples. These stories became embellished over the years. Somewhere along the way, these netherlands became associated with death and demons, with dragons and the supernatural—an association that prevails even in our high-tech age. Even as the human mind developed and reached far out to the stars, it never forgot the darkness at the back of the cave.

No one was more attracted to the romantic possibilities of life beneath the surface of the earth than Cyrus Read Teed, a New York–born botanist who began his metaphysical researches after experiencing a divine "illumination" in the autumn of 1869. In time Dr. Teed put forth his theory that the earth is practically stationary in time and space and exists as a concave sphere, with all life on its inner surface: a gigantic inverted cave. His controversial notion was outlined in a book called *The Cellular Cosmogony, or, The Earth in a Concave Sphere*, which he wrote under his adopted name of Koresh, the Hebrew name for Cyrus. The known world is on the inside of the earth's curvature, he explained, beyond which there is only the darkness of a void. At the center of the sphere, rotating in unison, are the sun, stars, and other planets. The vast internal cavity is filled with a dense atmosphere that screens the other side of the globe.

To prove his theory, Teed measured the curvature of the earth—a measurement that contradicts the Copernican hypothesis but which has yet to be disproved. In fact he offered ten thousand dollars to anyone who could prove his theory wrong. He found plenty of takers, but each time scientific measurements were taken, the results were the same as Teed's.

Buoyed by his findings and at the same almost consumed with his passion for religion, Teed decided he needed a quiet, isolated place to work and to establish his own concept of social order. In 1894 he found such a place on the banks of the Estero River in deep southwest Florida—a 300-acre tract of land he called the Koreshan Unity, Inc. He set out to build a new society dedicated to the principles advanced in his new cosmology. Bringing about two hundred followers from Chicago, he founded his new settlement, which he named Estero, believing that the news he preached would become one of the world's great religions and that Estero would grow into a great city. He and his followers spent the next decade building houses in the wilderness. They also built a thriving tropical nursery, a handsome Art Hall, churches, tennis courts, baseball fields, marinas, a general store, and even a museum—devoted to the display and interpretation of Teed's curious teachings and scientific research. Teed eventually abandoned his medical practice altogether and proclaimed himself the messiah of a new religion called Koreshanity. He launched a newspaper, *The Flaming Sword*, which helped spread his gospel until it ceased publication in 1949.

Teed's colony never reached the population of ten million converts that had been his goal. In 1908 the old visionary died, leaving behind his unfinished colony and a personal and professional legacy steeped in legend. Among the unanswered questions are: Where did he acquire the financial resources necessary to found his colony (although his father was a successful country doctor, young Teed had to quit school to help support his large family)? How was he able to convince scores of young women—many of them married—to abandon their families and join him on his crusading pilgrimage to Florida? Who supported his scientific research?

Teed's body was placed in an immense mausoleum guarded twenty-four hours a day by teams of young women and men. In 1921, the tomb was washed away by a hurricane. In 1961 the state of Florida turned his tract of land into the Koreshan State Historic Site. Although the last of the original disciples died in 1981, site volunteers offer guided tours and slide shows of the settlement. Many of the buildings erected by the Koreshans still remain, thanks to rehabilitative and restoration efforts in recent years. Of special interest is the site's Museum and Library at the World's College of Life—Koreshan United headquarters—on Corkscrew Road along U.S. Highway 41. Here many of Teed's original books and furniture are on display, as well as an exhibit showing in three dimensions how his radical "cellular cell" theory puts the surface of the earth on the inside of the globe.

Surprises in the Sea

IN THE SPRING of 1967, the deep-diving *Aluminaut* was on a routine exploratory mission a few miles off the coast of Florida when scientists on board spotted what appeared to be an enormous highway meandering along the ocean floor three thousand feet below the surface. Intrigued, the scientists moved in for a closer inspection. The submerged "road," which appeared to be paved with manganese oxide, seemed to be part of an elaborate undersea highway system. Special wheels installed on the *Aluminaut* enabled the tiny submarine to rumble along the subterranean roadway for some distance, much as a modern automobile motors down an uncrowded interstate.

Except that this interstate was more than half a mile beneath the sea.

Subsequent voyages of exploration have thus far failed to reveal the underwater highway's origin or terminus. Assuming the phenomenon is indeed synthetic and not the result of some natural geological force as suspected by some scientists, several important questions naturally arise. Who built the colossal undersea stoneworks? When were they built, and why?

To begin our search for answers, let's go back to 1968, one year after the startling discovery off the southern coast. On a solo flight off the Florida coast, Dr. J. Manson Valentine, an American zoologist and veteran deep-sea diver, noticed what looked like a "giant wall" of stone crisscrossing the shallow depths in a remarkably well-defined and geometric pattern. The structure, which was several hundred yards long and clearly visible from the air, consisted of massive stone blocks over sixteen feet square, some of which formed regular polygons, circles, triangles, rectangles, and dead straight lines extending over several miles.

Valentine, who had first noticed the formation while flying over the area ten years earlier, donned scuba gear and went down this time to investigate. He was joined by veteran French diver and engineer Dimitri Rebikoff, a pioneer of underwater photography and inventor of the Pegasus torpedo.

The two seasoned scientist-explorers were not prepared for what they saw flickering in the clear waters—the apparent remains of a long-drowned harbor, perhaps an entire city, that presumably had vanished beneath the waves countless centuries before. In the sparkling depths the duo found what may be platforms, roads, collapsed walls, and columns, some resembling the pre-Inca stonework of Peru, the pillars of Stonehenge, or the Cyclopean walls of Minoan Greece.

Carbon 14 datings of fossilized mangrove roots growing over the stones indicated the walls had been in place for at least twelve thousand years—long before the first Indians are believed to have arrived in that part of the New World. According to Valentine, the intriguing ruins consisted of

> an extensive pavement of rectangular and polygonal flat stones of varying size and thickness, obviously shaped and accurately aligned to form a convincingly artifactual arrangement. These stones had evidently laid submerged over a long span of time, for the edges of the biggest ones had become rounded off, giving the blocks the domed appearance of giant loaves of bread or pillows. Some were absolutely rectangular, sometimes approaching perfect squares.

Valentine went on to describe "avenues of apparently fitted stones, . . . mosaic-like pavements" and "three short causeways of accurately aligned large stones . . . of uniform width and that end in corner stones." From the air, Valentine said, "one can dimly make out, under their blanketing of dark algae, the huge individual stones that precisely border the margins of this geological or archaeological challenge."

Reacting to criticism from academic circles over his astounding find, Valentine said:

> My personal feeling is that this entire complex represents the intelligent utilization, by ancient man, of materials provided by nature and appropriate for the creation of some sort of ceremonial center. In this connection it should be remembered that certain ancient sacred sites, such as the Glastonbury Circle and the designs of the Nasca desert of Peru of lines and images of mile-long animals, traceable only from the air because of their gigantic proportions, have virtually no point of reference with our modern technology, as the purposes of these majestic artifacts are incomprehensible to us.

Soon after the discovery, hundreds of divers and scientists rushed to the scene, mapping, photographing, digging, and studying the ruins. Some observers considered them to be of natural origin, but many more argued that the artificial nature of the sprawling watery complex indicated it might have been constructed by an advanced civilization using superior engineering technology in remote antiquity.

For months the controversy raged. Hundreds of articles appeared in scientific journals as well as newspapers and popular magazines. Television crews from all over the world descended into the depths to probe with color cameras and stereophonic sound equipment. Rather than asking whether the ruins were synthetic, most investigators seemed more curious to know who had built the colossal structure, and when.

Predictably, archaeologists were very careful in offering opinions. Theories ranged from pre-Columbian builders—the Olmecs or possibly Mayans—to extraterrestrial connections. It was pointed out that the ruins were located in the vicinity of what has been called the Bermuda Triangle, a part of the Atlantic Ocean renowned for mysterious activity. It was inevitable that the name of Atlantis, too, would be invoked in attempting to solve the riddle of the undersea ruins. For years, searchers for the lost continent of Atlantis have looked to the warm, shallow waters between Florida and the Bahamas for clues to the sunken empire.

Most of what we know about Atlantis can be traced back to a couple of Socratic dialogues supposedly authored by Plato around 355 B.C. In *Timaeus* and *Critias,* Plato laid the basic groundwork for the theory of Atlantis, drawing upon blurry accounts handed down by questionable Egyptian priests. According to these stories, some of which were pure fairy tale, a brilliant civilization had once flowered "beyond the pillars of Hercules [thought to be the Straits of Gibraltar]," a civilization older and larger than North Africa and Asia Minor combined.

The Atlanteans, so the story went, were a "brave, handsome and virtuous" people who had achieved a high state of culture, excelling in finance, religion, the arts, and military prowess. Sometime around 12,000 B.C., however, a powerful earthquake, followed by massive volcanic eruptions and tidal waves, was said to have sunk the entire land mass in one day. Temples, palaces, fortresses, and houses toppled into the sea; overnight, millions of "proud, fair" Atlanteans were washed away, leaving only a handful of survivors who fled the devastation in swift-sailing vessels. These survivors reached the New World and either mingled with Atlanteans who had already migrated there earlier or introduced their culture into some areas for the first time.

Of the drowned "mother continent" not much more is known, yet legends of its existence persisted through the centuries. Generations of scholars since Plato have been unable to establish whether the story of Atlantis was a product of the philosopher's imagination or whether he was deliberately misinformed by his sources. Even skeptics do not rule out the possibility that the story of Atlantis might have been based on historical fact, but they stop short of embracing the idea due mainly to outrageous claims about the continent's antiquity.

Since the dawn of recorded history, the memory of disastrous floods has haunted the human consciousness, beginning perhaps with Noah's biblical account of the Great Flood. That episode was probably based on an even earlier Mesopotamian story told in the Gilgamesh epic, which might itself have been formed from yet a much older legend. In the New World, Indians living along the southern coast and eastern flanks of the Appalachians believed their ancestors had come from across the great sea. Farther south, the ancient Aztecs told the Spanish conquistadores that their grandfathers—the people of Az—had come from Aztlan, a sunken land in the east, and that the "fair god" Quetzalcoatl, a white-bearded teacher, had also come from a land "beyond the swelling waves." Could Aztlan have been ancient Atlantis? Is it possible that survivors from a catastrophic upheaval somewhere far out in the Atlantic made their way across the angry waves to the nearest safe ground— a refuge that would later be called the United States? Some scholars theorize that these scattered survivors who reached the southern coast of the New World settled along the coast of the Carolinas, Georgia, Florida, Mexico, Central and South America, and the islands of the Caribbean.

After marrying into local Indian tribes, these "superior" foreigners helped engineer the construction of dazzling cities of stone and colossal highways spanning Yucatan, some of which now lie buried and forgotten beneath the waves.

Supporters of the Atlantis theory point out that less than a century ago the cities of Troy and Mycenae were considered myths as well. Their discovery and subsequent excavation by the self-taught German scholar Heinrich Schliemann (1822-1890) has become a model for many champions of the Atlantis theme. In the words of Prince Michael of Greece: "The rehabilitation of Homer and the belated but definitive victory of those who believed him may give food for thought to those who doubt the existence of Atlantis."

To add to the lingering mystery of Atlantis, Edgar Cayce, the famous "sleeping prophet" of Virginia Beach, Virginia, in

1945 predicted that "in 1968 or 1969" a portion of Atlantis would rise from the sea off the Coast of Florida.

Cayce, considered one of the world's greatest clairvoyants until his death in 1946, claimed Atlantis was situated somewhere between the Gulf of Mexico and the Straits of Gibraltar. His colorful and detailed descriptions of the vanished continent, which came while the prophet was said to be in a deep trance, bear a remarkable resemblance to the southern United States as it is in the last quarter of the twentieth century.

Cayce himself, who professed to know little about history and even less about ancient civilizations, was surprised at his own repeated references to Atlantis. Commenting on one statement attributed to him during a hypnotic sleep, Cayce said:"I wonder where that came from and if there is anything to it?" In 1933 he predicted that "a portion of the temple [of Atlantis] may yet be discovered under the slime of ages of sea water—near what is known as Bimini, off the coast of Florida."

Seven years later his prediction was more precise: "And Poseidia [Atlantis] will be among the first portions of Atlantis to rise again. Expect it in 'sixty-eight or 'sixty-nine. Not so far away!"

When the underwater structure off the Florida coast was discovered in 1968—exactly as foretold by Cayce—waves of joy and satisfaction rippled through Cayce's followers. Vindication had never been sweeter for these die-hard devotees of the Virginia psychic, objects of considerable ridicule and scorn by the established scientific community. Their leader had been right all along, so they believed, and now the restless ocean was spitting up the evidence to prove it—just as Cayce had foretold.

Atlantologists and Cayce followers pointed to the stunning architectural features now emerging from the depths—eroded marble and stone columns, some with tongue-and-groove edges, traces of finely tempered color, and long rows of brooding stone blocks that could have only been chiseled and laid in place by refined engineering techniques. The subterranean finds, including the mysterious roadway off the southern coast, fired the imagination of Atlantologists around the world.

Shortly after the discovery, a group of English newspapermen voted the reemergence of Atlantis as the "fourth most important news story they could imagine—five places ahead of the Second Coming of Christ."

It was a remarkable time for believers in Atlantis. Textbooks would have to be rewritten to include whole chapters on the once-fabled civilization, now rising slowly from the depths of the ocean. Television documentaries were being released by the dozen; magazine and newspaper articles brimmed with illustrated references to the sunken continent. An entire generation was in the grip of "Atlantis fever" as new finds were brought forth from the deep.

In academic circles, however, the ivory towers remained drawn up tight, stoically warding off the flurry of unsubstantiated claims being hurled at them from advocates of Atlantis. At best, the established community said, Atlantis was only one of several possible romantic explanations for the existence of these peculiar undersea ruins.

"Official" theories as to the origin and nature of the stone walls ranged from Indian fish traps to underwater storage pens for conch shells, sponges, or turtles. One archaeologist suspected the stone walls were laid by local Carib Indians, even though it seems fairly certain that at the time of the discovery of America this tribe did not build in stone. Others have attributed the subterranean construction to Spanish explorers, calling it a "blockhouse" without revealing why it happens to be underwater.

The lack of records, oral or written, means that we probably will have to wait until more conclusive research is conducted before knowing for sure whether the undersea megaplex off the southern coast is some kind of weird but natural geological formation or the remains of a brilliant civilization that vanished thousands of years ago.

Voyagers
From Beyond

In Search of Cofitachequi

ALONG THE BANKS of the Savannah River in what is now South Carolina there once lived a people of uncommon grace and elegance. Their kingdom, known as Cofitachequi, or "Dog Town," consisted of several small villages and communities, most of which were constructed around a series of handsome, pyramid-shaped earthen mounds. Unlike most of their neighbors on each side of the winding river, the people of Cofitachequi were a peaceful lot, preferring to settle disputes by arbitration than with spears and tomahawks. They were ruled by a young queen whose stunning features and regal countenance were later compared to another great female leader, Cleopatra of ancient Egypt. The woods along the river fairly bristled with game, and the gentle climate was ideally suited for growing a variety of crops—including corn, squash, and golden stalks of tobacco. It was in many ways a paradise for the thousand or so Indians who called Cofitachequi home.

In the summer of 1540, no one had reason to think it would ever end. But a few hundred miles to the south, near what is now Tampa Bay, Florida, several "strange houses" that floated on water had been seen unloading more foreigners and their terrifying animals on four legs. The white-skinned strangers were said to be clad in shiny "skin" that burned like the sun, and they carried noisy sticks that made smoke and fire at will.

Still, in spite of such alarming reports, the gentle people of Cofitachequi had no reason to fear the far-off arrival of such outsiders. Life went on as before. The men fished and hunted;

the women cooked and tended the fields.

But the man called Captain Don Hernando De Soto would change all that soon. Already, as his gold-hungry conquistadores trudged north through the swamps of northern Florida, the tall, bearded Spaniard was dreaming of the fabled treasures that he knew awaited him at Cofitachequi.

Gold! The very sound of the word was enough to make De Soto's eyes light up. He trembled as he recalled the mounds of precious stones he had seized from the people of Peru only a few years earlier. Enough gold to fill up several rooms! Now he was about to add to his fabulous personal fortune. And it all seemed so easy. What was there to prevent him and his battle-hardened soldiers—six hundred strong of Spain's finest infantry, cavalry, and scouts—from taking what they wanted in this raw, untamed new world? Certainly not a few naked savages armed with spears and knives!

By any standard, De Soto was already rich. Most of his wealth had been attained during his participation in the bloody conquest of the Inca Empire in Peru. Not only had he been appointed governor of Cuba, he owned a handsome villa in Havana and several pieces of valuable property back in Spain.

But he was unhappy. He wanted more, lots more. His biggest dream now was finding Eldorado, the legendary city of gold which he believed to be somewhere beyond Florida, hidden in vast, wild regions that would later be known as Georgia and South Carolina.

Others had said the city lay in the deserts of the great Southwest. Rumors circulating in Madrid and Havana placed it first in Mexico, then Colorado, Arizona, and New Mexico. De Soto, however, had reason to believe Eldorado lay somewhere in the southeastern part of what was to become the United States of America.

On May 18, 1539, he and his hand-picked army had set sail in a large fleet for the northlands. A few days later they landed near Tampa Bay and immediately set off in search of the city of gold. Besides his soldiers, the retinue included twelve priests, four friars, two secretaries, servants, cattle, horses, mules, thirteen sows, and several boars—the first hogs to be seen on the American continent. De Soto also traveled with a pack of Irish bloodhounds. Whenever captured Indians wouldn't cooperate, he had them thrown to the vicious dogs for sport.

Before reaching Georgia, De Soto's army passed through Apalachee, near what is now Tallahassee, where they demanded to know from the local population the whereabouts of the lost city of gold. Whenever their questions went unanswered, the Spaniards would summarily execute Indians at random, enslave a few others, then burn down the village. On at least one occasion, the captain ordered a captured Indian to be burned alive for refusing to talk.

Finally, stories began to come forth from terrified villagers about the place De Soto was seeking. At swordpoint, these Indians were only too happy to describe a glittering city just beyond the forest, or just over the next ridge, a city said to be filled with the stones of gold he was searching for. Some even offered to show him the way—anything to rid their village of his cruel presence. More often than not, once the Spanish army was safely out of town, their volunteer guides would pretend to be so sick they couldn't go any farther. Some simply fled into the woods to escape.

Whenever they heard he was coming, some Indians would abandon their villages, preferring to let the fire-brandishing foreigner march through rather than risk confrontation. After the army had left, the villagers would safely return to what remained of their community.

Once the Spaniards reached southwestern Georgia, travel became extremely difficult. The forests were dark and thick and many of the rivers impassable. To make matters worse, hostile Indians constantly harassed the arrogant band of outsiders, shooting venom-tipped arrows at them whenever the opportunity arose.

Still the Europeans pressed on through the wilderness, guided by scouts who frequently took the wrong trail or deliberately misled them in other ways. The patience of the conquistadore was beginning to wear thin. Many of his men began to urge him to halt the expedition, to turn around now and go back home.

But they had come too far to go back home empty-handed. Surely, thought the commander, the city of gold was near. He could almost smell the glittering substance.

Finally, on May Day, 1540, Hernando De Soto and his weary, hungry, and footsore men stumbled from a dense pine thicket into a clearing along the Rio Dulce (Savannah River), just south of present-day Augusta, Georgia. Immediately they were greeted by four canoes carrying several young men and women. In one of the canoes rode the queen of Cofitachequi herself.

After formally welcoming the strangers with wreaths of flowers and strings of pearls, the "Lady of Cofitachequi" invited them into her city to eat and rest. On the way into town, the conquistadore was beside himself with joy. At last he had reached his Eldorado, the lost city of gold! But here it was known as Cofitachequi.

Rudely, De Soto began looking around for signs of the treasure. He ordered his men to search every hut and every mound in the village, to question every Indian—man, woman and child—about gold.

One is tempted to try to imagine what must have been going on inside the captain's mind that day. Visions of gold-bedecked villagers, such as those he had encountered with Pizarro in Peru so long before, must have filled his head. He probably remembered the jewel-encrusted tombs, the temples and government buildings laden with precious stones. Here, in this quaint little kingdom on the wild American frontier, he no doubt expected to find similar treasures.

Alas, not a single precious stone was to be found anywhere. There were no necklaces or rings of gold, no silver ornaments or ruby adornments. In fact, the Indians of Cofitachequi had never even heard of gold! The only valuables they had to offer were pieces of copper and mica and some glittering strands of freshwater pearls.

After a few uneventful days in Cofitachequi, De Soto had had enough. Accepting fresh supplies from the generous queen—tanned skins, blankets, strips of venison, dry wafers, and a large quantity of "very good salt"—he decided to push on, but not before first stripping the village of every strand of pearl in sight. Methodically his men went from house to house and temple to temple snatching anything they considered of value. Soon their pockets and satchels were bulging with shiny, round pearls, so many they didn't bother to collect those that spilled out onto the ground.

When the queen saw that the only way to spare her village from the torch lay in her cunning, she led the Spaniards to another town within her kingdom called Talomico, said to be a special religious center, where she allowed them to plunder a large temple mound decorated inside and out with strings of finely polished pearls.

Still not satisfied, and disheartened at his failure to find gold, De Soto resorted to one last dastardly act. When the queen told him—presumably in a desperate final attempt to rid her people of the Spanish scourge—that the golden metal he was looking for lay in another province a few days' journey from Cofitachequi, De Soto insisted she come along as a guide.

This action understandably angered the natives, but they were powerless to do anything but watch their beloved queen hauled away in chains before the marauding band of soldiers. A few miles downstream, however, she managed to escape, along with a couple of servants who had volunteered to accompany her on the forced march.

The Lady of Cofitachequi eventually made her way safely back home, but the tiny, once-tranquil kingdom would never be the same again. Besides looting their villages, the Spaniards had also infected the Indians with a plague-like disease, and soon the riverside empire of Cofitachequi disappeared, along with its legends of gold.

Do Soto continued marching north into North Carolina, eventually crossing the Blue Ridge Mountains into Cherokee territory, then beyond into Alabama, Mississippi, and Louisiana. But he never found his lost city of gold.

In May of 1542, almost two years to the day after plundering Cofitachequi, De Soto died, presumably from a fever contracted along the Mississippi River. Chroniclers of his adventures say he never got over his failure to find gold in Cofitachequi and died a broken man.

On the Trail of Prince Madoc

MANY STRANGE STORIES have been advanced to account for the origin and development of native American cultures. Some legends tell how fleeing survivors from the sinking continent of Atlantis made their way across the sea to settle in the wilds of the New World, where they spawned a new race of reddish-colored people. Others claim that centuries ago shipwrecked sailors from Iberia or Gaul somehow mingled with Indians already living along the southern coast to produce a noble stock of blue-eyed savages. Still other theories hold that it was the ancient Egyptians or Libyans who somehow survived perilous voyages across the ocean either to become the first Americans or at least to influence inhabitants already here. For years many scholars believed the Israelites might have landed on the North American continent, presumably in southern waters, where they intermarried with local tribes and eventually transferred aspects of their culture.

To defend their theories, scholars often point to striking similarities in languages, customs, dress, habits, and other cultural traits between native Americans and whatever group of oceangoing voyagers they happened to be favoring at any given point. In the eighteenth century, for example, a British trader named James Adair claimed he heard chanting Choctaw and Chickasaw Indians use the word "Jehovah" and other Jewish terms which suggested to him that the Indians were descended from the Ten Lost Tribes of Israel.

Adair's astounding claim was only one of many such tales

coming to light as European explorers and settlers pushed deeper into the southern hinterlands. Contact with the local inhabitants, whether friendly or hostile, always evoked the same question: Who were these red-skinned people and where had they come from?

Since there was no mention of them in the Bible, invading Europeans eventually declared them to be subhuman. Some even thought they were devils, outcasts after the Fall of humanity. And since such was the case, it seemed appropriate that they should be dealt with accordingly by superior, God-fearing Christian colonizers and conquistadores. That is, nobody—especially these half-naked, red-skinned savages—had any moral, religious, or legal right to stand in their way. And as soon as gold was discovered in the hills of southern Appalachia, this determination took on new meaning.

It was just such an attitude, which seemed to grow coarser with time, that helped to justify the Europeans' ruthless exploitation of the local inhabitants of the North American continent, as well as lands to the south. Besides, there was a war going on, an undeclared war to control territory and commercial enterprises in the New World. Anyone who interfered—and there was special reference to native Americans—had to be shoved aside to make way for expansion and development. Even when the Church officially recognized the unfortunate natives as humans after all, it still didn't alter the official policies of conquest, conversion, and extermination set into motion by the Spanish and continued by the French and English. Europeans arriving in North America still didn't know what to make of the strange, secretive, occasionally docile population they encountered.

As European exploration went on, stories began to crop up about a mysterious race of white-skinned Indians that lived just beyond some craggy ridge or forest. Crouched around a campfire late at night in the wilds of this strange new land, settlers found it easy to fantasize about the existence of such curious beings. If these "white" Indians existed, then the conclusion was obvious: at some time in the remote past, other European travelers had to have reached these lonely shores. If so, it was only natural that they would have intermingled with host tribes, either as masters or as captives.

From these modest beginnings, one of America's most enduring myths was born—that of a superior "white" race of Indian that supposedly ruled over portions of the New World long before Christopher Columbus's epic-making voyage in 1492. Even today, stories of blond, blue-eyed Indians live on in the folklore of the southeastern United States.

The search for white Indians began in earnest in 1666 after Morgan Jones, chaplain to the governor of Virginia, narrowly escaped death at the hands of a fierce tribe of "British-speaking" Indians while on an expedition in the Carolinas. Jones, a Welshman, said the group of Tuscarora Indians spoke in a tongue that sounded similar to that of his ancestral homeland. The Indians spared his life when they discovered they shared the same language.

Within a few years, fair-skinned Indians, many of whom were said to be fluent in Welsh, were discovered elsewhere in the Carolinas, Virginia, Kentucky, Tennessee, Georgia, Alabama, Florida, and other nearby regions. Daniel Boone himself told of coming upon a band of "blue-eyed" Indians who he thought spoke with a British dialect, probably Welsh, "though I have no means of assessing their language."

Perhaps the most popular "white Indian" tale of all centered around the mythological adventures of a young Welsh prince named Madoc, or Modoc, whose full name was Madoc ab Owain Gwynedd of Wales. According to several accounts, no doubt embellished over the centuries, Madoc led a convoy of settlers to the New World in 1170, arriving in Mobile Bay, Alabama, before fanning out with about 120 followers on expeditions that traversed several states in the Southeast.

No one is sure what brought the legendary Welsh prince to America in the first place. It is true that a bloody civil war was raging in his homeland at the time. Many Welsh families emigrated to escape the bloodshed, with most settling elsewhere in Britain and on the continent. There is no reason to doubt that Madoc, fleeing the turmoil for the same reasons, could have been blown off course, eventually landing in

America as legend purports.

It is also reasonable to assume that the prince would have had the nautical skills, and perhaps even the inspiration, to embark on a trans-oceanic voyage of such a magnitude. Though not exactly common, tales of a vast, uncharted land far to the west were being circulated among Welsh seamen and explorers as early as the twelfth century. Many of these stories, no doubt, had their origins in ancient Viking sagas.

According to historian Humphrey Lhoyd's *Historie of Cambria*, written in 1584, Prince Madoc not only discovered North America, but also returned home to round up "more of his own nation, acquaintance, and freends to inhabit that fayre and large countrie, [and] went thither again." The first voyage reportedly took the settlers as far as Mobile Bay, Alabama, where he immediately set out to explore lands to the west in Mississippi, Louisiana, Arkansas, and Texas, and as far east and north as North Carolina and Georgia.

Lhoyd claims that after the war in Wales had ended Madoc returned home and reported having found a fruitful land to the west where he had left some of his people. Then he collected ten more shiploads of colonists and went away for good. One version puts the number of ships at eighteen and the number of colonists at more than three thousand.

Later, when Spanish conquistadores captured Mexico, they learned from Montezuma that the imperial Aztec leader was descended from a mysterious race of fair-skinned people that had come "from a generation very far away, in a little island in the north." Wales, perhaps? What sounds incredible might not be so farfetched when one considers the research of Dr. Barry Fell, formerly a professor at Harvard University. In his book *America, B.C.*, Fell draws on hard evidence to support his theory that North America was visited not once but numerous times in prehistory by several groups of Old World sea voyagers, including Egyptians, Phoenicians, Iberians, Libyans, and perhaps even the Israelites. To defend his thesis, Fell points beyond the archaeological record alone to architectural, linguistic, religious, and other cultural similarities between American Indian groups and those of some ancient peoples.

For more than a century, archaeologists have indeed puzzled over the origin of several unexplained stone forts and buildings scattered throughout highland areas of the southeastern United States, particularly in Georgia, Tennessee, and Alabama. Old Stone Fort, near Chattanooga, Tennessee, for example, resembles a medieval castle—a Welsh castle, complete with walls and a single gateway and moat fed by the Duck River. The remains of Old Stone Fort, Fort Mountain, near Chatsworth, Georgia, and De Soto Falls in Alabama have intrigued visitors and scholars for years with their strange, zigzagging pattern of construction, isolated locations, and other traits that hint of pre-Columbian origin.

At Fort Mountain, bronze markers along the trail leading up to the fort make vague reference to the mysterious "moon-eyed" white people mentioned in Cherokee legend. They also mention other fanciful visitors to the area, including the legendary Prince Madoc, whose name has been linked to several other stone markings and petroglyphs in other parts of the Southeast.

Fort Mountain's 855-foot wall, which weaves back and forth along the rock crest of the mountain like a gigantic, petrified serpent, averages two to three feet in height and up to twelve feet in width. Archaeologists speculate that the circular wall might have been higher at one time—perhaps as high as seven feet. And this, many contend, rules out the possibility that local Indians themselves might have built the wall. Why? Simply because they lacked the tools or engineering technology necessary for erecting such impressive monuments and structures at that time in prehistory!

Unfortunately, there are few of these ancient stoneworks around to help shed light on pre-Columbian contacts with the New World. As a result, scientists often turn to the oral record left behind by the Amerinds themselves.

In his book *The Secret,* archaeologist Joe Mahan points to convincing evidence that the forebears of native Americans were radically influenced by contacts with ancient European voyagers. This evidence, handed down by the Yuchi Indians of the southeastern United States, strongly suggests that certain tribes—principally the Cherokees, Chickasaws, and Creeks—were descended from the "lost" Ten Tribes of Israel. Mahan also suspects that the Yuchi are a much older group of Indians than originally believed. He urges other scholars to step up studies of this remarkable group of people in order to better understand their dramatic legends and myths that link them with Old World cultures.

What are we to make of these old legends? Is it possible that "white-skinned gods" walked among the Indians of North American many thousands of years before Columbus's landing in 1492? Were these "gods" actually the shipwrecked survivors of ancient sailing vessels from Europe, Asia, or Africa, perhaps lost or blown off course? Did these survivors intermingle with the natives, influencing their cultural development over the centuries, as suggested by the likes of Adair, Fell, and Mahan? Or are these ancient trans-Atlantic voyages mere myth, myths spawned and perpetrated by self-serving Europeans who saw in them the ethnocentric ammunition needed to enslave a race of people, thereby aiding in their exploitation of the New World?

Some have carved their answers to many of these questions onto a bronze memorial tablet in Mobile Bay, Alabama. The tablet, erected in 1953, reads: "In memory of Prince Madoc, a Welsh explorer, who landed on the shores of Mobile Bay in 1170 and left behind, with the Indians, the Welsh language."

The Restless Skies

IT WAS A night of inky calm, a perfect night for flying. George Smith, a 22-year-old commercial aviator from Quitman, Georgia, a small town in the southwest corner of the state, had just finished dusting a tobacco field in a nearby county and was heading home. Five miles from the airport he happened to glance out his rear window. That's when he saw it—a bright, cigar-shaped light hovering over an isolated patch of woods.

"It was the most incredible thing I'd ever seen in my life," the young pilot later told a local reporter. "It just hung there over the trees, flashing like some kind of lit-up Christmas ornament."

The next day a farmer riding his tractor near Albany "nearly had a heart attack" when a shiny, round object the size of a motorhome whooshed by overhead. That afternoon two state patrolmen near Lakeland, Georgia, watched a mysterious object float slowly over the courthouse for about five minutes, then vanish in a puff of smoke.

In the days and weeks that followed, hundreds of such sightings were reported throughout Georgia, from the mountains in the north to the heavily populated coastal shores. Meanwhile, hundreds of other reports of unidentified flying objects (UFOs) were jamming telephone lines at police stations and military bases from Jacksonville, Florida, to Jackson, Mississippi.

That summer of 1974 was one of the busiest on record for UFO watchers in the South. Thousands of unexplained aerial phenomena were reported across vast areas of the region, primarily in Georgia, Florida, Alabama, Mississippi, and the Carolinas. Eyewitnesses included policemen, firemen, farmers, politicians, students, commercial and military pilots and at least one governor—Jimmy Carter of Georgia. The wave of sightings made front page news throughout the summer, as an aroused populace craned their heads skyward night after night in hopes of catching a glimpse of an extraterrestrial airship.

Although they are considered modern, unidentified flying objects are really nothing new. Sightings of strange objects dashing, darting, and dancing through the skies were reported in ancient times, beginning with the Egyptians and Babylonians. One of the first written accounts of a close encounter with what sounds like extraterrestrials, recorded on a 3,000-year-old papyrus scroll, is found in the annals of Thutmose III, who reigned over Egypt around 1504 B.C.

> In the year 22, of the 3rd month of winter, sixth hour of the day . . . the scribes of the House of Life found it was a circle of fire that was coming in the sky. . . . It had no head, the breath of its mouth had a foul odor. Its body was one rod long and one rod wide. It had no voice. Their hearts became confused through it; then they laid themselves on their bellies. . . .

The article goes on to describe how the scribes rushed to the Pharaoh to report the strange sight in the heavens, whereupon

> His Majesty ordered . . . an examination of all which is written in the papyrus rolls of the House of Life. His Majesty was meditating upon what happened. Now after some days had passed, these things became more numerous in the skies than ever. They shone more in the sky than the brightness of the sun, and extended to the limits of the four supports of the heavens.

In the Bible, numerous references are made to "flaming

chariots" and "burning lights" in the sky. Perhaps the most famous of all such sightings is found in the Book of Ezekiel, in which the prophet describes what clearly sounds like some kind of spaceship descending near the Chebar River in Chaldea around 592 B.C.: "As I looked, behold, a stormy wind came out of the north, and a great cloud, with brightness round about it, and fire flashing forth continually, and in the midst of the fire, as if it were gleaming bronze." The star-struck prophet continues to describe how "four living creatures" emerged from the strange craft, creatures who

> had the form of men, but each had four faces, and each of them had four wings. Their legs were straight, and the soles of their feet were like the sole of a calf's foot; and they sparkled like burnished bronze.
>
> Under their wings on their four sides they had human hands . . . Each had the face of a man in front: the four had the face of a lion on the right side, . . . the face of an ox on the left side, and . . . the face of an eagle at the back. . . . And their wings were spread out above; each creature had two wings, each of which touched the wing of another, while two covered their bodies.
>
> And each [creature] went straight forward . . . without turning as they went. . . . And the living creatures darted to and fro, like a flashing of lightning.

For centuries scholars have debated who—or what—the humanoid occupants of Ezekiel's vision might have been. Were they indeed angels descending from heaven, as the aged prophet believed? Or were they astronauts from outer space, clad in gleaming space-suits and brandishing unknown weapons?

The Swiss writer Erich von Daniken has become a millionaire selling books proclaiming that Ezekiel's visitors were indeed visitors from beyond the stars, returning to earth on one of their regular missions for reasons not yet clear. Other writers have compared the prophet's vision to countless other stories of aerial phenomena down through the ages and have come to the somewhat startling conclusion that these "living creatures" were actually stellar beings, sent to earth to help humanity along the road to civilization.

Ezekiel's disturbing account continues:

> Now as I looked at the living creatures, I saw a wheel upon the earth beside the living creatures, one for each of the four of them. As for the appearance of the wheels and their construction: their appearance was like the gleaming of a chrysolite . . . being as it were a wheel within a wheel. . . . The four wheels had rims and they had spokes; and their rims were full of eyes round about. And when the living creatures went, the wheels went with them; and when the living creatures rose from the earth, the wheels rose.

Throughout the 1800s, hundreds of reports of strange flying lights and cigar or barrel-shaped "airships" appeared in European, American, and Canadian periodicals. "Ghost rockets" were spotted over the northern regions of Europe in 1946. These unexplained airborne objects resembled "glowing vapors spewing a tail of smoke."

Norwegian airline pilots radioed control stations that they had observed "luminous missiles" emitting bluish-green flames and flying at speeds in excess of 6,700 miles per hour at altitudes ranging from 25,000 feet down to the level of tree-tops.

But the modern age of flying saucers actually began on June 24, 1947, when Kenneth Arnold, a civilian pilot from Boise, Idaho, saw nine gleaming objects streaking through the sky at an astonishing velocity of 1,600 miles per hour, nearly three times the capability of aircraft in those days. Arnold's detailed description of the aircraft—"flat like a pie pan and so shiny they reflected the sun like a mirror . . . flying like a saucer would if you skipped it across water"—gave rise to a new phrase in the English dictionary: flying saucer.

The years following the Korean War saw a surge in flying saucer sightings, from China to the Carolinas. The U.S. Air

Force was eventually prompted to form a special department whose sole purpose was to investigate and evaluate UFO reports. After thousands of case studies, however, Project Blue Book finally concluded in 1969 that UFOs posed no threat to national security and that there "was no evidence the sighted objects were of extraterrestrial origin." The government project was then terminated and all its files declassified.

That did not mean the end of UFO sightings. On the contrary, that same year—1969—the governor of Georgia stood on the doorsteps of a building in Leary, Georgia, watching what he and other eyewitnesses believed was a formation of unidentified flying objects streaking by overhead. About a dozen people were in the company of the governor at the time; all agreed they had definitely seen something mysterious.

In a newspaper article, Carter was quoted as saying: "I am convinced that UFOs exist because I've seen one. . . . It was a very peculiar aberration, but about twenty people saw it. . . . It was the darndest thing I've ever seen. It was big; it was very bright; it changed colors; and it was about the size of the moon. We watched it for ten minutes, but none of us could figure out what it was."

Four years later Carter filled out a detailed report form for the National Investigation Committee on Aerial Phenomena (NICAP) in which he described the object as having been erratic in flight, about 30 degrees above the horizon, and perhaps 300 to 1,000 yards distant.

A few months after Carter filed the NICAP report, the wave of UFO sightings in the South was on. Television stations, newspapers, and magazines carried daily stories on the sightings, while wire services broadcast the reports around the world. It was a time of terrific national and international tension. Watergate and Vietnam were still on the minds of most Americans, and the Soviet Union and United States had entered a new phase of the escalating arms race. Long gasoline lines at service stations and reduced speed limits were right around the corner.

People who study the UFO phenomenon theorize that most waves of sightings coincide with troubled times—wars, economic depressions, domestic turmoil. Others see a relationship between military buildups—especially of nuclear forces—and the frequency of reports of UFOs. The idea seems to be that extraterrestrial explorers orbiting the earth hail from civilizations far more advanced than ours and therefore possess the wisdom necessary to guide us through dangerous times.

In 1952, for example, at the height of the Korean War, dozens of UFO sightings were reported over Asia near the site of the conflict. But one close encounter in Florida that year was the first episode where a UFO left tangible evidence. It involved three Boy Scouts, their scoutmaster, and a lonely Florida road at night.

C.S. Desverges was driving the young scouts home from a camping trip when, about 9:00 p.m., on the night of August 19, 1952, he spotted a strange light hovering over a palmetto thicket just off the road. Desverges stopped the car, instructed the boys to run for help if he wasn't back in fifteen minutes, then set off to investigate. He carried only a flashlight and a machete, which he used to hack his way through the dense underbrush.

The scoutmaster wasn't prepared for the sight that awaited him in the woods. A large, flat object seemed to be hovering about thirty to forty feet above ground, supported by thin, metallic legs protruding to the ground. At that point he noticed a sudden rise in temperature and detected a foul odor. As he advanced toward the curious object, the heat became almost unbearable.

A few yards away, Desverges was able to make out the object's shape and density—large and disk-shaped, he later recalled, and its underpart concave. He noticed also a dome over the center of the strange craft, which he made out to be smooth and gray in color.

Suddenly he heard a sound "like the opening of a well-oiled door," and a tiny red ball that grew into a red, misty cloud drifted toward him. The instant the mist engulfed him, he fainted.

The scouts, meanwhile, had watched their leader march

deeper into the dark woods, following the sweep of light from his flashlight. Unable to see the large object occupying so much of Desverges's attention, they were startled when a bright red light exploded over the spot where they thought the scoutmaster might be. Frightened, the boys scrambled out of the car and raced to a nearby farmhouse for help.

Desverges had recovered by the time the sheriff's deputies arrived, but was found stumbling along the road, talking incoherently. As soon as his orientation returned, he led the officers to the spot in the woods where the strange red light had overcome him. Other than his flashlight—and a few flattened weeds—they found nothing out of the ordinary. On the drive back to town, however, Desverges noticed that the hair on his arms and hands had been singed. He also found slight burns on his arms.

An official investigation was conducted over the next few days, but whatever Desverges encountered that August night in 1952 remains a mystery.

The Colony of Rugby

ONCE UPON A time, on a high mountaintop in eastern Tennessee, there occurred one of the strangest colonization movements in American history. While wagon trains rolled westward and gunfighters shot it out in places like Dodge City and Tombstone, a group of English aristocrats, accompanied by lords, ladies, dukes, and representatives of the queen, moved into this rugged high country wilderness to carve out a new life. Instead of guns, plows, mules, and axes, they brought with them soccer balls, pianos, books, and banquet tables.

The unusual group of settlers, which began arriving in the late 1870s, was part of a bold new social experiment launched by Thomas Hughes, a nineteenth-century British author and social reformer. The colony, called Rugby, was Hughes's attempt to put together a new society in the American wilderness based on the utopian ideals of his time. In the decade that Hughes's community flourished, it was a cultural showplace. Famous artists, poets, writers, philosophers, and scientists from all over the world flocked to Rugby to participate in what Hughes proclaimed as the "new Jerusalem."

A prominent member of Parliament, judge, and queen's counselor, Hughes was also the popular author of *Tom Brown's Schooldays,* in which he criticized contemporary British society. His writings eventually helped bring about widespread changes in England's child labor practices and corrupt educational system. Hughes was also a spokesman for the Christian Socialists and founded the Working Men's College. At age sixty-two he founded Rugby, his utopian dream in the New World, the experiment he referred to as "my last castle in Spain." This dream was spawned at least in part by his concern for the plight of the younger sons of British aristocracy, victims of primogeniture, the social system in which all inherited estates went exclusively to the oldest son. Since manual labor was considered beneath them, the young squires had no choice but to enter already overcrowded professional fields or "starve like gentlemen." Many who followed Hughes to America were younger sons of wealthy families, who preferred to start anew in the wilderness rather than suffer the indignity of having to seek work at home. Others, perhaps, were bored with daily life as members of the privileged upper class in Victorian England, and were lured across the Atlantic by the call of the wild.

Hughes later wrote: "We are able to open a town here, a new center of human life, human interests, human activities . . . in this strangely beautiful solitude; a center in which a healthy, hopeful, reverent life shall grow." His plan was to establish a self-sustaining community in which people would carve their own estates out of the wilderness and still enjoy the "good life" associated with British learning and culture.

The community was founded atop a steep plateau surrounded by virgin timberlands and rushing river gorges, about seventy miles northwest of modern-day Knoxville. Originally named Plateau, the colony was renamed Rugby after Hughes's alma mater, Rugby School in England, and was dedicated on October 5, 1880. Its growth followed a sophisticated town plan that emphasized aesthetic rather than practical considerations. Eventually about seventy buildings graced the trim, well-manicured townscape, many with the high peaked roofs, gabled windows, and decorative millwork typical of the Victorian era. A tastefully designed and furnished hotel was built—the Tabard Inn, named after the inn in Chaucer's *Canterbury Tales*. A public library, with thousands of volumes donated by publishers and other admirers, was the pride of the colony. Tea houses were also planned, of course, as well as tennis lawns, theaters, elegant restaurants, and hotels with impeccable accommodations. Fancy clothing shops would follow, as would other trappings of a civilized society.

Elaborate gardens also abounded in Rugby. Park land was set aside for common use. Trails were built into surrounding river gorges. Lawn tennis grounds were established. Highways were laid out and given English names—Donnington, Farringdon, Reading, Longcott. The town also published its own newspaper, *The Rugbeian*, which was widely read throughout Europe and America.

Rugby quickly gained international attention, arousing curiosity among people who followed its progress through every crisis and triumph. Travel to the colony became fashionable as steamship lines devised and advertised excursions to Rugby from Liverpool, England, via Philadelphia and Cincinnati. Arriving visitors prepared to face a harsh environment were pleasantly surprised to discover just how much the wilderness had been transformed into a little "new England." There were riding and hunt clubs, comfortable country clubs, and teas galore. Literary and drama clubs had sprung up, as did a tennis team that competed against champions from England and elsewhere in the United States.

While other Tennesseeans snickered at their fancy new neighbors, the British colonists went about their carefree ways unruffled, day after day, year after year, season after season. They ate, drank, and played excessively, mimicking their contemporary counterparts back home. Just because they had chosen to live in the wilderness did not mean they had to give up the good life. So Rugby flourished for a decade, reaching a peak population in 1884 of 450.

But its early years were marked by adversity as well—severe winters, droughts, and, during the long summer of 1881, a typhoid epidemic that took several lives. Some townsfolk attempted to establish a tomato canning factory and a pottery business, neither of which succeeded. Efforts to raise livestock, grain, fruit, and vegetables met similar fates. From the beginning, the Rugby colonists were beset with problems, many stemming from the fact they would rather play than work. Priority was placed on cultural and recreational activities. Attending afternoon teas and tennis matches was preferable to plowing cornfields and mending fences. Fancy-dress balls were common, as was participation in social, musical, dramatic, tennis, soccer, and baseball clubs.

By 1887, the year of Queen Victoria's Jubilee Celebration, the colony had entered its twilight. *The Rugbeian* had ceased publication, several buildings had burned or collapsed, and settlers were leaving the colony for England or resettlement in the United States.

In spite of Rugby's numerous problems, however, Hughes cherished hopes for his colony's success to the end of his life. In 1896, in a letter to some Rugby friends, he wrote, "I may not see Rugby again. . . . I can't help feeling and believing that good seed was sown when Rugby was founded, and that someday the reapers . . . will come along with joy bearing heavy sheaves with them."

After the turn of the century, with most of the original colonists gone, Rugby settled into a small farming community of about 125 residents. Today the town has only about 70 inhabitants, some of whom are descended from the original colonists.

Seventeen of the original buildings still stand, and most of them open their doors to the public each July during the town's annual pilgrimage celebration. Visitors can stroll through the town's historic buildings, including Christ Church, Episcopal—with its original hanging lamps and 1849 rosewood reed organ, believed to be the oldest in the United States; the Thomas Hughes Public Library, unchanged since its doors opened in 1882; and Kingstone Lisle, the resort home built for Hughes. The library, containing seven thousand rare books, is considered one of the finest collections of Victorian literature in the New World.

Caves, Comets,
And Killer Storms

Last Island's Last Day

ON THE MORNING of August 9, 1856, early risers along the Louisiana coast marveled at a magnificent, copper-colored dawn breaking over the Gulf of Mexico. A few were reminded of the old mariner's adage: "Red sky at night, sailor's delight; red sky at morning, sailor take warning." Many had in fact heard troubling reports about a large storm brewing down in the Caribbean. But that was far away, hundreds of miles to the south, and since no order had come to evacuate their homes, they saw no real cause for alarm. They felt safe inside their long rows of tightly shuttered shelters built on poles high above the water line.

Just across Caillou Bay a few miles offshore, the tiny island resort of Île Dernière—or Last Island, to the English-speaking population—was gearing up for its biggest social event of the season, the ballroom dance. Hundreds of wealthy planters and tourists from all across the South had descended on the popular island for the occasion. Men, women, children, and servants had settled comfortably inside the grand hotel and its surrounding cottages in anticipation of the upcoming gala.

That morning, a few revelers out on the beach noticed something peculiar about the tide. The water seemed glassy, yet a series of choppy waves kept breaking higher and higher up the flat beach. Each time the breakers tumbled ashore, the frightened bathers and strollers backed playfully out of harm's way. They felt a trifle foolish, of course; that is, until they saw the mysterious mound of dark water forming far out at sea, about where the horizon line of the ocean collided with the cloudless sky.

Soon the beach began filling up with people wanting to know what all the commotion was about. Even at that early hour, they came dressed in their holiday finest—white coats and straw hats, hoop skirts and bonnets. Whenever their parents weren't looking, children carrying buckets and shovels scampered cautiously down to the water's edge.

Far out at sea, the monstrous wave seemed to be getting closer. The reddish glow in the sky had given way to grim overcast conditions. A light rain started falling, but mysteriously stopped before the first umbrella could be popped open. Seconds later, the sun broke back through the clouds.

The vacationers' fear gave way to fascination. Fascination soon dissolved into collective frustration—frustration that their wonderful seaside vacation might be interrupted by a silly storm!

Then, just as they were getting ready to trudge in and pack for a hasty ferry ride across the bay back to the mainland, the ominous wave subsided and the surf returned to normal. The people breathed a sigh of relief, then went on about their business, frolicking arm-in-arm down the glistening white strand.

What they couldn't see, and certainly wouldn't want to have seen, was at that moment a massive wheel of wind, wave, and cloud whirling furiously through the Gulf of Mexico. Mountainous walls of water rose and fell, collapsing against each other like tumbling skyscrapers, only to reconstruct themselves and fall again seconds later. Shrieking, clawing gusts of tropical air ripped at tattered clouds and spumes of spray and foam. Howling, moaning, hissing and hooting, the angry black storm churned steadily northward toward Île Dernière.

In those long, hot days before the Civil War, Last Island was the most fashionable and popular vacation resort in the South. Islanders especially liked to boast about their grand hotel— one of the biggest and most luxurious buildings in the Southeast. The sprawling two-story structure, surrounded by tennis courts, lawns, and flower gardens, could accommodate more visitors than any hotel in New Orleans.

Each summer the handful of permanent islanders—mostly farmers and fishermen—saw their population swell to nearly five hundred. That was just fine with most of them, because the influx of wealthy vacationers meant money in their pockets and spicy entertainment from sunset to dawn.

After dinner, merrymakers would gather in the grand ballroom to dance, drink, and eat until the wee hours. Concert music and recitals were provided by some of the top orchestral groups and individual performers of the day. Legend has it that on calm nights alligators and muskrats on the mainland bayous would crawl out of their swampy dens to listen to the sweet sounds floating over the bay waters from Last Island.

Ironically, the tragedy that would soon unfold on Last Island could have been averted. Had the islanders only paid heed to the signals—the strange, choppy surf, the eerie, whistling wind, and the clouds that seemed to gleam radiantly one moment, then dissolve into reddish puddles of fog the next— they could have climbed aboard the passenger ferryboat *Star* anchored behind the hotel and sailed away to safety. But later that night, while the waves rose higher and the winds grew stronger, the spirited vacationers preferred to dance their cares away.

The first to recognize that something was dreadfully wrong was the captain of the *Star* himself. Captain Abraham Smith had been around too long, weathered too many blows, not to sense that this was no ordinary storm. Why, he wondered, didn't the hotel authorities evacuate its occupants?

Even as his ship began to rock and grind dangerously against its moorings, he knew they still had time to climb aboard and make it across the bay to the mainland. If they waited much longer, it would be too late.

But they waited. And waited. The waves rose higher and the moaning winds became a tempest, a seething, slashing fury that blew into oblivion umbrellas, beach chairs, and anything else not tied or bolted down. Recognizing the danger, Captain Smith ordered his men to lash themselves to the deck. Seconds later, a powerful gust ripped his ship away from the marina. As the ship careened wildly away in the darkness, Smith knew it was every man for himself—and pity the poor devils on Last Island.

When the storm finally hit land, the first things to go were the crude fishing cottages and huts of the locals. Roofs, wrenched from walls, flapped away into the night like bat wings. Entire walls evaporated, along with carriages, barns, armoires, and shoes. Driven by the tempest, fenceposts and uprooted trees darted through the tumultuous darkness like missiles, striking and killing and destroying whatever got in their way—people, livestock, and other houses.

Only when a handful of terrified islanders rushed into the hotel did the music and dancing inside stop. Only then, when the orchestra had quietened down, did the gaily attired crowd hear the roar of the wind, the rumbling hiss of rising waters. Too late, the doomed men and women understood the extent of their danger.

Moving quickly to keep the crowd from panicking, the hotel managers spoke reassuringly about reinforced walls, stout timbers, and a strong roof. They explained that the unique design and construction of the hotel made it virtually hurricane-proof, that there was absolutely nothing to worry about, and that they should go back to the dance floor. Drinks and sandwiches were served on the house.

Sometime before midnight, as the smoke-filled ballroom reverberated with the brassy strains of the orchestra, someone saw a window full of water. She screamed. The music stopped and everyone watched as the dark, surging wall of debris-choked seawater strained against the delicate glass. Then, to their horror, they realized that water was rising above every window in the room!

At that moment, the huge building began to shake. The crystal chandeliers swung and jangled wildly, dishes rattled off food-bedecked tables, and guests began toppling to the heaving floor. The tall French windows disintegrated into jagged shards before the giant, crushing wave. Floor, walls, windows, and ceiling reassembled into surrealistic patterns, as bodies and furniture were swept outside into the marina and away into the sea.

All night long the storm pounded away at the island. Across the bay, along the marshy deltas of the mainland, people knelt and prayed inside their relatively secure homes for the poor souls out on Last Island.

Of the estimated four hundred people registered at the hotel that night, only forty survived the storm. Had it not been for the courageous actions of the ferryboat captain, who risked his own life to pluck dazed and bewildered survivors from the churning waters, it is probable that no one would have escaped.

When it was all over, nothing was left of Last Island—not a house, cow, or tree. In fact, the powerful storm had literally ripped the narrow island into two separate land masses. A deep channel, carved out by the killer storm that night in 1856, now flows between the two "last" islands—over the same spot where once stood the grand hotel.

The Carolina Bays:
Did an Ancient Comet Strike the Earth?

FOR YEARS, PEOPLE living along the Carolina coast have marveled at a series of oval-shaped depressions in the ground called "Carolina bays." From the air these shallow, marshy depressions and quivering sinkholes create a landscape that resembles the pock-marked surface of the moon; they crisscross each other in a chaotic tapestry. At ground level they are hardly noticeable, swallowed up by gloomy forests and lush, semi-tropical swamplands. Highways and modern housing developments have obliterated thousands of the bays, leaving them visible only to trained eyes.

It is estimated that no fewer than 300,000 such bays, ranging from a few feet across to almost two miles in diameter, dot the East Coast landscape from southern New Jersey to northeastern Florida. One source places the number at more than half a million. Few people outside the Carolinas have ever heard of the baffling depressions, apparently because the largest number of them are found in North and South Carolina—hence the name Carolina bays.

For hundreds of years the bays went unnoticed. The first white man to record notice of them was John Lawson, who, on an expedition down South Carolina's Santee River in 1700, wrote about a "prodigious wide and deep swamp" where there grew in great numbers a "tall, lofty Bay-tree, not the same as in England, these being in their Verdure all Winter long." Lawson called these gloomy regions "pocosins," an Algonquin name for bay-covered swamps. "Bay swamps," or simply "bays," remained the designated name for these formations as subsequent white settlers moved into the virgin backcountry.

On his wilderness trek to Florida, naturalist William Bartram wrote in his journal about the botanical wonders of the bays. Accompanied by his son John, he took time to explore several large bay lakes, including Waccamaw, the largest extant Carolina bay lake. In 1847 the state geologist for South Carolina, an Irish-born gentleman named Michael Tuomey, evaluated the bays' significance: "A peculiar feature of this sand-hill region is the number of circular depressions that are scattered over the surface," he wrote. "They are not deep and conical . . . but flat and shallow, at first reminding one of a circular race course. They have quite an artificial appearance."

Interest in these "artificial" bays continued to increase as the region became more populated. Numerous theories were advanced to account for the mysterious formations, some admittedly fanciful.

One of the most intriguing early suggestions was that immense schools of fish, now extinct but once resembling salmon and shad, had created the bays as spawning grounds in prehistoric times when a shallow sea covered much of the Atlantic seaboard. Another asserts that the depressions are actually the marks of ancient icebergs that grounded and melted in the warm seas tens of thousands of years ago.

It wasn't until 1933, however, that a couple of professors from the University of Oklahoma issued a radical new theory to explain the Carolina bays. According to Melton and Schriever, they are actually scars left by a "meteoric shower or colliding comet." After years of study, the scientists concluded that "since the origin of the bays apparently cannot be explained by the well-known types of geological activity, an extraordinary process must be found. Such a process is suggested by the elliptical shape, the parallel alignment, and the systematic arrangement of elevated rims" of the bays.

Today, the cosmic-strike theory is widely accepted among scholars and is the standard interpretation offered in textbooks and journals. In his book *The Mysterious Bays,* Henry Savage draws a vivid picture of the rain of fire that fell from the sky ages ago to create the Carolina bays:

> These half-million shallow craters represent the visible scars of but a small fraction of the meteors that fell to earth . . . when a comet smashed into the atmosphere and exploded over the American Southeast. Countless thousands of its meteorites must have plunged into the sea beyond, leaving no trace; while other thousands fell into the floodplain of rivers and streams that soon erased their scars.

The bays' appearance bears out this theory. From the air they resemble peculiar elliptical depressions, or oval craters, surrounded by low banks of earth—or rims—invariably elevated at the southeastern end. Each bay's long axis extends from northwest to southeast, suggesting that the comet or shower of meteorites struck from the northwest at an angle of 35 to 55 degrees. Melton and Shriever believed that meteorites streaking in from the northwest at such an angle blasted into the relatively soft earth, leaving elliptical outlines upon impact. The sand blown away by the strike created rims and would "account for their accentuation in the direction of the strike." The meteorites would have struck with terrific force; it has been estimated that a single falling meteorite striking the earth at ten miles a second would be about equal to nineteen times the explosive energy of its weight in nitroglycerin. The impact must have occurred some time during the Ice Age, because the bays contain considerable buildup of fossil-laden sand and silt which indicates that the region was covered by the sea during the terrace-forming glacial period.

Many of the physical scars from meteorites are long gone—eroded by water, wind, and shifting sands, or simply vanished beneath the foundations of modern buildings, shopping centers, and highways. Some remain, however, visible from low-flying aircraft: low, egg-shaped depressions resembling gigantic flat coins, scattered over acres of fields, streams, hills, and woodlands.

The Lost Sea

THIRTEEN-YEAR-OLD BENJAMIN SANDS of Sweetwater, Tennessee, had known about the cave all his life. Ever since he could remember, his father had taken him on arrowhead hunting expeditions inside the dark, gloomy hole in the mountain known locally as Craighead Caverns. On Saturday afternoons he and friends would slither through the cave's narrow entrance and scamper down the slippery rocks inside until they reached the bottom. There they would play among the weird stone formations and gushing underground streams.

It was on such a Saturday afternoon in the summer of 1905 that the Tennessee farm boy discovered a tiny opening in the back of the cave. Lantern in hand, he eased into the cramped, muddy passageway, squirming along on his stomach until finally emerging, dripping wet, on the other side of the rock wall. His wildest fantasies had not prepared the boy for what he saw. "It was like another world," Sands would later write. "I knew at that moment I had discovered another world deep within the earth."

Glistening in the dim light of his lantern was a vast underground lake. In the inky shadows the crystal-clear water sparkled like cut glass, stretching as far as he could see. The cave room itself was so big and the body of water so broad the light from his torch was swallowed up long before reaching the ceiling or far side of the lake. For the rest of his life, Sands delighted in describing how he threw mudballs as far as he could into the unearthly blackness, listening to nothing but unseen splashes echoing through the still, vaulted chamber.

Although he couldn't have known it at the time, Sands had discovered the Lost Sea, the largest underground lake in the world, according to *The Guinness Book of World Records*. The lake, which is about 800 feet long and 220 wide, is actually part of an extensive and historic cave system.

For millions of years the five-acre lake had been hidden from the outside world. While mastodons and saber-toothed tigers stalked through primeval forests overhead, the waters of the Lost Sea had flowed in total darkness. The only life forms known to have flourished in the lake were large rainbow trout, whose three-foot-long descendants still thrive in the cold waters. Today, these sightless fish (whose eyes did not evolve due to the total darkness of their habitat) glide eerily through the lucid depths, resembling torpedoes suspended in watery space.

One of the cave's first visitors was a giant Pleistocene jaguar whose tracks have been found deep inside the cavern. According to Lost Sea records, the cat, which weighed 500 pounds and measured eight feet long, apparently lost its way in the darkness about 20,000 years ago and fell into a crevice. Some of its bones, discovered in 1939, are on display in the American Museum of Natural History in New York. Others, along with plaster casts of the tracks, are among the exhibits at the Lost Sea's modern visitor center.

Known regions of the cave have been used since the days of the Cherokees, who held tribal council assemblies and ceremonial rites deep in the interior. Nearly one mile from the entrance, in a room now known as the Council Room, a wide range of artifacts has been found, including arrowheads, pottery, and jewelry.

Ever since the first white settlers pushed into the area, there had been rumors of a large body of water hidden somewhere inside a local mountain. But nobody—not even the Indians—knew for sure. These rumors probably referred to the backwaters of a large spring running through the cavern, and not the actual lake itself. Officials at Lost Sea Inc., the company which now owns and operates the underground lake, believe the

Cherokees "conceivably" could have known about the lake, but there are no records of any human's having seen it until Sands's discovery in 1905.

In the early nineteenth century, white settlers used the cave as a kind of colonial deep-freeze, having discovered that their produce would stay fresh longer in the cool air. The abundance of saltpeter (potassium nitrate) in the cave also contributed to keeping the vegetables fresh. During the Civil War, the cave was heavily mined for saltpeter, a principal ingredient in the manufacture of gunpowder.

In 1915 the cavern's owner built a large dance floor inside the cave after expanding the entrance. But the "cavern tavern" concept soon fizzled when too many intoxicated revelers started loosing their way—and footing—among the slippery foot trails leading in and out of the bleak, subterranean passage.

Some eighty years and two million visitors later, the Lost Sea is one of east Tennessee's biggest tourist attractions. The Lost Sea Inc. was formed in 1964. A year later, the first group of visitors was escorted through the caverns and across the lake in a small boat. Scientists, explorers, and curiosity-seekers from all over the world flock here each year to stroll along the lonely shores of the lake and to glide across the surface in glass-bottomed boats powered by electric motors. The caverns are particularly appealing to cave climbers, who often book months in advance for an opportunity to explore the more remote regions. Spelunkers enjoy prowling the depths of the cavern, never knowing what wonders might lurk around the next corner or just beyond the flickering shadows.

Deep inside the yawning darkness, where temperatures can suddenly plunge twenty degrees or more, time seems to be suspended. The landscape is the stuff of nightmares and Hollywood science fiction. There are constant surprises: one moment you are trudging straight across a narrow rock bridge, past strange geological formations; the next, out on the smooth, silvery lake, a dangerously long fish swims right up to your boat. The surrealistic imagery is now intensified by green lights submerged along rock walls just below the lake's surface. Boats, people, and fish seem to drift through time and space, while the hollow whisper of a tour guide's voice echoes strangely through the semi-darkness. On thirty-minute trips through the cave, visitors can observe at close range several displays of rare crystalline structures called "Anthrodites"— fragile, spicy-spelling clusters commonly known as "cave flowers," found in only a few caves around the world.

It is a spectacular place, and as the guide's reassuring voice reverberates through the heavy air, one is reminded of a passage in Jules Verne's classic tale of subterranean adventure, *Journey to the Center of the Earth:* "My hair stood on end, my teeth chattered, my limbs trembled," declared one of literature's most famous cavers upon entering the shaft of a volcano that would lead him on a perilous nether journey.

Today, no one knows just how deep or far back into the mountain the lake flows. Teams of divers armed with modern exploration equipment have probed visible portions of the lake, but accurate dimensions have been difficult to map due to dangerous undercurrents and forbidding geologic formations. Beneath the calm waters of the lake itself, divers have discovered an even larger series of rooms completely filled with water. More than thirteen acres of the lake have been mapped so far and still no end to the main body of water has been found. As exploration continues, so does the cavern's intrigue.

The Mystery of Rock Oven

DEEP IN THE rugged Altamaha River Swamp in south Georgia, only a few miles downstream from the Edwin I. Hatch Nuclear Power Plant, is a rock formation known locally as Rock Oven. The limestone ridge is punctuated by a series of deep, winding tunnels and caves, which are thought to have once sheltered an enigmatic tribe of Indians and might even contain treasures left behind by early Spanish explorers.

Tradition has it that the gloomy lagoons surrounding Rock Oven are haunted by the spirits of Indians who left behind subtle reminders of their mortal presence—beautifully crafted arrowheads, cooking utensils, and pottery. Oldtimers who have hunted and fished this region for years swear they've heard strange voices echoing through the woods, seen eerie green lights, and glimpsed the wispy forms of Indians dancing around the entrance of the cave. Some think that devil worshippers are conducting their rituals there. To this day, some people around these parts won't venture near the caves, even in broad daylight.

One such person is Benny Coursey, a commercial fisherman whose riverfront cottage is located a few miles upstream from Rock Oven. Coursey, who used to raft timber down the Altamaha River to the sawmills on the Georgia coast near Darien, said the Rock Oven place is haunted.

"There's something down there that's awful strange," he said late one afternoon. The ninety-year-old grandfather was sitting on his boat dock, tending to some fish traps set out earlier that day. A breeze drifted in from the river, rustling through the bushes alongside the steep, muddy bank. Coursey smiled as he spoke. "I've heard fellows tell me they've seen ghosts around those old caves. And heard voices, like babies crying or a woman screaming. Of course, that might have been a panther they heard, who knows? But what was it they *saw?*"

Dr. Ray Crook, an assistant to the state archaeologist at West Georgia College, said the swamp, where the Altamaha River winds through southeastern Georgia on its way to the sea, has never been properly excavated. "We don't know a lot about the area," Crook said. "To my knowledge, there's never been a professional archaeological investigation."

Generations of spook-hunters have sought unsuccessfully to unravel the secrets of Rock Oven. Hikers and amateur pot-hunters have dug, scraped, probed, and climbed throughout the wet, slippery chamber of rocks in search of clues to the cave's mysterious past. In spite of their efforts the mystery remains—who built Rock Oven? When? And why?

The huge limestone wall, which snakes across a low-lying ridge overlooking a lagoon leading to the river, was formed millions of years ago when most of south Georgia was covered by a shallow sea. According to Dr. William McLemore, a state geologist in Atlanta, Rock Oven itself appears to be about twenty-five million years old, based on the type of ancient marine organisms found embedded in the rock. Limestone is made up of seashells, coral debris, and other marine deposits and takes millions of years to form. "There are limestone units [like Rock Oven] scattered throughout the area," McLemore said. "Ninety percent of these formations are derived from ancient organisms."

A few miles up the river, just west of the sprawling nuclear power plant on the Appling County side of the Altamaha, a team of commercial archaeologists recently uncovered artifacts thought to be several thousand years old. A spokesman for the Altamaha Area Planning and Development Commission in nearby Baxley said the archaeologists found pottery shards, flint arrowheads, and other evidence indicating the presence of Indians at least a thousand years ago. But some fiber-tempered pottery also was discovered in the area, lending support to theories that Indians lived along the river as long as four thousand years ago—much earlier than originally believed.

Rock Oven got its name by the main cave's charred interior—evidence, say local residents, that Indians cooked meals there a long time ago. Yet history tells us little about exactly what native Americans these might have been. Early Spanish missionaries mentioned "secretive" Indians who hunted and fished the wilderness area along the river, but little else. They used to pass these Indians on their way up-river from the coast to the fall line near Macon, where there lived a powerful tribe that developed one of the most elaborate civilizations in the Southeast. Known as the Ocmulgee Indians, these aboriginals built massive earthen mounds and traveled far and wide until, with the coming of whites, they vanished.

But Crook said little more is known about the Rock Oven people, referred to as the "Tama" by neighboring tribes. "We don't know exactly who these Indians were or where they may have lived," he said.

In spite of the region's spooky reputation, the caves have long been a popular place for picnicking, hunting, and fishing. There is real danger, of course; rattlesnakes, moccasins, panthers, wildcats, and bear do inhabit the gloomy swamp. But scenic rewards make the rugged trek worthwhile—virginal stands of sycamore, sweetgum, bays, and pines; palmetto thickets, clusters of flowering tangles, and gushing streams. Locals believe that this wild seclusion probably prompted early Spanish missionaries and explorers to hide their treasure from British as well as Indian attackers. Buried amid the damp bogs and quivering pools of quicksand are thought to be gold-laden chests, weapons, and other valuables worth a fortune. To this day, no sign of the treasure has been found, but many believe it's only a matter of time until some lucky pot-hunter strikes it rich.

"One thing's for certain," said Coursey. "There's a lot of

things about this old place that we'll never know. If we did, it wouldn't be a mystery anymore."

Unearthly Oddities

Gifts from the Sky

STORIES OF DELIGHTFUL or not-so-delightful objects showering from the sky are as old as recorded lore; they have always had their skeptics and their hot defenders.

The first documented skyfall in the southern United States occurred on Friday, March 3, 1876, when bits of pleasant-tasting meat plummeted down onto the Kentucky home of Mr. and Mrs. Allen Crouch of Bath County. The portions measured up to four inches square and resembled fresh beef. According to a couple of volunteers who tasted it, the substance was "either mutton or venison."

The next year, on a hot Sunday afternoon in 1877, the city of Memphis, Tennessee, was caught up in a wave of hysteria when a rain of living snakes suddenly started falling over the downtown area. Thousands of reptiles, some measuring more than eighteen inches long, terrified eyewitnesses for several days until the snakes could be collected and destroyed. Special church services and prayer meetings were held following the aerial invasion, as scientists rushed to the scene from as far away as New York and Boston.

The mysterious "rain of snakes" was officially attributed to a freak storm that had sprung up over a nearby swamp, sweeping up the snakes and depositing them over the city. However, the official explanation failed to satisfy several pressing questions: Why did the storm gather only snakes, and not squirrels, rabbits, turtles, and other light animals that cohabit the swamplands with the serpents? Why was there no wind accompanying the snake-storm? Perhaps most puzzling of all, how was it that thousands of snakes fell from the skies that day, a number that in all probability exceeded the local population of serpents?

On August 31, 1886, the city of Charleston, South Carolina, was jolted by an earthquake that rattled buildings and caused local creeks to overflow their banks. Soon afterward, reports of "warm stones" falling from the sky went around town. Three of the incidents had happened in front of the local newspaper office. The shower of bricks had actually begun about an hour after the earthquake, lasting for several minutes with each occurrence. Reporters and editors arriving at work at 7:30 the following morning gave alarming accounts of how they had to run and duck to avoid being struck by another barrage of stones.

Another shower of "grape-sized" rocks fell outside the news building at 1:30 that afternoon. Personnel inside the news offices who witnessed the phenomenon agreed that the stones seemed to fall from somewhere directly over the building, striking the pavement with such force they gouged out huge holes.

In 1901, a flood of small catfish, perch, and trout poured over Tiller's Ferry, South Carolina, causing a mild panic in some parts of the rural community. Three years earlier, something described as a "sulphur rain" had fallen on Mount Vernon, Kentucky. The foul-smelling substance was found to be highly flammable.

Occasionally, skyfalls occur in perfectly clear weather in full view of witnesses. Such was the case on October 23, 1947, when a deluge of freshwater fish—largemouth bass, sunfish, hickory shad, and minnows—drenched the town of Marksville, Louisiana. Although some fog was reported in the area at the time, the weather was calm and visibility excellent.

The aerial assault in Marksville began about 7:00 a.m., just as residents were rising and going to work. At first they didn't know what was hitting them. The fish continued falling for several minutes, striking a number of people scurrying to get out of the way. According to a local newspaper story, the fish were "absolutely fresh and fit for human consumption." A few appeared frozen; most were merely cold, but very much alive.

Another incident in Louisiana rocked the state with excitement when, on July 12, 1961, carpenters working on the roof of a house in Shreveport had to take shelter to escape a bombardment of golfball-size peaches. Some of the workers said the peaches looked as if they were being "tossed" out of a large cloud. Town officials speculated that a strong wind had swept up the fruit and dropped them on the workers. However, the local weather bureau dismissed that possibility, saying the wind that day was not strong enough to transport peaches through the air.

One of the most bewildering episodes involving skyfalls in Dixie was reported in August 1962. Grady Honeycutt, a farmer from Harrisburg, North Carolina, had spent the afternoon fishing on a small pond near his farm. Just as he was getting ready to head home, he saw something strange streaking down from the sky.

Honeycutt, who had read a lot about meteorites, watched the shiny globe plunge into the shallow pond, causing a loud splash that nearly swamped his small boat. As soon as his nerves had settled, he paddled over to the spot where the ball of fire had struck the water and peered down.

Resting on a muddy bed about seven feet below his boat was a "round and shiny" object unlike anything he'd ever seen before. He later described the thing as "looking a lot like a bowling ball that glittered strangely." He also said it had short spikes protruding from its smooth surface.

Honeycutt wasted no time contacting the local authorities. By the time the sheriff arrived, however, the mysterious object had disintegrated into a "tangle of shiny wires." Next morning, army divers were brought in to search for missing parts. Nothing was found—except for a few strips of aluminum foil, the kind used by the air force to help distort radar systems.

The Honeycutt case was officially closed but placed in the "unsolved" file in the sheriff's office.

Flaming balls of fire zipping through the night sky; showers of living fish and snakes; "hot bricks" and hailstones the size of softballs falling from the heavens. What are we to make of these strange gifts from the sky? Explanations range from the scientific to the supernatural, from black holes and extra-dimensional connections to poltergeists and otherworldly mischief. Chances are we'll never know, and that's probably just as well. A wise man once said that explanations can be a dangerous thing—unlocking doors to secrets and mysteries better left unknown.

Human Torches or Fire from Heaven?

ON A CHILLY autumn afternoon in 1952, police were summoned to the home of an Algiers, Louisiana, man who neighbors suspected might be the victim of foul play. No one had seen 46-year-old Glen B. Denney, owner of a local foundry, in days. When a woman next door smelled smoke coming from his house, she feared the worst.

After forcing the door down, investigators made a grisly discovery. In the middle of the living room floor, heaped between two chairs, were the charred remains of Denney's body. Flames, so hot firemen had to don protective clothing to smother out the blaze, still engulfed the blackened corpse.

Nothing else in the room had been damaged by either smoke or fire. Except for the smell, the only physical sign of the conflagration was Denney's badly burned body.

An investigation was launched to determine the cause of death. If it was suicide, as some authorities initially speculated, the victim must have used a lot of kerosene or gasoline to create such an intense fire. But not a drop of combustible fuel was found in the house—not even a match, lighter, or cigarette.

It appeared that Denney had simply died, "struck down by a fire from Heaven," in the words of one witness.

"In all my experience, I never saw anything to beat this," commented Louis Wattingney, a special agent called in to investigate the case.

Twelve years later, in October 1964, 75-year-old Olga Worth

Stephens of Dallas, Texas, was sitting in her car in a parking lot outside a grocery store when witnesses saw her suddenly burst into flames. The former actress was dead before anyone could reach her. Police investigating the incident reported no damage to the car, not even to the seat where she was sitting. Nothing was found in the car that could have started the fire.

Three decades earlier, on a cold January morning in 1932, Charles Williamson of Bladenboro, North Carolina, was lying on the sofa listening to the radio when he suddenly heard his wife scream for help. His daughter heard the scream too, and together they rushed upstairs to the bedroom to find Mrs. Williamson on fire. Father and daughter quickly ripped off her flaming cotton dress with their bare hands. Mrs. Williamson had not been standing near any kind of flame, nor had her dress been in contact with any kind of flammable substance.

Two days later, a bed caught fire in the same bedroom, as did the curtains in an unoccupied room. Soon after that, a pair of Mr. Williamson's pants hanging in the closet burst into flames.

Arson experts were called in to investigate the bizarre series of "spot" fires which broke out over a five-day period. The results were inconclusive. A local newspaper stated: "The fires started, burned out and vanished as mysteriously as if guided by invisible hands. There has been no logical explanation."

For more than three centuries, coroners, police, and pathologists have been intrigued by the curious phenomenon known as "spontaneous human combustion," or SHC. The scientific world has been reluctant to accept seemingly indisputable evidence that incidents of spontaneous combustion in humans might have occurred. Invariably, such cases have been simply dismissed as "puzzling" or "unsolved." Occasionally an accusing finger is pointed toward the investigators themselves, charging them with careless or "not thoroughly sufficient" work.

Thoroughly sufficient or not, the fact is, more than two hundred well-documented cases of SHC have been reported since 1670, many of them occurring in the United States within the past five decades. According to studies made at independent laboratories and at several universities in the United States and in Europe, the fatality happens to people of all age groups and in all walks of life, but seems disposed toward elderly people who drink a lot of alcohol. In the early days, people who died by spontaneous combustion were believed to have brought on their own demise by drinking, dancing, committing adultery, or other licentious behavior. Their cruel fates were presumably divine retribution, sent down from heaven in a shower of holy flames.

One of history's most bizarre cases of spontaneous combustion occurred on July 2, 1951, when Mrs. Mary Hardy Reeser, a 67-year-old widow, was visiting her son and grandchildren in St. Petersburg, Florida. Dr. Wilton M. Krogman, a physical anthropologist and world-renowned expert on the effects of fire on the human body, called the Reeser case "the most amazing thing I've ever seen. As I review it, the short hairs on my neck bristle with vague fear. Were I living in the Middle Ages, I'd mutter something about black magic."

No one really knows what happened to Mrs. Reeser that morning in 1951. The best that can be said is that she somehow caught fire and died before she could get to a window or door for help. The worst, however, is that it must have been agonizing death, the cause of which will probably never be known. Based on reports by witnesses and investigating officers, here are the details:

Early that morning, a friend of the victim's had gone to the Reeser home to deliver a telegram. Mrs. Reeser's son, Dr. Richard Reeser, and his children had gone to the beach, leaving the elderly Mrs. Reeser alone in bed. When the neighbor, Mrs. Pansy M. Carpenter, knocked on the door, her knuckles were scorched by an intense heat radiating from within. Alarmed, she stepped back and called for help. Two painters working across the street heard her cries and ran over to help. Smelling smoke, they broke down the door and were immediately struck by a blast of hot air.

While Mrs. Carpenter called the fire department, the painters searched the house for Mrs. Reeser. She was nowhere to be found. Other than the smell of smoke and a scorched overhead beam, the house seemed to be free of danger.

When firemen arrived later, one of them made an astonishing discovery. In a corner of the den was a charred area roughly four feet in diameter. Within that blackened area were a number of chair springs and the ghastly remains of a human body—consisting of a charred liver attached to a piece of spine, a shrunken skull, one foot wearing a black satin slipper, and a small pile of ashes. The slipper belonged to Mrs. Reeser, as had apparently the foot protruding from the grisly pile of ashes.

Suspecting foul play, the family called in the FBI, along with top arson experts from the National Board of Underwriters. Tests conducted at the scene indicated it would have taken an enormous, white-hot fire to have incinerated the victim so quickly and thoroughly. A blaze somewhere in the range of 3,000 degrees Fahrenheit—the same temperature range used by modern crematoriums—would have been necessary for the bones and tissue in Mrs. Reeser's body to lose their shape.

The remaining slippered foot was a mystery in itself. How could an entire human body be so thoroughly incinerated, yet one of its feet scarcely singed by the inferno? Apparently the foot was unburned because it was outside the circle of incineration. Mrs. Reeser had been known to suffer from leg pains, causing her to often extend her left leg out and away from her body. This extension, suggested forensic experts, probably prevented the foot from being consumed by the same fire that cremated the rest of the victim's body.

A number of theories were advanced to explain Mrs. Reeser's death. Lightning was ruled out, since there had been no electrical activity reported in the area that morning. One possibility, ventured an arson specialist, was that the woman had taken sedatives, making herself so drowsy she failed to realize she had set herself on fire with a cigarette. However, neither the gown she was wearing nor the chair she was sitting in was particularly flammable. Besides, there was not enough material available in these items to produce the intense heat necessary to reduce a human body to ashes.

Another speculation, that the fire might have been caused by some failure in the electrical system, was also ruled out by the experts: the fuse would have blown. Murder and suicide were also discounted. Eventually Dr. Krogman admitted defeat. In his official report he stated: "I have posed the problem to myself again and again of why Mrs. Reeser could have been so thoroughly destroyed, even to the bones, and yet leave nearby objects materially unaffected . . . ."

Nor could he understand the shrunken condition of Mrs. Reeser's skull: "The head is not left complete in ordinary burning cases. Certainly it does not shrivel or symmetrically reduce to a much smaller size. In presence of heat sufficient to destroy soft tissues, the skull would literally explode in many pieces. I . . . have never known any exception to this rule. Never have I seen a skull so shrunken or a body so completely consumed by heat."

A number of other physical causes for spontaneous combustion in humans have been suggested, including fireballs, lightning, internal atomic explosions, laser beams, microwave radiation, high-frequency sound, and geomagnetic flux. Intestinal gases are also known to be flammable; fats and oils, which the human body contains in abundance, make excellent fuels as well. Static electricity sometimes produces sparks that could, under certain conditions, set a body on fire.

But no model has yet been constructed to demonstrate the accuracy or reliability of such theories. The mystery of spontaneous human combustion's "fire from heaven" may never be solved.

Paul Redfern's Final Flight
and Other Vanishing Acts

ORION WILLIAMSON WAS not a rich man, but he had everything he wanted—a loving wife, a healthy child, and a good farm. He was proud, too, having worked hard to save up enough money to buy his little spread on the outskirts of Selma, Alabama, and now he planned to make something of his life. Early on a July morning in 1954, as he set off from the house to fix a fence on the far side of the field, he thought he was the luckiest man in the world. When he got to the gate, he looked back and saw his wife and child waving from the porch. "Be back before lunch," he shouted, waving back.

Those were the last words Mrs. Williamson would ever hear her husband speak. Seconds later, he vanished before her eyes, right in the middle of the field. As it happened, two neighbors riding by in a buggy had also greeted Williamson a split-second before he disappeared.

Stunned, the two men stopped the buggy and raced out into the field to investigate. They were joined by Mrs. Williamson, who frantically shouted her husband's name over and over.

"It's no use, Mrs. Williamson," one of the men said after searching for more than hour. "He's gone."

Later that afternoon, dozens of searchers combed the unplowed field and nearby woods for the missing farmer. Bloodhounds were brought in, but their nosing around did not bring any luck. Newspaper reporters, including the young Ambrose Bierce, got wind of the story and conducted their own search of the premises. Bierce would later write about the incident in his short story "The Difficulty of Crossing a Field."

Orion Williamson had simply vanished from the face of the earth. Not a trace of him was ever found, not even the clothes he was wearing nor the tools he was carrying in his hands.

Twenty-six years later, on September 23, 1880, Williamson's disappearance was recalled when David Lang, a young farmer living near Gallatin, Tennessee, vanished before the eyes of his startled wife and two visitors who happened to drive up in a buggy at that very moment.

Lang had just left his house and was walking across a field to hitch up a mule for plowing. About halfway across the field, near the barn where the mule was corralled, he waved to the couple of neighbors approaching up the far side of the road. The two men in the buggy—Judge August Peck of Gallatin and the judge's brother-in-law—waved back.

A split-second later, Lang disappeared in full view of his wife and both men. Astonished, the visitors climbed down from the buggy and set out to search for the missing farmer. Lang's wife joined them, running first around the barn, then meeting the two men on the far side of the field. Thinking there might an unknown sinkhole or cave on the property, the trio continued searching until dark, then resumed the futile hunt the next day with several other neighbors.

As with Williamson, however, nothing was ever seen or heard from Lang again. He too had simply vanished.

Each year, thousands of Americans vanish into oblivion without a trace. In an age of computerized records kept from the cradle to the grave, it is difficult to comprehend how living human beings can suddenly and unaccountably fade or plunge into the unknown, leaving no trail or clue to their whereabouts. Of the estimated ten million Americans who are reported missing each year, about 95 percent eventually return or are accounted for within a few days. Five percent vanish forever.

Vanishing without a trace in the nineteenth century was one thing, but when wealthy, sophisticated people suddenly disappear in the middle of a modern American city in the 1980s, it's something else. Such was the tragic case of an elderly New York couple, who checked into a motel in Brunswick, Georgia, on the night of April 8, 1980, and were never seen again.

Charles R. Romer and his wife, Catharine, had made the long journey between their New York home and their apartment in Miami many times. They knew the route well, and often stayed over in Brunswick, the first overnight stop on the way. The Romers liked Brunswick, a bustling seaport city just across the causeway from Sea Island and St. Simons Island.

On the night of April 8 they checked into a local Holiday Inn along busy Highway 17. A little later a state patrolman spotted their black Lincoln Continental parked along the road near a cluster of restaurants. The officer theorized they were going to a restaurant for dinner.

If so, the couple never arrived. The Romers and their late-model luxury car simply disappeared.

In spite of a nationwide search, no trace of the couple was ever found. At first police considered murder as a motive, but since no bodies were found, there was no evidence to support the claim. One other possibility was kidnapping. Still, when neither the couple's car nor their bodies were ever discovered, investigators looked to other causes for their disappearance.

One baffled police officer suggested that the Romers had run off the road into a swamp while driving through the countryside. That theory seems highly improbable, however, since their suitcase and other belongings were left behind in the motel room.

Like Williamson, Lang, and others, Charles and Catharine Romer had simply vanished without a trace.

One spectacular disappearance in the South that stands apart from all others involved Paul Redfern, a young pilot from Sea Island, Georgia, whose ambition was to be the first person in the history of aviation to fly nonstop from the United States to South America. On August 25, 1927, his small, brightly painted monoplane, named *Port of Brunswick*, was loaded up with enough provisions for the long trip, and a crowd of several thousand onlookers gathered at the beach runway to see him off. Amid the fanfare, twenty-five-year-old

Redfern hunkered down comfortably inside the cockpit, waved goodbye, and taxied for takeoff. The pilot had to be in a fine mood that hot, humid August morning as his 5,500-pound monoplane skimmed along the beach, then lifted gently into the powder-blue skies over Sea Island. Down below was his wife of six months, along with several financial backers of the expedition and a swelling crowd of spectators. After a ceremonial dip of the wings, the *Port of Brunswick* droned off into the clouds.

Except for a few reports that his plane had been spotted flying on course over the Caribbean, then once more over the city of Ciudad Bolívar in Venezuela, nothing else was ever seen or heard of Redfern. He and his plane had simply vanished. Occasionally, reports still trickle in from the jungle claiming that the wreckage of Redfern's plane has been found, invariably in a remote, inaccessible region. As of this writing, no conclusive evidence has been forthcoming, in spite of hundreds of search party operations—including one led by the swashbuckling movie idol Errol Flynn.

One modern adventurer claims to know where the plane went down but says it would cost a fortune to reach the spot and retrieve the wreckage. "We're talking about true dinosaur country," said retired commercial airline pilot Robert Carlin, who has spent decades researching the Redfern story. "Steel wool jungle, pristine. Not even any Indian trails. . . . The plane was apparently hanging up in the trees for a great number of years. And I know the plane can be found. I could take you to the spot."

Redfern's destination was Rio de Janeiro, about 4,600 miles away from Sea Island, almost twice the distance of Charles Lindbergh's 2,500-trip from New York to Paris three months earlier. His flight plan was to take him from Georgia to the Bahamas, across the Caribbean and then over Puerto Rico, on past the tropical islands of Grenada, Tobago, and Trinidad, past the coast of British Guiana (now Guyana), and across Dutch Guiana (now Surinam) and northern Brazil to Macupa on the north bank of the Amazon.

Aboard his Stinson-Detroiter airplane, loaded down with

about 550 gallons of fuel, he carried a two-gallon container of drinking water, enough emergency food to last ten days, and complete survival equipment for ocean or jungle, including a pneumatic air raft, a small distilling outfit, mosquito netting, quinine, and a collapsible rifle and ammunition. Since radio instrumentation was not yet available, pilots in Redfern's day were alone among the clouds.

The mystery of Paul Redfern's final flight would soon be overshadowed by that of another ill-fated pilot—Amelia Earhart, who disappeared in 1937 while on a record-breaking round-the-world voyage. Like Earhart's last flight, Redfern's has found a lasting place among the unsolved mysteries of aviation history.

What happened to Redfern? Over the years, numerous theories emerged to account for his disappearance, many of them predictably fanciful. One had him crashing into a jungle and becoming head of a tribe of Brazilian Indians. Another said Redfern was captured by a hostile tribe that used spears to discourage rescuers from reaching him. Some reports said he was alive and well; others said he had been badly crippled by the accident, but chose to remain in the jungles rather than return to civilization.

Whatever happened, Redfern's widow finally gave up hope. Seven years later she had her husband officially declared dead. "If anyone had seen my husband and had been with him, as some of these people say, I would think he would have given them something to prove his identity."

South Carolina's "Healing Springs"

LUTE BOYLSTON LOVED the land. As a farmer, born and bred in the South, he saw the fields and woods surrounding his South Carolina homeland as God's gift to the people—a reward, he felt, for honest, decent folk who worked hard and led righteous lives.

It annoyed him when friends and neighbors abused God's gift. For years, the Barnwell County planter watched his beloved land slowly deteriorate—first from careless agricultural use, and later from the encroachment of civilization. When houses, shopping centers and parking lots began gobbling up great chunks of virgin territory, Boylston began to worry. Where would it all end? How much land would be left to his grandchildren? His great-grandchildren?

For years he stood helplessly by while developers, outdoor recreationists, and even other farmers pillaged the countryside. Then, one warm summer day in July of 1944, he did something a bit unusual to protect his farm. He climbed into his pickup truck and drove into town, stopping to collect his attorney and then heading to the courthouse to file a new property deed.

In that deed—still on file in the Barnwell County Courthouse—the 76-year-old farmer gave explicit instructions that upon his death part of his property would be deeded over to God. After all, reasoned Boylston, it had been God's land in the first place. In the unusual bequest he stated that he didn't believe "the white people who dispossessed the Indians ever appreciated the value of God's will sufficiently to help in any way preserve for posterity this gift of God Almighty to mankind."

The piece of land deeded over to God happened to be the site of Barnwell County's famous "Healing Springs." For decades, men, women and children from across the country had been flocking to the springs to drink, bathe, and play in the cool, clear waters bubbling from the ground. Many of those who did so claimed the waters possessed miraculous healing powers.

Boylston himself recognized the divine power of the springs as well. In his deed of land to God, he made it clear that "the Almighty had intended the cool waters of the wells to be a source of comfort to the afflicted. . . . I return to Him the most treasured piece of earth that I have ever owned or possessed."

The farmer's princely act earned him a big blue and white sign posted beneath several huge trees and a granite marker beneath a clump of oak trees surrounding the springs. Waves of people continued to enjoy the springs, which now, officially, belonged to God—the only piece of land on earth legally deeded so.

Indians had been the first to know about the mystical little patch of ground. Local legends suggest some of these Indians worshipped the waters—or at least spirits in the waters. Early settlers drank from the springs as well, and the mystical tradition continued. During the Revolutionary War, soldiers often camped around the springs to rest, bathe, and—according to some accounts—help heal wounds suffered in combat.

By the middle of this century, the Healing Springs had become a favorite destination for thousands of travelers from all parts of the country—even Canada and Europe. Eventually the springs were named an official state attraction. (This well-intended act probably has old Lute Boylston turning in his grave.) On any given Sunday, gangs of visitors descended on the one-acre plot of land to sip from the springs and splash their faces and arms. They came armed with plastic jugs and glass jars, metal buckets and wooden barrels—anything that would hold the life-giving waters from the Healing Springs.

Inevitably, the garbage began piling up. Plastic candy and cigarette wrappers. Beer cans. Discarded human debris which occasionally reached unmanageable proportions. Boylston's quiet little spring in the woods, the spring he had returned legally to God, was rapidly becoming a dumping ground for human refuse. Ironically, many of the people who came to the springs for comfort and healing were the same ones causing most of the mess. In stepped the state of South Carolina. If Barnwell County didn't take action soon to clean up the springs, the popular tourist attraction would lose its official status.

Disgusted by heaps of debris left over by man and nature, groups of concerned citizens joined forces to restore "God's little acre" to its former pristine condition. Spearheaded by the local chamber of commerce, the cleanup campaign was a roaring success. Healing Springs regained favor with the state and is still a state tourist attraction. Thousands of people still come here each year to partake of the waters' mysterious properties.

One such visitor is Sammy Lee Dunn, who claims to have been making the 150-mile round-trip to Healing Springs for the past fifty years. The 82-year-old Saluda County retiree believes the spring water is filled with "the Lord's mysterious powers. It's in there. And I ain't about to quit coming as long as the Lord will let me."

Sounds from Beyond

RABUN COUNTY IN the northeastern corner of Georgia is one of the most ruggedly scenic regions in the southern Appalachian mountains. This is true *Deliverance* country, made famous in the early 1970s by novelist James Dickey and the movie by the same name. In the old days Rabun County was a remote, unspoiled place where adventurers could ramble for days without so much as hearing the sound of another human voice. Towns like Clayton, Dilliard, and Mountain City seemed cut off, isolated from the rest of the world, until modern roadways began slicing through these hills in the early 1930s. Then came the tourists, trickling up and down Highway 441 which winds through the Great Smoky Mountains. It was only a matter of time until the first row of condominiums popped up on the side of a Rabun County mountain.

But in spite of new condominiums, shopping malls, and superhighways, Atlantans' vacation homes and Floridians' retirement centers, a sense of wilderness prevails. There are still places in Rabun unmarked and unseen by human eyes. Certain backwoods trails lead toward remote ridges and caverns, unvisited for hundreds of years. Some who have ventured down such trails swear they just disappear—vanish into smoky mists rising from deep within the earth. Indian legends claim that fire-breathing demons once dwelt among these lonely hills and woods, and that "little people" or "little demons" stood guard over sacred caverns and curious stone assemblies hidden in the forest. Occasionally, outsiders trekking through the backwoods report hearing strange sounds—sounds that over the years have come to be known as "music of the Bald."

For more than a century now, the music of the Bald has tantalized generations of Rabun Countians. According to those who have heard, the sound is less like music than like trees falling or boulders crashing far off in the woods. Some say it even sounds like cannon firing in the distance. A few, whose testimony has gone on record, swear the sounds are always preceded by screeching, or noises like babies crying in the night. Although they are most often heard at night, many people claim to have gotten an earful in broad daylight.

The first written account of the sounds appeared in an issue of the *Monthly Weather Review,* published in 1897. Two "reliable gentlemen" were reportedly camped on top of Rabun Bald, the highest peak in Rabun and one of the loftiest in the southern Appalachian range. About ten o'clock that night, they were awakened by sounds which reminded them of cannons being discharged in the distance. The booming noises went on for several minutes, echoing through the dark, lonely woods. Soon, however, they noticed that the sounds appeared to be issuing from the ground, from a ridge southwest of the mountain. According to the report, the men were perplexed, but "not badly frightened," even though at times the sounds seemed to proceed from the ground beneath their feet. At any rate, they sat up until the wee hours listening to the eerie booms.

When the two campers confronted the local sheriff with their experience the next morning, they were told that the sound might have been caused by bears rolling small boulders off the mountainsides in search of worms and snails. In those days, black bears were plentiful in Rabun County. Pioneers would often come upon the beasts pushing with their enormous paws and noses at rocks and boulders, apparently to get at edible goodies beneath. Sometimes the boulders would roll downhill or off cliffs, creating explosive sounds as they shattered on the rocks below.

The sheriff's explanation satisfied those two campers. But the sounds continued into the twentieth century, long after most of the bears had been killed off or driven to higher ground. Homesteaders sometimes were awakened at night by inexplicable noises. Hunters and trappers told about "eerie, haunting melodies" drifting through lonely glades and down the mountainsides. These sounds were attributed to the ghosts of two men murdered on Rabun Bald back in the late 1860s.

Scientists called in to investigate the noises generally attributed them to settlings within the ground, or boulders and rocks shifting on their own accord. As for the haunting screams heard by others, they were dismissed as screech owls or other wild birds and animals. Perfectly convincing, unless you happened to be the hiker who once felt the hot breath of "something evil and strange" on the back of his neck. According to a report by Barry C. Hawkins in the *Monthly Weather Review*, "some have heard these sounds so near them in the woods" that they had to run to escape a powerful presence that came over them.

Another enigma that has intrigued Southerners for years are the so-called "Seneca Guns": eerie booms echoing just off North Carolina's southeastern coast. These sounds, described as a cross between an earthquake and a sonic boom, usually are heard during daylight hours. Whenever they occur, houses shake, windows rattle, and nerves tingle.

Jim Lanier, director of the North Carolina Aquarium at Fort Fisher, says he has heard the sounds several times. He said, "It was pretty dramatic. It sounds exactly like artillery fire, artillery guns."

Investigations, however, have revealed no military activity in the area at the time of the sounds. Scientists called in to probe the phenomenon frequently point to another possibility—chunks of the continental shelf dropping off a cliff under the Atlantic Ocean. This latter theory is "a total misconception" of the shelf or the slope, according to Lanier, who has spent a lot of time studying the strange rumblings. "It's very gradual in this area," he said. "The continental shelf and the slope are quite gradual and there's nothing there that could break off and make this kind of rumbling noise."

But whenever buildings start shaking and windows start rattling for no apparent reason, a lot of local residents think it's time to call in a squad of ghostbusters.

"I hear it all the time," said Susan McClain, a dispatcher at the Southport Police Department. "There's no pattern. It's something between a sonic boom and an earthquake." Ms. McClain, who noted that the offshore booming has been going on since she was a youngster, said, "We've had people call and say it shook windows and knocked things off the shelf. Some days it's heavier than others."

Even Lanier admits the noises are a mystery.

"We had a funny instance where they had been going off a few times, and it sounded like one morning that someone had been rolling heavy equipment over the exhibit room floor," he explained. "There was a rumbling and you could feel the building shake, just slightly, not alarming, but the way it would shake when a jet broke the sound barrier. Of course people go and check it out and no jet broke the sound barrier in the area and the military disclaims any knowledge of any explosions going on and then people start speculating about what it is."

The mysterious noises have never been reported after dark. Some locals who claim to have heard the sounds numerous times don't recall ever having heard them on a Sunday either. Could it be that the good Lord may not want to disturb things on the Sabbath Day?

That's a question a lot of people would like to answer.

But answers—comforting answers, anyway—appear to be no nearer today than they were when the first odd sound was reported earlier this century, to the dismay of people living along the coast. "It's a little frustrating for all of us in that we don't have an explanation for it," said Lanier. "Under those circumstances, it's understandable that there's a lot of misinformation around."

At least one official believes that whatever is causing the offshore noises is also causing the beach to erode. "Ever since that started, this beach has been going," huffed Roby Osborne, police chief in Long Beach.

Screams echoing across a lonely mountaintop in Georgia, and eerie rumblings off the North Carolina coast; these are only two of the more disturbing phenomena in nature's storehouse of mysteries in the South.

The Man Who Wouldn't Die

YOUNG WILL PURVIS had proclaimed his innocence all along. In court he swore he was nowhere near the Mississippi farm owned by a man he was accused of having murdered the previous year. So when the jury returned a verdict of guilty, Purvis was stunned. He dropped to his chair, rubbed his head, and began softly sobbing. When the judge asked him to rise for sentencing, Purvis turned toward the jury and in an icy tone said: "I'll live to see the last one of *you* die!"

On February 7, 1894, the sheriff came to take him to the gallows. It was a gloomy day, but even the threat of rain couldn't keep away the 3,000-plus spectators gathered on the courthouse lawn to watch the hanging.

The sheriff, a burly fellow toting a shotgun, escorted Purvis up the rickety flight of steps leading to the hastily erected gallows where a hooded hangman and a preacher waited. A light rain had begun to fall and Purvis watched waves of umbrellas pop out in the huddled crowd below.

Some of the onlookers waved. A few fought back tears as they watched the doomed man trudge across the scaffolding. Many still believed him innocent. As the noose settled over his neck, Purvis whispered to the priest: "I am innocent of this crime. I did not kill anyone." With that, the trapdoor swung open and wide and Will Purvis, gagging and kicking, plunged into space. For a few horrible seconds the crowd gasped while his 140-pound body twitched and fluttered on the end of the thick rope.

But suddenly Purvis's body crashed through the platform to the wet earth below. Above his head, swaying in the chill afternoon breeze, was the rope. It had apparently come unknotted during the hanging, allowing the condemned man to slip through. On the ground below the gallows, Purvis picked himself up. Aside from one small cut on his cheek and some bruises around his neck and shoulders, he was unharmed.

For several seconds the crowd was quiet. Then a low murmur began to sweep through the pressed ranks, followed by whistles, clapping, and cheers. "We knew you were innocent," shouted several in the crowd.

But the sheriff, a stern-faced man clad in a large gray overcoat and wide-brimmed hat, was unimpressed. He had been hired to hang a man, and hang he would. Without further ado, Purvis was led back up the steep flight of steps to the scaffolding a second time. A thin trail of blood trickled down his cheek as he stood over the trapdoor, waiting for the noose to be reknotted and placed over his head.

But the crowd had seen enough. Convinced they had witnessed a miracle—and of the young man's innocence—the entire audience began singing, shouting hallelujah and praising the Lord. They demanded that the prisoner be released.

Utterly bewildered, the sheriff consulted with the clergyman for a moment, then reluctantly led Purvis back to his cell.

"Don't get any funny ideas. We ain't done yet," the sheriff snarled in Purvis's face.

In the weeks following, attorneys for Purvis launched a barrage of appeals with the Mississippi State Supreme Court, but to no avail. A new execution date was set for December 12, 1895. Purvis's friends, however—and many others who had witnessed the "miracle"—had other ideas. A few nights before the scheduled hanging was to take place, a group of disguised men and women stormed into the jailhouse, tied up the sheriff's deputy, and escaped with the prisoner. Warrants were issued for his re-arrest, with a bounty this time, but Purvis was nowhere to be found.

For months the young outlaw remained in hiding, confident that a new governor would be sympathetic to his cause. When a new chief executive was finally elected later that year, the now-famous fugitive turned himself in. Instead of being treated like a criminal, however, he found a hero's welcome.

Thousands of letters had poured into the state capitol demanding a full pardon for the crime Purvis swore he didn't commit. Toward the end of 1898, almost four years after the date he was to have hanged, an official pardon was issued by the governor.

Twenty years later, a dying man named Joseph Beard confessed to the murder of the Mississippi farmer and Will Purvis was finally exonerated.

The story doesn't end there, however.

During his trial in 1894, Purvis had told the jury repeatedly that he was innocent, that to send the wrong man to the gallows would be a mortal sin. When his pleas had fallen on deaf ears, he vowed before the judge to outlive them all, just to prove his innocence.

On October 13, 1938, twenty-one years after his exoneration, Purvis died—three days after the death of the last juror.

Specters And Spells

Miracle in the Clouds

ON THE AFTERNOON of August 15, 1988, a crowd of about twelve thousand gathered on the grounds of a small Catholic Church in Lubbock, Texas, to witness a miracle. For days they had been drifting in from all corners of the globe. Some brought sleeping bags and tents to stay in while awaiting the event, while others arrived in four-wheel drive vehicles and sleek motorhomes. The occasion was the Feast of the Assumption, one of the Roman Catholic Church's holiest festivals, which celebrates the day the Virgin Mary ascended into heaven. But this was to be no ordinary celebration of the feast.

Television cameras and reporters swarmed among the worshippers. Helicopters buzzed overhead. A small contingent of police had been stationed nearby, just in case they were needed. In the midst of the congregation stood Monsignor Joseph James, charismatic leader of the St. John Neumann Catholic Church, a huge underground structure located on the outskirts of town.

Breathlessly the people waited. Necks craned toward the heavens. Many wept and prayed. Others recited prayers on their knees, from the back of pickup trucks or from lounge chairs. Even above the roar of helicopters and the murmur of the crowd, the rattle of rosary beads could be heard.

The fact is, nobody really knew what to expect. They had been told only that something "miraculous" was going to happen on the church grounds soon, probably on the sacred day itself. Monsignor James had prepared his people well.

After a trip to Medjugorje, Yugoslavia, a few months earlier, he had experienced visions of the Blessed Mother of Jesus, and he was confident that she was at last going to reveal herself to his congregation—at least in signs, if not in spirit. At regular services during the past few weeks, hundreds of worshippers had heard fellow parishioners transcribe special messages— messages from the Virgin Mary which supposedly had come to them in a series of prayer-induced visions. Hastily scribbled down in the notebooks of parishioners, these words had come to a selected few who knelt on the altar as the congregation recited the rosary.

"My dear little children," one of the messages said. "Listen to me, your mother. I want to help you. I want you to be in Heaven, where we can pray and serve our father for all eternity. Yes, my dear ones, you must have signs and you will have these signs . . . but it will be up to you to believe."

Another message promised salvation to the pure of heart and to those who believed in the messages: "My children, do not be sad. Have joy in your hearts, have peace. Listen to the prayer that you ask for, the Lord will give it to you."

Most of the supernatural utterances were received by three regular churchgoers—Mike Slate, a retired air force officer; Mary Constancio, a former hospital therapist; and Teresa Werner, a housewife and mother. The three recipients would reportedly go into a trance following several minutes of prayer by the congregation, then automatically begin "receiving" the holy communication while fellow parishioners looked on in reverent silence.

When news of the messages broke, thousands of believers rushed to the church to see the miracle for themselves during regular and special services. The church wasted little time capitalizing on the series of reported miracles. More than fifty thousand books containing the messages were rushed off the presses and into circulation throughout the South. Plans were being made for additional volumes as the number of visitors swelled. Promises were made that a major miracle would occur soon. Many churchgoers, including the Monsignor, believed that all the signs pointed toward August 15, the annual celebration of the Virgin Mother's miraculous ascension into the clouds. As wire services and newspapers picked up the story, followers from around the world began making plans to attend the heralded manifestation. At one point it was estimated that at least thirty thousand people would descend on the little church to witness the miracle that the faithful believed would transform their lives forever.

August 15 was a warm, muggy day, but a breeze stirred through the chanting, singing crowd. One newspaper reporter said there "was electricity in the air. . . . You could almost sense something great was about to happen, even though in your mind you knew it wouldn't. Still, you wanted something to happen—anything, an unusual cloud formation to develop, a freak thunderstorm, a hailstorm, even a tornado. Anything to kindly reward these patient, God-fearing people."

Sometime during Mass that afternoon someone spotted a strange cloud high overhead. Then another. And another. Soon several unusual cloud formations seemed to come together to form a portrait of Jesus. A few seconds later, some of the astonished onlookers recognized the holy face of the Virgin Mary herself riding high in the clouds.

A calm prevailed as thousands of trembling fingers pointed skyward and faces grew warm in the glow of the late afternoon sun. Many in the crowd claimed that the sun appeared to dance in the sky, while multicolored lights and shadows played in the shimmering clouds. Some in attendance that day swore that their silver-colored rosaries turned a golden hue.

Whatever it was that had happened that warm August day in Texas, it was over in a hurry. No one heard the rustling of wings or the blaring of trumpets; not a single person in the crowd claimed to have been "illuminated" or caught up in any special rapture. There were just the faces in the clouds that seemed to smile down for a few seconds, then dissolve into a spectacular display of lights.

Many—especially those who had driven far and were probably doubtful anyway—were disappointed. But for untold thousands of others, those who wept and prayed and cried out for signs from their heavenly redeemer, the signs had been there. They had seen the face of Jesus in the clouds, along with that of the Virgin Mary. They were convinced they had witnessed a miracle. Some people reported that their ailments mysteriously cleared up. Bob Golec, who journeyed to the service from Midlothian, Texas, said his chronic knee problems disappeared after Mrs. Werner relayed a message from Mary to him and the church pastor included his name in a healing prayer.

Maybe it was mass hysteria that caused the collective "visions," as skeptics were quick to point out. But what caused the color change in the rosaries? Who could explain the overwhelming sense of calm that prevailed in those few dramatic minutes while more than twelve thousand people watched and waited—then observed—what they firmly believed were divine wonders?

Immediately following the August 15 feast, a panel of Texas bishops was appointed to study the charismatic church and its reports of miracles. Lubbock Bishop Michael Sheenan asked the National Conference of Catholic Bishops to assist him in investigating the event. But a spokesman for the conference in Washington said the organization would stay clear of such a probe.

"He [Sheenan] is free to set up his own investigation and ask experts in on his own, but the national organization [prefers to have] nothing to do with that," said Joe Lipovsky.

Sheenan, who called on Monsignor James not to continue promoting or printing the books until the investigation was concluded, warned that people shouldn't assume anything supernatural ever happened at the church.

"I take a cautious attitude about the rosary messages spoken about by several parishioners at St. John Neumann," he said a month before the feast day in August. "I neither encourage people to participate in the events nor do I discourage them."

Voodoo and the Walking Dead

INTO THE NEW World they came, untold thousands of them, not as conquering heroes or divinely charged pioneers, but as simple slaves and servants to work the fields and woods. They came from the west coast of Africa, kidnapped from their villages and rounded up like cattle, then packed aboard cramped, disease-ridden ships for the long voyage across the ocean. Chained, shackled, and beaten into submission by their white overlords, these unfortunate souls were forced to draw upon secret inner strengths if they were to survive the horrors of the southern plantation.

Such secrets had been handed down from generation to generation, along with other customs, traditions, and ancient tribal beliefs.

One of those secrets was the mystical power of Voudou, or voodoo, as it came to be called in America. In time the practice of this enigmatic religion, blended with elements of the Roman Catholic faith, would become the dominant religious force among transplanted Africans in the South. Voodoo offered hope and the promise of supernatural rewards to its gangs of followers who often congregated in the dead of night.

No one really knows how voodoo became so widespread in the Southeast, especially near New Orleans in the eighteenth and nineteenth centuries. The religion, which focuses on the magical powers of a serpent god kept in a box, was first prevalent in Haiti, probably brought over from Africa's Slave Coast. Eventually it was introduced to slave communities living in the southern United States, where it took root and blossomed.

In a world of unspeakable hardships for African slaves, voodoo provided its followers a badly needed spiritual outlet. While practicing their age-old faith, slaves as well as later generations of free blacks could suspend their troubles, if only temporarily, and concentrate on a world beyond. Often that world was not so divine. Frequently, it became a place of unrelenting horrors, a nightmarish realm suspended somewhere between reality and the imagination.

Today the ancient religion is still celebrated in song and dance. Its arcane practices have been the subject of numerous television specials, and practitioners, in a sense, have become celebrities in the wake of frequent appearances on talk shows and interviews in major newspapers and magazines.

Spells are still cast, curses are frequently heard, and the mystical protection of charms remain a fundamental part of traditional voodoo enclaves in the South. Just as they did in the old days, voodoo kings and queens see to it that their "favorites" receive all the protection they need from evil spirits, while blasphemous enemies are dealt with accordingly through powerful mumbo-jumbo and an occasional sacrifice.

The word "voodoo" itself has long been enough to conjure up sensational images of naked, writhing bodies dancing wildly around a roaring fire, enraptured by the steady beat of drums and chanting worshippers. Such scenes often depict trance-induced dancers swirling around with increasing frenzy until finally they collapse, moaning and groaning, to the ground. Snakes are usually shown hissing and coiling around attractive young women, while muscular, half-naked men dance and gorge themselves with the bloody entrails of mutilated sacrificial animals.

Practitioners of voodoo insist that such cinematic treatments of their ancient art are not far from the truth. In fact, say some who have observed or participated in the ceremonies, movie-makers would be shocked at just how accurate many of their celluloid portrayals actually are.

Sacrifices—human and otherwise—were not uncommon in

the early days, and whispers of blood-letting ceremonies are still heard in the bayou backcountry of Louisiana and Mississippi. Chickens and roosters are usually the preferred sacrificial animal. Blood smeared on the floor and on the lips of worshippers who sit cross-legged in a circle is seen as one of the secret ingredients needed to unlock the doorway to a variety of mystical powers.

Of all the voodoo queens in New Orleans, none was more feared nor respected than Marie Laveau, a large, mustachioed woman said to have the devil's strength and an angel's charm. Laveau, who reigned as the supreme voodoo queen during the years of the American Civil War, possessed extraordinary powers of conjuration. On St. John's Eve, the most sacred of all spectacular voodoo celebrations, Laveau would retreat to a hidden bayou along Lake Pontchartrain. Crouching before an altar, the mulatress would clutch a serpent and chant:

"L'Appe vinie, li Grand Zombi
L'Appe vinie, pour fe gris-gris!"
("He is coming, the great Zombi
He is coming to make gris-gris!")

Then into the clearing would leap a tall Negro brandishing a small black coffin. At the sight of him the celebrants, gathered around a cauldron seething with witches' brew, would bound into the air, screaming, "Li Grand Zombi! Li Grand Zombi!" At the conclusion of the chant, the contents of the cauldron— live pigeons and chickens torn limb from limb—would be distributed until faces and teeth and hands and bodies were smeared with blood. Then the voodooists would dance and whirl and scream until many fell to the ground unconscious.

Public pressure targeted against such bizarre rituals eventually drove voodoo underground. Voodoo ceremonies, though still common, are today a closely guarded secret. It is hard, though not impossible, for the uninvited to witness a ritual. In New Orleans and other cities in the South where there are large concentrations of blacks, one may buy the same kinds of charms and powders and lotions used in Laveau's day. If you know where to go, there are stores offering Love Powders, Get-Together Drops, Boss-Fix Powder, Easy Life Powder, Come To Me Powder, Devil Oil, Controlling Oil, and Dice Special.

Many educated blacks—and whites—are still careful not to cross anyone said to be possessed with an "evil eye"—a strong indication that person is a sorcerer or enchantress and is likely to be equipped with the skills necessary to cast powerful spells at will. Foremost among those to be feared are the voodoo kings and queens and their representatives.

Today, voodoo rituals take place in private homes, in the middle of dark forests or swamps, on street corners, and even in cemeteries. Followers of the ancient religion believe that by heeding a list of strict rules, they can summon and win the favor of a particular *loa,* or god. Loud, exotic ceremonies are usually required to get the loa's undivided attention, hence the pulsating dancing, singing, and music-making at regular rituals.

However, smaller requests can be made in the privacy of one's own home, simply by purchasing or assembling a charm and by following a list of grisly instructions from the head queen of a region. Even today these queens are both respected and feared for their far-reaching supernatural powers. Such powers enable them to conjure up spirits to punish or reward, depending on the circumstances, and members of a voodoo community see to it that they always remain in good favor with the Head Queen.

Most voodoo practices today are curious blends of Old World rituals and established Christian teachings. Congregations sing Protestant hymns accompanied by clapping hands and stamping feet. Members "fall out" and "talk in the unknown tongue" while church leaders summon the ghosts of departed relatives and heal ailments. Many church leaders do a brisk business in gris-gris on the side.

No discussion of voodoo would be complete without mentioning zombies, dead people called back from the grave by either a priestess or priest called a *houngan.* These nightmarish creatures, whose souls have been stolen by the houngan, are reanimated as mindless robots—zombies—and are required to follow its creator's instructions. Belief in zombies, or the walking dead, is a central feature of voodoo and was the subject of a recent popular movie, *The Serpent and the Rainbow.*

Despite their history of suffering, African-Americans have contributed much to New World culture: backbreaking labor, ingenious skills, and wonderful customs, artistic works, and inventions. But not all these gifts have been sunny and straightforward. Voodoo must be counted among them—one of the more mysterious and macabre strains of the ancient, proud black heritage.

The Surrency Haunting

WAY DOWN IN south Georgia, in a railroad settlement on the edge of the Altamaha River Swamp, people talk about the Surrency ghost as if its reign were only yesterday. But it was more than a century ago, in the late 1870s, that the hotel-home of the Allen Surrency family—the family for whom the town was named—became center stage for one of the most spectacular hauntings in American history. In less than a decade, news of the strange goings-on at the Surrency home had spread all across the country, with thousands of journalists, scientists, and curiosity-seekers pouring in to investigate.

Diaries, books, newspaper and magazine reports, and hundreds of personal accounts vividly describe the unearthly activities that occurred in that old house: tables and chairs flying through the air, mirrors exploding in hallways, clocks running wild, hot bricks raining from the sky, mysterious lights flickering in the dark, and the noises—bloodcurdling noises ranging from sorrowful weeping to sadistic bursts of unexplained laughter.

Only a handful of oldtimers are still around who actually saw the house; fewer still are alive today who witnessed the spooky manifestations before the structure went up in flames early one Sunday morning in 1925. Those who remember speak nostalgically of their town's infamous ghost, pleased at the attention their community once received.

Phillip Dukes, who ran a local grocery store until his death in 1985, did not believe in ghosts. But in an interview with an

Atlanta newspaper right before he died, the elderly Surrency native said he didn't "doubt for a moment" the veracity of accounts handed down to him from his grandmother. "She used to spend the night at the house often, because she was Mrs. Surrency's sister. A lot of times when she put her shoes under her bed at night, she'd wake up next morning and find them out in the hallway. That happened so many times she came to expect it every night. She never figured out what caused it, so she thought it must have been the ghost."

The late Hershel Tillman, a longtime postal carrier for the Surrency district, was also convinced that ghosts were responsible for the haunting. As a boy he visited the Surrency house many times, but it was stories related to him by his father, uncle, and other relatives that convinced him there was more to the Surrency ghost than just talk. "No doubt about it, a ghost was involved," Tillman said. "I wasn't old enough to understand, but the poor people who lived in that house always had trouble going to sleep once the ghost invaded the place."

Nearly every person in town has his or her own tale about the Surrency ghost—tales invariably handed down from grandparents or great-aunts and -uncles who had visited the house in times gone by. Most stories center around the mischievous activities of a poltergeist—a restless spirit that supposedly derives pleasure from wreaking havoc in the lives of its mortal hosts.

According to Rev. Henry Curtiss Tillman, the supernatural forces haunting the Surrency house rarely disappointed visitors. Tillman said his father, the late Eason F. Tillman of the Ten Mile Community near Surrency, often described how plates, cups, and saucers would dance on the table at mealtimes, bedcovers would roll up and down at night, and glowing red lights would hover over the railroad tracks directly in front of the two-story house. "My daddy was one of the most honest men who ever lived," Tillman said. "When he said he saw those things, he really saw them."

Newspapers during the late 1800s and early 1900s were full of disturbing stories about the ghost, many written by journalists who visited the house and witnessed firsthand the sightings they recorded. Appearing in the *Savannah Morning News* on October 28, 1872, was an article purporting to be a "reliable report of the mysterious Surrency phenomenon."

A reporter had arrived at the Surrency home by train late one afternoon, and had just settled down for a smoke and interview with his hosts. As he scribbled notes on a pad, his attention was drawn toward a large, handsome wall clock in the parlor.

> The clock was hanging on the wall in the parlor, and had ever been characterized by the correctness of its time. Suddenly with a weird, buzzing noise the hands began moving around with exceedingly rapid motion, the hour hand exactly five minutes ahead of the minute hand. In this singular position they continued to move for seventeen minutes, in which time it had described five hours and each time as it arrived at the twelve o'clock mark, it would pause and strike, one hour for another, such as twelve for one, etc., and at the end of the five hours ceased its wild movements.

The same writer told of books mysteriously falling off the library shelf, bottles of oil leaping off a table and onto the floor, fire logs rolling repeatedly out of the fireplace, hogs suddenly appearing in the living room, and unearthly screams floating down the lofty old corridors. "The whole thing is clothed in darkness and . . . bears the spirit of the supernatural," the writer concluded.

Eager to rid their home of their unnatural guest, the Surrency family sought the help of scientists, ministers, mediums, and psychics. The hauntings coincided with a wave of interest in psychic phenomena sweeping the country and Europe, and the twenty-year period before the close of the century was the heyday of "spirit investigations," including such celebrated cases as the Fox Sisters' séances. Mediums had become as popular as modern athletes and movie stars, and more than a few "specialists" were brought to Surrency to investigate the ghost.

111

Efforts to drive away the ghost—or ghosts—were unsuccessful, however. If anything, they seemed to make matters worse. Windows suddenly began to shatter at random, doors refused to stay closed—even when locked—and scissors and irons flew across the room. Perhaps the eeriest phenomenon is described in the following article from the *Baxley News Banner*:

> On the day of the ghost's first appearance, Mr. Surrency had gone to Macon to purchase some supplies. A minister who was visiting in the home that night and one of the older sons were sitting in a room when they heard a loud thud on the front porch. The boy got up and went outside to see what was happening, and discovered the noise was caused by bricks falling on the porch, and he also found they were hot.

Another shower of hot bricks descended on the Surrency home later that same night.

In the months and years that followed, similar incidents continued. Relatives and neighbors took turns staying with the Surrencys, partly to lend moral support and undoubtedly in hopes of witnessing the events themselves. An estimated twenty thousand people visited the haunted house during those troubled years, the majority of them given free room and board by the Surrency family.

Tradition has it that a murder was behind the Surrency hauntings. One story tells of a trunk that was found in a bedroom, stuffed with a corpse. Another points to Allen Surrency himself, charging the wealthy landowner and farmer with foul play in the death of a man who once had owned the property on which the house stood. One surviving witness, who wished to remain anonymous, described Surrency as a "sick, sadistic fellow possessed with sorcery-like talents." The witness recounted how Surrency had once supposedly demonstrated his arcane powers by running a broom twig completely through his head without spilling a drop of blood!

Some investigators theorized that the disturbance at the Surrency house could be explained scientifically. An unusually large magnetic field was believed to be located beneath Surrency, possibly triggering physical reactions. A more modern explanation centers around a peculiar geologic formation situated in the earth's crust nine miles below the town limits. Geologists suspect this formation, known locally as the "bright spot," might be an ancient reservoir formed more than 500 million years ago by the collision of the North American and North African continents.

Internal pressures from this subterranean pool of fluid, trapped for millions of years following the awesome collision, conceivably could be responsible for strange physical phenomena, such as the baffling events at Surrency. "It might have something to do with Surrency's ghost," thinks Mayor Stanford Tillman.

For years, until the fire put an end to its controversial existence, the Surrency house stood as a landmark next to the Southern Railway Line that splits the small town. The house served both as home to the Surrency family and as a hotel for overnight train travelers.

In those days, before the turn of the century, Surrency was a bustling little town full of promise. Its position on the railroad line, plus its booming naval stores industry, assured the town of continued growth into the twentieth century. But that was not to be. Baxley, ten miles up the road, soon took the lead, and Surrency's population began rapidly declining. Today, fewer than five hundred people call Surrency home, and the crossroads community is little more than a ghost town.

In the beginning, the Surrency family was terrified by the ghost occupying their home. On many nights it was impossible to sleep in certain bedrooms because the beds would "hop up and down like rabbits," covers would fly off the bed and dangle in the air, and articles of clothing would mysteriously disappear, only to be found weeks later at the same spot where they went missing.

Gradually, however, family members grew accustomed to the eerie antics of their visitors from beyond. But when they moved to another house not far away, the ghost went along.

Hershel Tillman, who watched the old house go up in

flames early one Sunday morning in 1925, said: "That thing haunted Old Man Surrency until the day he died. But when he was buried, the haunting stopped."

And what became of the ghost?

In an interview with the *Atlanta Journal* in 1929, Hampton W. Surrency, brother of Allen, said its own popularity probably contributed to the phenomenon's demise.

It is a mystery. We might almost say that it was killed by too much popularity. People came from everywhere to see it. The railroad advertised its presence and ran special trains at tourist rates to bring visitors to Surrency. The village was small, and hotel accommodations were not sufficient to care for such large crowds. My brother realized the danger, and knew that it would ruin him, as he was a very hospitable man who made every effort to assure comfort to the multitudes who came.

So he decided to move to another farm he owned six miles out in the county. . . . The ghost was never again seen at the big house. It appeared to have vanished as suddenly and mysteriously as it had come.

Fin, Fang,
And Fantasy

The Sea-Maiden of the Biloxi

ENCOUNTERS WITH STRANGE sea creatures were nothing new to Robert Froster, a thirty-five-year-old professional scuba diver from Australia. Over the years the Aussie had tangled with sea snakes, sharks, poisonous eels, barracuda, and even a giant manta ray. Still, none of his adventures had prepared him for what came charging at him through the clear blue waters of the South Atlantic one afternoon in 1988. Although he survived without a scratch, the ordeal has left him with emotional scars and a deep fear of the sea. Since the incident he refuses to go back into the water.

It all began with a request from a friend to help explore and photograph some strange rock formations several miles off the coast of Florida. Froster had probed the shallow continental shelf there several times before, because he too believed that the mysterious undersea formations might be the ruins of an ancient city—perhaps even Atlantis.

On this particular afternoon, however, Froster was diving alone. He knew he was violating the most sacred rule in his dangerous business—always dive with a buddy—but when his companion had been unable to accompany him on the trip, he decided to go it alone. It was a decision that nearly cost him his sanity—and his life.

Everything had been going fine until he noticed a disturbance in the water behind him. When he turned to look, he saw a vague, shadowy figure slashing toward him. All around him the water had begun to churn wildly, and clouds of

116

sediment were swirling.

He knew it wasn't a shark; the creature was too lean, too lithe. As it rushed toward him, it appeared to undulate, rather than glide directly like a fish. When the fast-moving form got within twenty yards of him, he noticed something else odd about it. Appendages, like arms, seemed to be reaching out toward him, and at the end of each arm appeared to be sharply taloned hands.

Seconds later the creature came into full view. That's when Froster saw the unmistakable pair of breasts, long flowing hair, smooth skin, and scaled tail from the waist down. Froster nearly dropped his mouthpiece.

"The thing came straight at me," he told a Florida newspaper. "It was a mermaid, all right—half woman and half fish, with female breasts and upper torso and a fish-like tail below. That creature had one thing on its mind—to kill me because I had seen it. I've never seen such evil hate in the eyes of any human or animal before."

Before the apparition could reach him, however, Froster shot up toward the surface. Several times before he reached the boat, he thought he felt the curl of cruel talons on his flippers and ankle. Fortunately, he was able to scamper over the side of his craft to safety. He never saw the creature again.

"But it's still down there, I suppose, guarding the secrets of that ancient city," theorized a bewildered Froster.

Froster's amazing confrontation with what he believes was a mermaid resembles other encounters reported by sailors, divers, and swimmers down through the years. Legends about mermaids, or mermen, exist in nearly every country and culture in the world, from landlocked desert kingdoms to communities along inland rivers as well as on the coast.

In most tales, they appear as beautiful young men or women whose haunting melodies, when heard ringing out over the waves of lonely rivers or the ocean, are usually interpreted as a sign that danger or death is at hand for listeners. They are rarely friendly to humans, except when trying to lure them to their doom.

The fact that no flesh-and-blood mermaid or merman has

been captured or washed ashore on some uncrowded beach does not diminish the possibility of their existence, at least in the eyes of believers. However, scientists who have studied the phenomenon have offered some plausible explanations, ranging from manatees and sea-cows to seals and floating pieces of driftwood. Seen lolling near the surface or flippering along through the waves, these sea creatures and objects often bear an uncanny resemblance to human forms.

One of the most famous descriptions of a mermaid in southern waters was provided in 1614 by Captain John Smith. Upon spotting the strange creature, Smith said the "upper part of her body perfectly resembled that of a woman, and she was swimming about with all possible grace near the shore." His meticulous observation continues: the sea-beast had "large eyes, rather too round, a finely shaped nose (a little too short), well-formed ears, rather too long, and her long green hair imparted to her an original character by no means unattractive."

Like sea serpents, the legendary mermaid, whose enchanting beauty and powers of seduction most certainly have kept her in our favor down through the ages, figures prominently in our literary and artistic record. Plays, poems, books, movies, and other significant works of art have been spawned by our fascination with this mythological wonder-beast. Once exposed to its mystical lure, one cannot escape seduction, whether far out at sea or landlocked in a library or movie theater.

In Louisiana, legend has it that an entire Indian tribe—the Biloxi, also known as the Pascagoula—marched into a raging river at the command of a mermaid-like sea-goddess and drowned. True or not, the fact is that the Biloxi Indians did suddenly and inexplicably vanish during the early sixteenth century, only weeks after a white, bearded priest had appeared to them with a crucifix in hand demanding that they abandon their superstitious belief in an underwater goddess.

The Biloxi lived on the banks of the River Pascagoula between New Orleans and Biloxi, Mississippi, and worshipped a beautiful mermaid deity, whose statue was housed in a handsome temple. On moonlit nights they held rituals at river's edge while listening to the sweet stirrings of the mermaid's music. The music was said to be so sweet that brave warriors would weep under its spell. Sometimes the men would dance adoringly around the goddess's sacred idol while womenfolk played strange instruments to accompany her bewitching sound.

But sometime in the year 1539 a Catholic missionary came to dwell among them and attempted to turn them against their pagan ways. Apparently the priest had some success, because eventually the peace-loving Biloxi tore down their temple and threw their idols into the river.

Not long afterwards, according to tradition, the river-goddess rose from the boiling depths and, amid a towering column of waves and the sound of rushing water, commanded her people to join her in paradise.

"Come to me, come to me, children of the sea,
Neither bell, book, nor cross shall win ye from your Queen."

Unable to resist her siren call, the Indians went into a frenzy. Around the flickering flames of a ceremonial bonfire, they danced and drank and shouted out their ancient goddess's name. Then, one by one, they plunged into the murky river and perished. The next morning, there was not a single man, woman, or child left in the land of the Biloxi.

Even today the Pascagoula is known as the Singing River, because according to a newspaper writer's account, on warm, summer nights "people hear a low humming coming from the river," as if hundreds of voices were chanting in unison below its waters.

The legendary mass suicide of the Biloxi tribe has intrigued historians and archaeologists for years. There is some evidence suggesting such a mass extinction, but a few scholars theorize the action came not from the mythological summons of a water demon but at the hands of a more powerful tribe, perhaps the Choctaw. Romantic versions of the story insist,

119

however, that it was the haunting lyrics of a mermaid that drove the Indians to their watery deaths.

Some experts who accept the mass-suicide theory have linked the tragic episode with that of another, equally baffling case involving a group of African slaves freshly arrived in Georgia. Although no mermaid was involved, the story of the Ibo tribe's mysterious fate on St. Simons Island is equally fascinating.

According to a tale circulated among black Seminole Indians in Florida, the West Africans had been en route to Charleston when they made a stopover at St. Simons, a sizable coastal island near Brunswick. While there, the shackled slaves somehow learned of the fate awaiting them at the hands of white plantation owners in South Carolina. In slavery, they would no longer exist as human beings. Families would be split up, perhaps never to see one another again.

A great sadness prevailed over the hundred or so Africans that night as they pondered their uncertain future aboard the cramped, disease-ridden vessel. Finally, a tall chieftain stood up and announced he had a plan. Rather than submit to a life of bondage, the proud Ibo tribesmen should take their own lives.

The chief's radical proposition was not immediately well-received among the Africans. When the chief assured his subjects, however, that happiness and freedom awaited them in "the world beyond time," the tribe decided death was better than slavery, especially if they were all going to be together with their loved ones in paradise.

So beneath a pale, full moon they marched, the entire group, their chains clanking and clattering in the muted southern night, and the echoes of their soft chanting ringing through the gloomy oak forest along Dunbar Creek. One by one they shuffled into the swirling depths of the creek, and one by one their black, naked bodies vanished beneath the waves.

Nowadays condominiums and a waste treatment plant are located along the creek where the Africans are said to have drowned. But on still summer nights, when the moon is shining bright over Dunbar Creek, islanders claim they can still hear the rumble of low chanting and the grind of metal chains echoing beneath the waters.

Behold the Fanged Serpent

NATIVE AMERICANS PROBABLY invented tall tales about giant rattlesnakes to enhance their own religious experience. Over time, these myths became part of the their belief system. Winged serpents and hissing water demons existed at the top—and bottom—of early American religious pantheons, and in between was their symbolic, though very earthly agent, the fanged rattlesnake.

The first Europeans to arrive in the New World heard terrifying tales about these strange creatures. Rattlesnakes the size of trees were said to lurk in the southern swamplands. Reports of snakes large enough to swallow a man whole were not uncommon.

Such exaggerated accounts were in all probability spawned by local Indians who resented the encroachment onto their lands by these pale-skinned strangers. The stories were intended to frighten gullible explorers, traders, and settlers hacking their uninvited way through the wilderness. Their impact upon our ancestors cannot be measured, of course. But for anyone huddled around a smoldering campfire in the wilderness or the flickering embers inside a lonely log cabin, the tales must have been effective.

Gradually, the mythological rattlesnake became ingrained in our folk tradition. As more and more settlers poured into the virgin wilderness, tall tales about rattlesnakes began to get even taller. Each harrowing encounter seemed to become even more harrowing with embellished treatment. Overblown accounts eventually reached all the way back to the relatively civilized coastal regions, and from there even to the courts of England.

For example, the story is often told of the unfortunate homesteaders in Kentucky who happened to build their cabin on top of a snake den. Soon after settling in, the pioneers built a glorious fire and began celebrating their new way of life with a housewarming. But that night, as the story goes, thousands of warmed-up rattlesnakes issued forth from the ground and caused what must have been no little consternation in the occupants.

Such incidents could have really happened. Rattlesnakes do occasionally den up in large numbers, and it is just possible that cabins and houses could have unknowingly been erected on top of an underground nest. However, the "cabin over the den" legend probably began when a couple of rattlesnakes slithered innocently through some cracks into a house, understandably startling the owners.

By the late 1700s it had become almost impossible to separate myth from reality. Snake lore seemed to grow as fast as the young territory, and no region of the South lacked bone-chilling tales about monstrous aggressive rattlesnakes. Size figured most predominantly in these stories.

In 1714, for example, several rattlers were killed that were longer than 17 feet.

In 1750, a rattler killed in Virginia was said to have stretched to 18 feet.

In 1753 a group of traders killed a rattler that measured 22 feet—minus the head and rattles. The snake had reportedly attacked without provocation before it was killed with several musket balls and a well-thrown hatchet.

In Mississippi, a man swore he was chased by a 16½-foot-long rattler that he had mistaken for a dead tree. In 1872, a Georgia farmer couldn't believe his eyes when he saw a snake, which he thought to be a rattler, stretched across the two-lane road—a distance of about 15 feet.

The mangled carcass of a giant rattlesnake struck by a train in Washington County, Alabama, reportedly had 53 rattles and measured 13 inches across the middle of its body. The *Dallas Weekly Herald* of July 28, 1877, reported that an 18-foot-long rattlesnake had been killed in the Cherokee Nation, near Eufaula. "Thirty-seven distinct rattles" were on its tail.

More recently, the *Texas Game and Fish* magazine ran a story in October 1954 about a "giant rattlesnake" that measured just over 11 feet long "without its head and rattles."

Even today, newspapers and magazines occasionally carry articles about huge rattlesnakes that have either been spotted or killed—usually in a garden behind the house or crossing a highway. These stories may be accompanied by a black-and-white photograph of a portly farmer or hunter holding the dead snake up by the tail for all the world to scrutinize. Rarely, however, do we find the outlandish, diabolical dimensions reported by our ancestors!

Why? What happened to the giant serpents of old? If you ask a herpetologist, the answer is usually simple: stories about rattlesnakes longer than eight or nine feet are just that—stories. Some time in the past, for reasons already discussed, it probably became fashionable to "exaggerate" the size of snakes, especially rattlesnakes. After all, it's only human nature to stretch the truth—as well as the snake hide—a wee bit every now and then. Cowboys bored from a day out on the range, or explorers weary from their travels through wilderness, were certainly not above spinning a good yarn whenever the situation called for it—such as when a tenderfoot happened to be bunking down nearby. A three-foot rattler that slithered inside a sleeping bag might somehow become a ten-foot killer; a coiled serpent at the back corner of a barn might turn into a forked-tongue monster packing fifty rattles and a button.

Such embellishment was usually harmless, of course, perhaps even therapeutic in a rough-and-tumble sort of way, but over the years reality became fuzzy.

The size and aggressiveness of rattlers were only a part of the snake lore rapidly seeping into frontier consciousness. Yarns about other snakes, even harmless varieties, began to flourish around rural country stores and barbershops.

The hoop snake of the southern United States, for example, is alleged to have attacked unwary travelers by "rolling" into them and pricking them with its tail. It supposedly accomplished this miraculous feat by scooping up its tail in its mouth and twirling along like a hoop after its intended victim. Within striking distance, it released its tail and hurled its body—tail first—inflicting a deadly sting with the tip.

Another much-maligned creature was the coachwhip snake, said to have been another vicious attacker in Southern folklore. This speedy snake was supposedly faster than a horse, and once it caught its victim would stick its head inside his mouth so he couldn't scream, then proceed to "whip" the hapless individual to death with its tail. The mature coachwhip snake, which can grow to five feet and more, apparently earned its name because its streamlined body resembles a slender, braided whip.

Along the marshy streams and ponds of the Southeast lives the much-feared cottonmouth moccasin, so named because, when frightened or agitated, its "cotton-white" mouth opens wide to reveal a set of glistening, deadly fangs. Although cottonmouths do not grow very long—three to four feet is the average length—they often exhibit aggressive behavior, and will attack even if unprovoked. Many are the woeful stories about careless victims wandering into the squirming coils of these creatures, hanging from tree limbs and bushes in the swamps. Fishermen wading along riverbanks are particularly careful not to disturb these easily annoyed snakes, whose bite can kill or cripple.

No account of snake lore in the South would be complete without mentioning the legendary black racer, rumored to be the fastest snake in the world. Every boy who grew up on a farm has his own story about these long, lithe serpents that prey on mice and birds around barns and old houses. Also known as black snakes, these swift reptiles are said to be able to keep up with a car going thirty-five miles per hour! Ironically, the black snake is one of the rattlesnake's closest companions. During hibernation, it's common to find dozens of these non-venomous reptiles coiled up inside a den alongside their more dangerous cousins.

It is easy to understand the human fascination with snakes. They are creatures both lovely and loathsome; the sight of them can strike terror in the hearts of many of us, while others regard them as a blessing in our rodent-plagued ecosystem. We like to talk about snakes. At any zoo, the snake department is always the most popular. Yet ask any one of us to touch a snake—that is, actually reach inside a cage and pet one, even a harmless grass snake—and watch the reaction. Invariably it is one of repulsion, revulsion, and unrelenting fear.

Too, we are intrigued by the unique physics of their earth-bound form—flickering tongues, glassy eyes, sinuous coils, venom-dripping fangs. At the same time, we see them as the essence of evil, possessed with mystical powers that go beyond mere rat-catching dynamics. After all, didn't Satan tempt Eve while in the guise of a serpent in the Garden of Eden?

But snakes—especially rattlesnakes—seem to trigger within us all some deep, emotional antipathy—a chilling response that harks back perhaps to a time long ago when our barefoot ancestors shared the earth with these great lords of the forest floor.

The Shadow of the Beast

ON THE NIGHT of June 10, 1988, seventeen-year-old Christopher Davis was driving through Scape Ore Swamp, a dismal bog near Bishopville, South Carolina. It was late and the boy was tired, having moments before driven his date home. He was heading east along the narrow road when he heard a pop, then felt the car lurch out of control to the right.

A flat, he groaned, dreading the thought of having to stop in the middle of the swamp to change the tire. Not that he was afraid; he knew these woods like the back of his hand. He and his buddies had fished and hunted these parts since he was a kid.

But as he pulled his car off the edge of the road, he did feel suddenly alone. And afraid. It was way past midnight, with not another car in sight. The moon was high, but dark, gloomy shadows pressed in from the deep woods, scattered every few yards by moonbeams. Stepping outside the car that night was like stepping into another world—an uninviting world of shifting shadows.

Then Davis realized how quiet it was. There was no sound, not even the chirp of a cricket or the croak of a bullfrog. That's odd, he thought, popping the trunk open and hauling out the spare tire and jack. Usually this time of night the swamp was jamming with all kinds of grunting and groaning. Why was everything so quiet?

He didn't like it.

To calm his nerves he started whistling. It was a hot, humid night, typical for that time of year, but a pleasant breeze stirred through the moss-draped oaks and pines. He pulled off his shirt and slung it inside the car.

Dead, he thought. Maybe everything in the swamp was dead. Maybe some toxic nerve gas or other chemical junk had been dumped into the swamp and all the animals had belly-upped beneath the lily pads.

It was only a joke. But somehow he didn't feel like laughing.

He worked quickly, first removing the flat tire, then replacing it with the spare. At the back of his mind was a wish—that he could see the headlights of another car approaching up the highway. That would be a welcome sight. He vowed never to complain about traffic again.

The tire changed, young Davis wiped his hands and looked around before stepping back into the car. That's when he heard the noise off in the woods. A shuffling sound, like that of a large animal dragging itself slowly toward him through the bushes. He was reminded of the sound skin divers make when they try to walk on dry land with flippers.

Swish! swish! swish!

Without a flashlight it was impossible to see what was making the noise. Not that he really wanted to. But something had come over the boy, and he found himself unable to move. Large drops of sweat broke out on his forehead and the palms of his hands felt like jelly. He stood there for several more seconds, glued to the spot, listening to the swishing sound advance steadily closer. His heart was pounding inside his chest like a jackhammer. Sweat poured down his face.

Then he saw the creature. It stood less than ten feet away from him, a tall, slimy hulk that looked like some kind of weird cross between a man and an ape. In the pale light of the moon, Davis estimated the thing stood at least seven feet tall and appeared greenish-black.

For several seconds boy and beast stood on the lonely highway at the edge of Scape Ore Swamp staring at each other. The boy was the first to move. He moved fast, leaping into the car and slamming the door shut behind him. Mercifully, the car's engine roared to life. As it did, the creature sprang.

"It was strong and it wasn't an animal and it wasn't no man," Davis later told Sheriff Liston Truesdale.

The lizard-like monster first grabbed the door, then started banging on the roof. Frantically, Davis put the car in gear and accelerated, the creature hanging onto the hood. Davis had to swerve several times along the road before the creature finally lost its grip and tumbled off the car into the dark. To the young man's horror, however, the thing managed to keep pace with him at about thirty-five miles per hour.

Davis's ordeal was the first known encounter with South Carolina's now-famous "Lizard Man." It was not to be the last. In the days and weeks that followed, dozens of other people reported seeing a large, reptile-like animal loping through the rugged woods and fields of rural Lee County, South Carolina. Most of the sightings occurred in or near Scape Ore Swamp, a particularly gloomy region which got its strange name in Revolutionary War days. According to one legend, the name was shortened from Escaped Whore Swamp, so called because a group of British soldiers had escaped from an American ambush there.

Most descriptions of the monster matched Davis's, down to the "red eyes, lizard-like skin, and greenish-black color." One farmer near Brownville said something resembling the creature broke into his hog pen and "caused all kind of ruckus" before he chased it away with a shotgun blast. The thing he saw had a long, thick tail which it used to help climb over a fence and escape. There were bloodstains all over his hog pen the next day.

The "Lizard Man" of Brownville, as the creature soon came to be known, spread terror throughout this rural region as more sightings were reported. Sheriff's deputies were pressed into round-the-clock action as alarmed citizens began stocking up on guns and ammunition. Investigators combed the county for clues, escorted by volunteer hunters armed with high-powered weapons.

Before long, the entire country knew about the monster. Network television crews swarmed into town, along with reporters for national newspapers, magazines, and wire services. Everybody from Seattle to Seneca wanted to know more about the monster said to be haunting the lonely Lee County countryside.

But what was it? Nobody seemed to know. There were theories, of course, many of them wilder than descriptions provided by eyewitnesses. Explanations ranged from the plausible to the fanciful. Some said it was a bear. Others insisted the thing had to be an escaped gorilla. A few thought it was a hoax—maybe a man, decked out in a weird outfit, going around scaring people for kicks. At least one investigator claimed the monster was another Bigfoot, the legendary ape-man said to roam the higher elevations of the Pacific Northwest. The description did match those of recent "Bigfoot" sightings in other southern states, notably Florida, Georgia, Louisiana, North Carolina, and Alabama.

One of the most incredible accounts came from Florida in the mid-1970s when a deputy sheriff by the name of Joe Simboli reported an encounter with a seven-foot-tall hair-covered creature just north of the Everglades. One year later, a "large, hairy animal" reportedly killed and ripped apart a horse and beheaded a calf on the farm of Debbie and Michael Polenek in central Florida. An investigation revealed that tracks around the slaughtered animals resembled those of Bigfoot, or Sasquatch, the name given by the Indians to the creature.

Stories about fantastic creatures roaming the backwoods of North America are nothing new. Early pioneers pressing into the wilderness from the East Coast told of hair-raising encounters with giant bears, bear-men, wolf-men, and similar creatures. One of the most widespread legends, which probably had its origins in Indian mythology, centered on the "Wampus Cat," an impossibly hideous critter said to have the head of a man, the body of a wildcat—only larger—and the soul of a demon.

Like Bigfoot, the Wampus Cat was said to lurk among the gloomy river bottoms of the South and to take fiendish delight in preying upon hunters, fishermen, and others who strayed too far off the beaten path. Whereas Wampus Cat stories eventually petered out around the turn of the century, however, tales of harrowing run-ins with Bigfoot creatures continue to this very day.

Along the Mississippi River, and all across the arc of the Gulf Coast, numerous legends still exist about another dangerous creature, one the Cajuns call "Loup-garou." Half-man and half-beast, these hairy bipeds—which bear a remarkable resemblance to the Wampus Cat—are thought to be responsible for kidnapping children and livestock. In all, more than thirteen states, many of them southern, have reported sightings of incredible beasts such as Bigfoot, Loup-garou, or the Lizard Man.

As soon as stories about Lee County's own "Bigfoot" made the network news, it was only a matter of hours before curiosity-seekers swarmed into town. Along with the visitors came more sightings of the creature, which soon started being officially billed as the "Lizard Man" because of its reptilian characteristics.

A few days after Davis's initial sighting, another Lee County citizen reported shooting something that resembled the boy's description. The fellow even offered the local sheriff some scales and blood for proof. That proof, however, resulted in the shooter's receiving a citation. A crime lab analysis revealed the scales and blood apparently came from a dead fish.

Another couple camped near the swamp blamed the critter for battering their car and pulling wires out of the engine. That same day, a carload of visitors from Charleston claimed to have spotted a "large, ugly, gorilla-like thing" scurrying across a field about six miles from Bishopville.

In spite of the testimony from several respected eyewitnesses, local authorities continued to dismiss the Lizard Man as a hoax. Wildlife biologists called in to study a set of plaster casts made of the creature's footprints determined that at least some of the tracks were man-made. Those results, plus additional laboratory findings on what was said to be the creature's hair, worked to quiet the "lizardmania" that had swept through this small farming community of 3,500 people. Law enforcement officers, weary from answering calls at all hours of the night from frantic citizens claiming to have spotted the creature, were relieved when things settled down a few months later.

But late at night, when the moon is high and a curious kind of silence stalks the clammy darkness, folks around these parts have become accustomed to thinking twice before getting in the car and driving through Scape Ore Swamp.

"Thou Shalt Take Up the Serpent!"

THE RITUAL BEGINS with a medley of old-timey preaching and gospel singing, followed by prayer and a round of frantic hand-clapping. Then, as the preacher walks down the aisle, sweat dripping profusely from his furrowed brow, chanting men and women in the packed congregation begin to sway.

With eyes closed and teeth clenched, the minister reaches inside a wicker basket and slowly withdraws a large rattle-snake. The audience gasps, responding in a raw chorus of "Hallelujah!"

The chanting subsides as the preacher, a stocky man in his late fifties, reaches into another box and pulls out a tangle of dark, hissing coils. Draping the venomous reptiles across his shoulders, he closes his eyes and lifts his head heavenward.

"Thou shalt take up the serpent, and neither fire nor harm shall come to thee." The sound of his voice bellows above the weeping crowd.

At that point a hysterical shudder sweeps through the rows of mostly middle-aged and elderly men and women, and eager hands reach out to fondle the poisonous swirl of rattlesnakes, cottonmouths, and copperheads clutched between the preacher's outstretched arms. In the front row, a woman dressed in a flower-print dress leaps from the pew and begins jerking violently, her slender arms twitching around in circles.

As if on cue, other members of the congregation follow suit, and above the impassioned strains of "Praise Jesus!" and "Amen!" they start speaking in tongues—high-pitched, rapid-

133

fire bursts of incoherent exclamations. Cymbals clash, tambourines jangle, and a foot-stomping choir commences with a resounding rendition of "Nearer My God to Thee."

For the fifty or so members of Dolley Pond Church of God With Signs Following, it's just another Sunday night in Grasshopper Valley, Tennessee. The hour-long service will end with more shouting and the usual healing ceremony as backaches disappear and unneeded wooden crutches are cast aside. By the time the last stanza of "Just As I Am" is sung, the hysteria will have passed, and the dangerous snakes will return to their baskets and boxes to await the next meeting.

The Right Reverend George Went Hensley knows it's been a good night, and he smiles as the congregationists file past, offering spirited handshakes and hugs. As the church's controversial founder and spiritual leader of the southern snake-handling cult, Hensley has come a long way. In spite of jail cells, threats, fasts, and hundreds of snakebites, Hensley has catapulted his unique brand of evangelism into the nation's limelight.

On this particular night—January 14, 1945—Hensley is undoubtedly the most talked-about evangelist in the southern foothills of Tennessee. From his tiny church here in Grasshopper Valley, the minister has spread the word far and wide, claiming converts from as far away as Florida and the Midwest.

It had all happened so fast—almost like a dream, he would later recall. And Hensley—the Right Reverend George Went Hensley, as he insisted on being called—never missed an opportunity to talk about that dream.

The vision had come to him on a lonely mountaintop in east Tennessee one hot summer day in 1906. For years, young Hensley had been puzzled by certain scriptures in the Bible. Particularly troublesome was a passage in the Book of Mark, verses 17 and 18, which read, "And these signs shall follow them that believe: In my name shall they cast out devils; they shall speak with new tongues; they shall take up serpents; and if they drink any deadly thing it shall not hurt them; and they shall lay hands on the sick, and they shall recover."

Jesus had spoken these words shortly after the Resurrection and before the Ascension. As Hensley pondered their meaning, a vague idea for putting his faith to the test began to take shape in his mind. Suddenly, pieces of the eternal puzzle of life and death came together. All it involved was a literal interpretation of the scripture as written by St. Mark. In a blinding flash of inspiration, he walked across the mountain until he found a rattlesnake sunning on a rocky ledge. Trembling, but resolute in his determination to stare Satan down, he picked up the snake.

Convinced it was his faith that protected him, Hensley marched down the mountain with his rattler. His first stop was at a local evangelical prayer meeting where he feverishly related his revelation to friends and neighbors. At first the group was skeptical, less than inclined to allow a dangerous serpent into their church, let alone handle the thing.

After repeated demonstrations, however, and readings from St. Mark, a few bold members reached out and touched the viper. Instant jubilation exploded in the aisles as the hardscrabble assembly of dirt farmers, factory workers, and mill hands realized that God's power stood between them and the serpent's deadly fangs. A new American religion was born.

In the years that followed, hundreds of rural churchgoers converted to Hensley's bizarre form of worship. Snake-handling soon became a common practice at small churches, private homes, and wooded gatherings throughout backwoods regions of the Bible Belt. In his book *They Shall Take Up Serpents,* Weston La Barre describes such a meeting, based on a newspaper story filed by the *St. Louis Post-Dispatch:*

> The snake-handling lasted about half an hour, but the service went on for an hour or more. To the singing of such songs as "Jesus Is Getting Us Ready for the Great Day," several female communicants, eyes shut, hands waving, . . . moved their feet in a rhythmic step and wheeled slowly in backward circles. Frequently their bodies would jerk as if the spine were being snapped like a whip.

Some of the men also performed this jerk. Fire-handling by male saints was also performed; their hands, held in the flames of a kerosene torch and a miner's acetylene lamp, were blackened by smoke but otherwise appeared unhurt.

The rattlesnake cult was still largely unnoticed by the outside world. Michael Jenkinson, who investigated the snake-handlers in his book, *Beasts Beyond the Fire,* attributes this fact to the worshippers' relative isolation, rather than to some deliberate desire for secrecy.

By the 1930s, the use of rattlesnakes in church services had spread into several neighboring states. Virginia, West Virginia, Kentucky, the Carolinas, Georgia, Alabama, and Florida all reported snake-handling activities, usually in remote pockets away from the ridicule of bigger churches and the long arm of the law. Most people who attended these services were deeply religious and undoubtedly sincere in pressing their faith to the prescribed limits. However, the congregations must have included at least a few skeptics, curiosity-seekers, and even detractors.

In the early 1970s, the sheriff of Berrien County, Georgia, told a local newspaper that the cult had a "wide number of followers" in his territory as well as in nearby counties. Sheriff Walter Gaskins recalled an instance in the mid-1960s when a local pastor had been tried for murder after a snake bit a worshipper. The sheriff grimly told of other instances where "ignorant people" had been fatally struck while handling snakes at rituals.

In 1985 the pastor of a church in Cartersville, Georgia, died from the bite of a snake he had stroked during services. The pastor had refused medical treatment, believing until the end that the power of the Almighty would intervene and protect him from death. At his funeral, mourning members of the congregation explained that "God's will has been done."

The Cartersville pastor's death was only the latest in a long string of deaths and near-deaths linked to snake-handling. At least fifty persons had died either of snakebite or from drinking "salvation cocktails"—liquid laced with venom or strychnine, kept on hand in some churches in case a member felt compelled to make a particularly powerful statement about his or her faith. It is not known how many other deaths and injuries have gone unreported.

Some leaders will apparently go to any length to prove their belief in the power. When a young congregationist named Lewis Ford was fatally bitten by a rattlesnake at the Dolley Pond Church, the story was picked up by wire services and broadcast across the country. The pastor of the church, Tom Harden, saw in the tragedy a chance to advance his cult's cause. Jenkinson wrote,

> Now that his [Harden's] church was in the public eye, he saw an opportunity for gaining converts within the city limits of Chattanooga, which to the pious hill people was a fortress filled with all kinds of wickedness. Harden, accompanied by cult founder Hensley, set up a tent with an oil drum altar. Word got around. A curious crowd gathered and traffic was blocked. Harden and Hensley, to their delight, were taken to the city lockup. They likened their persecution to that suffered by the Biblical prophets.

While church members and other followers waited outside the jail to pray for their leaders, Harden and Hensley led inmates and jailers in singing spirituals aimed at driving out demons. The two men refused to pay a fine, insisting they had been called on to do God's work; their defiance won them a three-day stint on the local chain-gang pounding rocks.

Many snake cultists at that time viewed their leaders' release as "divine intervention," but the Tennessee legislature thought otherwise. A bill was soon approved outlawing the handling of venomous snakes during worship services. Other states soon followed suit.

Predictably, the new law did little to curb the illegal practice, which continued to flourish in out-of-the-way communities and hamlets from Arkansas to Kentucky. Authorities seemed caught between a rock and a hard place. On one hand, they were compelled by the court to arrest violators of the law; on the other, they were reluctant to impose restrictions on worship services, even though people continued to die from the fangs of serpents.

Today, the controversial rattlesnake cult of the Holiness Church and other denominational offsprings continues to thrive amid backwater draws of the Deep South, Midwest, and remote mountain regions of southern Appalachia. Despite dozens of snakebite deaths and crackdowns by the law, this strange religious practice appears to be a favorite among some fundamentalist churches whose communicants believe the Holy Spirit confers supernatural gifts, such as the ability to speak in tongues and to heal by prayer, the laying on of hands, and anointing with oil. The exact number of snake-handlers is not known, since records are rarely kept. But some mainstream clergymen estimate that "thousands" of people risk life, limb, and persecution by law for the privilege of handling dangerous serpents at meetings.

Many states still provide snake handlers with a vague form of protection from legal interference. An amendment in Georgia's state constitution is typical of these go-easy laws: "No citizen shall be molested in person or property . . . on account of his religious opinions. . . . All men have the natural and inalienable right to worship God . . . according to the dictates of his [sic] own conscience and no human authority should in any case control or interfere with such rights."

There is no specific reference to snake worship in the United States Constitution, and many attorneys feel the law is so nebulous that a court would have a difficult time making cult services cease.

Mainstream clergymen generally show little tolerance toward snake-handlers, although opinions are mixed about where to draw the legal line. Most view the dangerous ritual as a "gross misinterpretation" of St. Mark's scripture. "They [the cultists] have taken literal words and fashioned their own meaning from them," is how one Methodist minister in Georgia put it.

But another pastor in Alabama said, "God didn't intend for such sensationalism and foolishness to come into the churches. . . . Handling snakes and drinking venom to express one's faith in Christ is ridiculous."

One is tempted to wonder whether snakes used during services have been "doctored" to render them incapable of striking. Studies provided by churchgoers and outside witnesses show that these reptiles are not drugged, de-fanged, or gassed to make them less dangerous. Nor are the snakes "trained" not to bite, as are some poisonous serpents in circus sideshows. The many bites suffered by worshippers over the years seem proof enough to dispel any lingering doubts about the danger of the snakes. Fatalities continue to occur, even among the most experienced leaders.

In 1951, Ruth Craig, a veteran handler, held a small service at her home in New Hope, Alabama. Midway through the meeting, she pulled a writhing rattlesnake out of a glass jar and proclaimed, "I'm going to handle the snake and anyone who doesn't believe had better leave." Minutes later the horrified crowd watched the large snake bite their leader four times in rapid succession on the arms and shoulder. She collapsed into a coma and died the next day.

Three years later, Reece Ramsey of Rising Fawn, Georgia, was struck on the side of the head by a large diamondback he was holding at an open-air service. The elderly cultist smiled when offered to be taken to a doctor, but refused, confident that the Lord's healing power would soon cleanse away the devil's venom now coursing through his veins. Ramsey strolled toward the preacher, staggered, then fell down in front of the altar. While the congregation sang "I'm Getting Ready to Leave This World," the old man died in the arms of the preacher.

In 1965, fifty-nine years after founding his controversial religion, George Went Hensley was the guest speaker at a small, open-air service in Altha, Florida. At seventy-seven, the preacher and prophet still moved easily before the packed crowd of wide-eyed visitors, casually fondling a small diamondback rattler draped across his forearm. He was happy to be there, he told the clapping congregation in his trademark baritone voice, happy to be among God's children and the devil's own tempters—a reference to the hissing mass of rattlesnakes writhing around inside glass cages near the altar.

About fifteen minutes later, just as he went to put the snake away, it reached up and struck him on the wrist. It was only a sting, and Hensley proudly waved the wounded arm around for the crowd to see.

"Nothing to worry about," he assured the crowd. "It's just Old Satan knocking on the Lord's heavenly door." The evangelist reminded the audience that snakebites were nothing new to him. Over the past four decades, he said he had been bitten at least four hundred times. God would bless this bite too, and the evil fluid would be sucked out by an angel's kiss.

He could already feel the angel's heavenly breath brushing against his skin as he put the snake back into its cage and closed the door.

A few minutes later Hensley's skin turned purple and began to swell. Excruciating pain racked his body and he found it hard to breathe. He lost his balance, stumbling to his knees, trying unsuccessfully to smile.

Silence descended like a pall over the small audience as they watched their leader struggle to regain his composure. Finally, a couple of men on the front row rushed to his aid.

But it was too late. The snake had struck hard, burying its inch-long fangs into the preacher's veins and squeezing out a full load of venom. Now that pool of "evil fluid" was sweeping through his paralyzed body toward his heart.

The next morning George Went Hensley, "God's own anointed disciple of serpents," went into shock and died.

Monsters of the Deep

IN THE SUMMER of 1962, Edward McCleary and three companions from Miami were skin-diving off the coast of Florida when they noticed a disturbance in the water behind them. Because of a fog rolling in from the open ocean, the men—all experienced divers—were unable to make out the long, shadowy form slithering through the dark waves toward them.

When they finally saw the beast approaching, it was too late. The creature struck swiftly, devouring one of McCleary's companions in a single gulp, then dragging the other two kicking and screaming to their deaths below the surface. McCleary survived the ordeal by scampering into the group's anchored cabin cruiser. For several minutes he watched in horror as the monster circled the small boat, its green eyes glistening and turtle-shaped head reared high above the foaming waves. It finally gave up, however, and sank beneath the surface, never to reappear.

Surprisingly, the tragic encounter between McCleary and the sea creature received scant attention from the news media. There were a few headlines, but officials theorized that a large shark, probably something in the range of a twelve-foot hammerhead, had attacked the men. The skeptics said that the divers might have paddled into the middle of a shark breeding ground or even a feeding frenzy. Ridiculous, argued McCleary, who to this day vehemently denies that allegation, insisting instead that it was some kind of sea monster that killed his friends and terrorized him that foggy summer day long ago.

Encounters between people and dangerous sea life are nothing new in the warm coastal waters of the South. Several species of killer sharks are known to thrive there, as well as barracuda, sting rays, giant jellyfish, and numerous other potentially life-threatening creatures such as eels, whales, oarfish, and groupers.

Rarely does a summer pass without at least one shark attack report, barracuda bite, or severe jellyfish sting. Fortunately, the likelihood of bumping into one of these predators of the deep is quite remote. And a sea serpent? What are the odds of running into one of these fabled fellows, so dreaded and feared by seafaring voyagers down through the ages?

Pretty high, if you ask Dr. Berard Heuvelmans, a Belgian zoologist who has spent a lifetime investigating and writing about the sea serpent phenomenon. In his classic study of the subject, *In the Wake of the Sea-Serpents,* Heuvelmans came up with 587 reported sightings of sea monsters between the mid-seventeenth and mid-twentieth centuries. Of these, he determined that 121 were vague or doubtful, and another 50 or so others were hoaxes, many identifiable by their excessive detail. (One overheated account described a 200-foot specimen sporting a bright green handlebar mustache; another gave precise coordinates placing the observer in the Libyan desert.) Another 50 looked like mistaken identities—a train of playing porpoises, a flight of skimming sea birds, a mass of seaweed, or, if the sighting was of a stranded, rotting carcass, a basking shark.

Heuvelmans settled with 358 sightings that he considered fairly reliable, based on a number of factors—the number of witnesses and their credibility, location, time of day or night, weather, and physical descriptions.

The zoologist, who spent ten years researching and writing the book, was able to pin down seven distinct types of sea serpents. Their "convenient, informal" names are: Long-Necked, Merhorse, Many-Humped, Many-Finned, Super-Otter, Super-Eel, and Marine-Saurian. Part of what makes

Heuvelmans's work so fascinating is his use of modern scientific methodology in collecting and evaluating data—data which he feels proves conclusively that sea serpents are real. "The existence of the sea-monster, commonly known as the sea-serpent, is no longer in doubt today," Heuvelmans quotes Professor Leon Vaillant of the French National History Museum as reporting in a scientific journal shortly after the turn of the century.

For centuries, tales about such creatures have circulated. In ancient times sailors voyaging into uncharted waters fought "many-armed hydras," while accounts of similar marine behemoths continued to be handed down by seamen during the Middle Ages. Hundreds of sightings of unknown sea animals infesting southern waters have been documented through the years, starting with the first Spanish explorers. Some Indian tribes living along the coast also believed that horrible water demons dwelled offshore. Vikings who sailed south more than a thousand years ago kept a constant lookout for dangerous sea monsters. Even early French and English explorers surveying coastlines from Louisiana to Virginia left records detailing bizarre encounters with large, serpentine denizens of the sea.

But it wasn't until the modern era, when newspapers and magazines started carrying written accounts in the early nineteenth century, that news of sightings and even attacks became common. In 1830, for example, a Charleston, South Carolina, newspaper carried this story about a sea serpent attack:

> Captain Deland with the schooner *Eagle* ran into Charleston on the 27th of March, from Turtle River, and with his crew is willing to confirm by oath the truth of the following declaration: On the 23rd day of March, at one o'clock A.M., at about a mile from Simons Bay, we perceived at the distance of about 300 yards a large body, resembling an alligator, which sometimes moved with the vessel, sometimes lay motionless on the surface.

Captain Deland . . . approached the animal, loaded a musket with a ball, and steered so that he approached it within 20 or 30 yards at a moment that it lay quite still and apparently careless. Capt. Deland aimed with great sagacity at the hindpart of the head, the only part that was just visible, and the ball . . . struck.

The ball apparently only grazed the creature, which "suddenly grew angry" and turned on the boat. First, the monster rammed the wooden vessel with its enormous head, then began smashing into the craft with its flat tail. The report went on to say that as soon as the men realized the reptile was about to attack them inside the ship, they scrambled to safety atop masts and below deck. Those on deck were able to view the creature at close range and later gave vivid descriptions of the monster as it thrashed furiously in the water, repeatedly charging the boat.

Later, when the threat was over, the men agreed the creature was "about 70 feet long, had a body as thick as a 60-gallon keg, was gray in color, eel-shaped, without visible fins and was covered in greenish scales." Some of the sailors also said the creature's back was "full of joints or bunches, the head and back resembled an alligator's, and the skull was about 10 feet long and as big around as a hogshead." A smaller serpent spotted undulating through the waters a small distance away had been chased off by a couple of marksmen.

When the ship finally limped into port, an inquiry was held to assess damage to the ship and to determine what manner of creature had attacked it. One official who attended the meeting later dismissed the incident as a hoax, claiming, "It is not the habit of the sea serpent to attack a ship after having been struck by a ball, but to plunge down and disappear."

Another bizarre creature washed ashore at St. Augustine, Florida, on December 1, 1896. The find was hailed by investigators, the media, and the public as final proof of the existence of sea monsters. A professor sent down from Yale University to examine the octopus-like specimen determined that it had weighed over six tons when alive and measured 25 feet around its middle, with 75-foot-long tentacles dangling from its thick, dark mass.

A story which appeared in the *New York Herald* on January 3, 1897, reported that the beast had been dead for some time when found, and that scavengers had mutilated much of its decomposed body.

> Its head was nearly destroyed, and only the stumps of two arms were visible. The body, as it lies somewhat embedded in the sand, is 18 feet long and about 7 feet wide, while it rises 3½ feet above the sand . . . the weight of the body and head would have been at least four or five tons. If the eight arms held the proportions usually seen in smaller species of the octopus, they would have been at least 75 to 100 feet in length and about 18 inches in diameter at the base.

A half-century later, on a fine December day in 1947, the Grace Line's *Santa Clara* was sailing off the North Carolina coast when the startled cries of a Third Officer pierced the air. Thinking something must be horribly wrong, fellow officers and mates rushed to investigate.

What they saw, undulating close astern, was carefully described in the following radio message: "LAT 34.34 N LONG 74.07 W 1700 GCT STRUCK MARINE MONSTER EITHER KILLING IT OR BADLY WOUNDING IT PERIOD ESTIMATED LENGTH 45 FEET WITH EEL-LIKE HEAD AND BODY APPROXIMATELY THREE FEET IN DIAMETER PERIOD LAST SEEN THRASHING IN LARGE AREA OF BLOODY WATER AND FOAM . . ."

The decade of the 1940s witnessed an upsurge of monster sightings, the largest number appearing along both sides of the Florida peninsula. One such group of sightings occurred near Clearwater and was reported in detail by the local newspaper. "Tales of a sea monster's tracks about Clearwater and the beaches increase," screamed the headlines after a set of strange tracks was found on a remote Clearwater beach.

As soon as news of the tracks broke, frightened citizens started complaining of being chased by a "sea creature–like thing" along the beach. One investigator who studied the tracks in the sand said they matched those made by unusual three-toed creatures he had once seen in the silt marshes of Cuba. The newspaper quoted the man as saying:

> This critter walks on his hind legs, leaving three-toed footprints. . . .It has a head similar to a crocodile, but a much shorter jaw. The critter has large teeth. I am convinced that the tracks found on the Clearwater beach are not those of a human prankster because where would you find a man with an eight-foot stride? And if a prankster were using stilts he would have to have about three times his own weight added to them to get the depth of the footprints found.
>
> Moreover, the tracks on the beach showed where their maker had upset the lifeguard stand in front of Everingham's Pavilion and left evidence that some large, rough-skinned animal had rubbed against the wood of the stand. That doesn't seem to be the work of a prankster.

Similar tracks were found on the beaches at nearby Dan's Island and Honeymoon Island. "From Tarpon Springs," reported the *Clearwater Sun*, "comes the unconfirmed story that a sponge boat crew battled over 12 hours with some large denizen of the deep recently when it attacked some of the boat's divers."

Later that year, four pilots flying together claimed they watched a marine animal wallowing in shallow waters near Clearwater. They said, "It had the shape of a hog, was over fifteen feet long, and moved in a clockwise direction." In an interview with the *Sun*, they said that the creature "was only a few feet off the north end of Clearwater Beach, and was easy to see because of the white, sandy bottom. We're positive that it was furry and its legs or flippers were white with the ends cupped like hands." The report again described the creature's head as "hog shaped."

The Clearwater creature remained in the news for several more months, attacking bathers and occasionally crawling onto beaches and frightening residents of the coastal community. A county highway patrolman dispatched to the scene of one attack found a "near-panic . . . among residents of that beach area north of the Indian Rocks Hotel by the appearance of a sea monster which chased one individual, identified as John Moore."

Then, in 1952, the Clearwater monster returned, causing considerable excitement throughout the state of Florida. Huge tracks were once again found on the beach, this time by a local Coast Guard Commander. About forty feet of deep tracks led from the water's edge to a low sea wall, prompting investigators to decide that whatever had made them weighed over a thousand pounds. Long rows of claw prints preceded each set of tracks, measuring one foot long and seven or eight inches wide.

One marine expert theorized that the tracks indicated the creature's legs were about a yard apart—too wide, it would appear, and too deep to have been made by an ordinary 200-pound man.

Strange, serpentine creatures have also been reported in the backwaters of tidal rivers and lakes in other parts of the South. One such creature was spotted several times in the Altamaha River near Darien, Georgia, several years back; a "long, green, snake-like critter" chased a woman along the banks of the Savannah River near Augusta, Georgia, in the late 1800s.

The deep waters of the South are filled with a variety of forms of life. As we probe the depths, who knows what creatures wait there?

The Devil's Brother
And Other Strange
Travelers

The Goat Man of Dixie

FOR OVER FIFTY years he traveled the lonely backroads of the Deep South: a whistling, happy-go-lucky vagabond who enthralled small-town youngsters from Virginia to Florida with his tales of adventure on the open road. His name was Charles "Chess" McCartney, but everybody knew the bewhiskered old man driving a team of goats as the "Goat Man of Dixie."

Clad in his familiar overalls, boots, and scruffy cap, the Goat Man would pull into town, unhitch his team of goats, set up camp, then proceed to entertain wide-eyed crowds with his yarns. Huddled around a campfire, he would often stay up all night spinning tales about life on the road. "Would you like to hear about the time that old panther chased me through the swamp?" he'd ask, drawing dramatically on a large black pipe while poking the flames of his campfire with a knotty stick. "Or would you rather hear about the gang of outlaws that got after me in Kentucky? Later, I can tell you about the Indians who came after my scalp, and about that old grizzly bear who wanted me for breakfast . . ." He could carry a tune too, and the crisp night air often rang with his deep, rich voice—a voice that some said seemed to echo out of a turpentine barrel.

At the time of this writing McCartney was rumored to be in his 108th year. Until he retired his scraggly team of goats and old wagon a few years ago, he was a familiar sight in Arkansas, Texas, Louisiana, Mississippi, Alabama, Georgia, Florida, the Carolinas, Virginia, Tennessee, and Kentucky. He also traveled in the North some, but found the warm climate and "hospitable nature of southern folk" more to his liking.

So many stories have cropped up over the years about him that it is difficult to separate fact from fiction. Some accounts claim he is a self-made millionaire, with sizable estates and mansions strung out all across the country. Others contend he was once a Russian spy, sent over to this country to keep count of the number of automobiles and trucks on the highways. In the 1950s, one story circulating in some parts of the South was that the Goat Man was the son of a famous Civil War general, some said Robert E. Lee himself. Another version linked him with General Ulysses S. Grant. It was this alleged association with the famed Union leader that earned him the wrath of a group of rowdies in Alabama back in the late 1940s.

"I had just pulled into this small town near Selma—I can't remember its exact name—and had unhitched the goats and built up a big, roaring fire," the Goat Man explained, tugging at a long, mossy beard swirling around his thin face. "A group of young'uns recognized me and came over to hear some stories. Well, as soon as I mentioned a part about the fighting between the states, some adults walked over and started calling me Yankee names.

"I knew I was in trouble, for no reason, and had to get out of there fast. They yelled at me as I hitched those goats back up and threw some rocks and bottles as I rolled away. Fortunately, none of my goats got hurt that night."

The fact is, McCartney was born in the North, in Iowa, to be precise, some time before the turn of the century—he won't say just how long. At the time of this writing he lives with his son, Albert Gene, in a converted school bus along Highway 80 in rural Twiggs County near Jeffersonville, Georgia. They moved into the bus a few years ago after their two-room shack was destroyed by fire.

The goats are long gone, given to a zoo in Florida in 1979. But McCartney misses his animals, especially on winter nights.

"You see," he said, blowing into his crusty palms, "I'd sleep with my goats if it got real cold. If it was a fairly cool night, I might get between two or three. But if it got nasty cold, it might take four or more to keep me warm. My goats are the finest electric blankets I can find. The colder it gets, I cover up with more goats—thirty degrees is a one-goat night; twenty degrees is a two-goat night; and below zero is a five-goat night."

McCartney said that during his long years on the road he camped in every state on the continent and often journeyed to Canada and Mexico. His box-shaped wagon pulled by a team of twenty goats was much heralded in many a small town along the way.

Children gathered around the Goat Man's camp often saw him as some larger than life hero, a rowdy, restless, rough-and-tumble adventurer whose pioneering spirit reminded them of Davy Crockett and Daniel Boone. Even adults who met McCartney in those years were awed by his wit, style, and storytelling ability.

Many people who knew the traveler idealized him, but others viewed him as a harmless old crank, a no-account drifter and potential troublemaker. Whenever it was rumored that the Goat Man was on his way to town, the sheriff would usually warn parents to keep a close eye on their children and valuables, just in case. "He's no better'n a gypsy," snarled one Tennessee lawman. "You have to keep a sharp eye out for the likes of these bums."

When the Depression hit his family's farm in Iowa during the 1930s, young McCartney decided to move south. Like many other Americans displaced by the economic crash, he became a hobo and soon learned how to profit from his misfortune.

He dressed in goatskins to draw a crowd during his travels, and soon found that people would flock around him to stare at his goats and even buy postcards he had made up. Along the way he met a woman, Saddie Smytheart, and the couple soon had a child, Albert Gene. Encouraged by the crowds—and the money they were willing to pay to see him—the Goat Man and his wife adorned their small son in goatskins and moccasins and had him pose for the people who swarmed around their caravan at every stop.

"I got the idea from Daniel Defoe's character, Robinson Crusoe," explained McCartney. "Dressing up the boy like that when he was just learning to walk was a real crowd-pleaser. It worked! They would buy our cards, and that money helped us work our way back and forth across this great country of ours, whenever and wherever we wanted to go."

But eventually Saddie Smytheart became weary of the rigors of the highway, and Albert Gene had to go to school. "This left me alone on the road with the wagon and the goats. Me and my team continued to go on, traveling here and there, far and near, always getting in trouble, but never having to go to jail."

In his heyday McCartney, who once preached the gospel as an ordained minister, was compared to another itinerant wanderer, Johnny Appleseed. The cheerful vagabond enjoyed that comparison, often remarking that he and the legendary Appleseed would have made a good team—"He a-doing the planting, and me a-doing the talking." McCartney estimated that he and his team of goats trekked more than 200,000 miles, camped at least 900,000 times, and burned "well over" a million junk tires to keep warm. In all that time, he never once slept in a bed nor in a house.

The old man tells of fighting off outlaws in Kentucky and California, Indians in Arizona and Texas, and a group of Ku Klux Klanners in Mississippi. Once he had to climb a tree to escape a grizzly bear in the Rocky Mountains. "I've met some mean hombres in my time—those that walk on two legs and those that walk on four," he said. "The ones that gave me the most trouble were up North. I ain't had a lot of trouble down here in the South. These are good people."

Nowadays, when he has to travel, the Goat Man goes by airplane or train. "It's a lot more comfortable. No use wasting what precious time is left in my life on a wagon."

And with his vagabond days behind him, the Goat Man— who says he's had four wives—wants to marry again and settle down.

"I'm gonna be around a long time to come. The devil ain't ready for me and the good Lord don't want me just now."

The Devil's Brother:
Blackbeard, Scourge of the Spanish Main

ABOUT THE ONLY good thing that could be said about Edward Teach, better known as Blackbeard the pirate, was that he was born an honest man. But a profitable lifestyle while privateering for the crown during Queen Anne's War probably convinced this swashbuckling rogue that it was easier—and more fun—to earn a living looting treasure and lopping off heads than working a regular job.

So, when the war ended in 1713, the greatest sea bandit of them all ceremoniously unfurled his black flag and launched his long and bloody career. In his day, Blackbeard captured or sank scores of ships, stole millions of dollars in treasure, took dozens of women as his wives, and left the mutilated bodies of thousands of victims who got in his way along the Atlantic coast from New England to Florida. But it is the memory of the pirate's treasure, more than his despicable deeds, that endures today. Although some of the loot has reportedly been found, untold fortunes in silver, gold, and jewels may remain buried beneath coastal sands, awaiting some lucky one's spade or metal detector.

Did Blackbeard himself leave any clues as to where his treasure was buried? It is said that on the eve of his last battle, one of Teach's henchmen questioned him about it. The pirate's swaggering reply was typical: "Nobody but the devil and myself know where my treasure is, and the longer liver of the two shall have it all."

Predictably, legends galore have sprung up about this formidable character. In real life he was an abnormally big man, but the impression he made on people was so much larger than life that some considered him to be the devil incarnate—a description he mastered at cultivating throughout his career on the high seas. Tall, well-built, and phenomenally strong, he wore a long, braided beard deliberately fashioned to unsettle friend and foe alike; according to tradition, the wiry swirls of luxurious growth covered every inch of his face, growing up to his eyelids and over his ears. Legend relates how he enjoyed setting off small charges of gunpowder in his beard that enveloped his head in a halo of black smoke. As a finishing touch to his satanic mien, he also drank his rum laced with flaming gunpowder.

A particularly gruesome example of Blackbeard's talents occurred shortly after he turned to pirating full-time, when his dreaded ship *Queen Anne's Revenge* came upon a commercial vessel off the Florida coast. First, his scruffy crew swung aboard the *Great Allan*, slew anyone who resisted, and grabbed the ship's supplies. After setting the ship ablaze, Blackbeard threw the remaining victims overboard in shark-infested waters. He is said to have roared with laughter as the sharks slashed into the helpless victims—men, women and children—and the sea turned red with blood.

On another occasion, he killed the fiancé of a woman he desired (reputedly the daughter of North Carolina Governor Charles Eden), cut off his hand, then presented the grisly gift to Miss Eden in a small silver casket. According to the story, the girl cried out in horror, fell into a swoon, and died within a month.

Soon after embarking upon his new profession, Blackbeard fell in with a certain gentleman pirate known as Major Stede Bonnet, a wealthy Southerner who had adopted pirating as a relief from boredom. The diabolical combination of talents resulted in a virtual wave of terror upon the high seas, with no port or sea lane safe from the double scourge. In two days alone they captured five vessels off the coast of Charleston, South Carolina, practically closing the port down. No captain in his right mind would take to the open water with the "devil incarnate" roaming the bounding main.

In his book *True Tales of Buried Treasure,* Edward Rowe Snow describes why many, including a number of his own crew, referred to Blackbeard as the very devil:

> One night soon after his successful exploits at Charleston, the pirate decided to give an exhibition of his Mephistophelean qualities. He took three of the more venturesome members of his crew aside, and, fixing his ferocious black eyes on them, told of his scheme. "Come," he roared, raising himself to his full height, "let us make a hell of our own and try how long we can bear it."'
>
> "All four men then descended into the hold." After Blackbeard had closed the hatches, he filled several large pots with brimstone and set them on fire. The four pirates remained in the cramped hold, breathing the suffocating smoke into their lungs until all but Blackbeard shouted for air. Then he released the hatches and allowed the others to pull themselves up on deck, not a little pleased that he had held out longer than any of his men.

Another illustration of Teach's particular brand of wickedness came when he tricked three hundred of his men into waiting for him on a small island. The marauding band of pirates had just returned from a profitable raid, and Blackbeard had promised them all their fair share of gold and silver bullion. Since the ship was overloaded with the ill-gotten booty, he told the men to wait behind, that he would return for them once the treasure had been safely deposited at a nearby hideout. After hand-picking a small crew to go with him, he waved goodby and set off, leaving the stranded men to their doom.

The strange relationship between Blackbeard and the North Carolina governor has tantalized historians for more than two centuries. Eden, an otherwise honorable man, apparently became involved with Teach after the pirate told him he had found several ships adrift at sea. The governor seems to have swallowed the story and, for a share in the booty, permitted the sea bandit to sail on his way.

On subsequent occasions, when Blackbeard sailed into port, Eden granted him full protection and even wined and dined openly with the cruel bandit. Some say Blackbeard had threatened to kidnap or murder the governor's young daughter unless he cooperated. Others claim the royal official was corrupt and had been in cahoots with the notorious pirate all along.

Records show that periodically Blackbeard would sail into Bathtown to declare his intentions of going straight. On one occasion, Eden called together a Court of Vice Admiralty and arranged a full pardon for the villain's nautical crimes. The meeting was adjourned after Edward Teach had been declared an honest privateer again.

In North Carolina, rumors still persist that Teach had secretly been in love with the governor's daughter and that she helped him import piratical spoils into the Eden household for safekeeping. This was accomplished by means of a tunnel, supposedly leading from a secret harbor directly to the governor's mansion. Some historians dispute this theory, pointing out that Miss Eden would probably have been too young for the likes of Blackbeard at the time.

During Teach's long reign as the undisputed leader of the sea pack, other pirates, many of them equally fierce and successful in snatching unwary ships, roamed the sea lanes of the Atlantic between the Indies and New England. The thickly islanded coastal areas of Virginia, the Carolinas, Georgia, and Florida furnished excellent retreats for the buccaneers as well as homes for their stolen goods. José Gaspar (otherwise known as Gasparilla), Captain Kidd, Jean Lafitte, and Nasty Ned Lowe were among the dozen or so swashbucklers known to have cruised the area.

Nearly every coastal town and island has its own legend about buried treasure protected by phantom guards, usually in the form of bearded pirates armed with cutlasses and flintlock pistols. It is true that many secluded barrier isles along the Atlantic seaboard were visited by pirates and may still hide fabulous fortunes. It would have been easy for ships flying the feared skull and crossbones banner to slip unseen into tidal creeks, rivers, and inlets and dispose of their blood-stained booty.

One island in particular that stands out as a possible treasure dumping ground is Blackbeard Island, located a few miles off the Georgia mainland. Named after the notorious pirate himself, Blackbeard Island was known to be a frequent haven for Teach and his band of swarthy outlaws. Numerous local legends tell how Teach buried a king's fortune in gold somewhere amid the island's gloomy forests, planning to return one day to claim his illegal loot. Before departing the island, he appointed a young sailor to guard the treasure with his life.

Over the years, there have been reports of a headless ghost, pistols and knives tucked in a sash, wandering the beaches of Blackbeard Island.

In 1718 the British government decided it had had enough of the pirate. After posting a reward of one hundred pounds for his head, it dispatched a fleet of ships under the command of Captain Robert Maynard to hunt down and capture Blackbeard—or kill him, whichever seemed most expedient. Because Governor Eden of North Carolina could not be trusted to take action against his friend and former confederate, an arrangement was made for Governor Alexander Spotswood of Virginia to oversee Maynard's operation. At Ocracoke Inlet, thirty miles southwest of Cape Hatteras, North Carolina, Maynard's expedition finally caught up with its legendary quarry.

As Maynard approached Blackbeard's clearly marked vessel, the following conversation is said to have taken place:

Blackbeard: "Damn you for villains, who are you? And from whence come you?"

Maynard: "You may see by our colors we are no pirates."

Blackbeard: "Send your boat on board so that I might have a look and see who you are."

Maynard: "I cannot spare my boat, but I will come aboard

you as soon as I can with my sloop."

Blackbeard: "Damnation seize my soul if I give any quarter or take any from you!"

Maynard: "I expect no quarter from you, nor shall I give any."

In spite of his strong words, Maynard knew he and his men were up against the scourge of the Spanish Main, the most feared and ruthless pirate of all time, the man who had personally murdered hundreds of innocent men, women, and children in cold blood. He could expect no mercy from such a beast, nor should he allow himself to give any.

Maynard's hopes soared when he realized his enemy's ship had run aground in the shallow waters. Wasting no time, he tried to maneuver into a better position, angling toward a favored engagement of cannon. Unfortunately, just as the barrage was about to begin, the tide came in and freed the ship's murderous crew.

Teach was the first to attack. Without warning, a battery of cannons opened fire on Maynard, killing or wounding about thirty men. The desperate captain realized he was in a fight to the death and only trickery would get the best of this madman!

Quickly, the captain ordered most of the survivors to hide below the deck, to make their attackers think only a handful of sailors had survived the bombardment. As smoke swirled around the creaking deck and tattered canvas sails, Blackbeard's voice boomed across the narrowing waterway: "Look at 'em! Why, there's only three or four of 'em left alive! All the rest are knocked on the head. Let's jump aboard and cut the others to pieces. Let no one live to see the sunset!"

With a bloodcurdling whoop, he led a rampaging charge onto the smoke-filled ship. Quickly the hidden soldiers dashed out on deck, and a gory free-for-all ensued. Sabers clashed and knuckles cracked against bony flesh. Suddenly both captains spotted each other. Their eyes locked as they quickly drew their pistols and aimed. The crack of pistol fire was hardly audible above the roar of muskets and clattering of steel sabers. Seeing that both balls had gone wide of their mark,

Maynard and Blackbeard scrambled across the tilting deck toward each other, cutlasses swinging wildly.

In a flash they were upon each other, flailing with cleaver-like strokes of their swords. Blackbeard's heavier blade crashed against Maynard's smaller, regulation saber, shattering the flimsy metal down to the hilt. With a roar of demonic laughter, the pirate raised his blood-stained weapon high, preparing to decapitate the young captain with a single swipe. At that instant, however, a British comrade rushed up behind him and slit the pirate's grizzled throat.

That brave action slowed down the giant, but only for a moment. Staggering backward against the railing, Blackbeard regained his balance and took stock of the situation. Without hesitating any longer, he fell upon Maynard with a howling vengeance. Five more volleys of gunfire erupted over the ship, now littered with the bodies of dead pirates. Five steel balls slammed into Blackbeard, knocking him backwards and into the slashing swords of government seamen.

Edward Teach, riddled with bullet holes, was dead.

Not taking any chances, Maynard grabbed a sword from one of his men and cut off the pirate's head—proof that Blackbeard had at last been conquered. Without ceremony, his crumpled body was thrown overboard to the sharks.

And what about Governor Eden, Teach's partner in crime?

As soon as Captain Maynard reached shore, he marched up to the governor's house, confiscated a considerable quantity of stolen goods, and placed Eden and his staff under house arrest. However, the crafty governor managed to withstand the storm of adverse publicity that followed and remained in office. Fourteen of the captured pirates were hanged; a few were pardoned, including Israel Hands, Stevenson's character in *Treasure Island,* who sailed back to England and spent the rest of his life as a common beggar.

Blackbeard's "skull" continued to surface in taverns and fraternity houses in North Carolina and Virginia for a number of years. The grisly relic became a favorite among rowdy collegians who dared drink their beer from its gargantuan cavity. Some who have drunk from the skull claim to have been possessed with newfound vitality and strength.

Others who had trouble growing beards swore they soon sprouted luxurious new growths of thick, healthy hair swirling around their faces . . .

Is Napoleon's General Buried
in North Carolina Grave?

IN A GRAVEYARD in the North Carolina backwoods, a moss-shrouded mausoleum towers over jagged rows of tombstones and simple wooden crosses. Its inscription, tarnished with time, reads: "In memory of Peter Stuart Ney, a native of France and soldier of the French Revolution under Napoleon Bonaparte, who departed this life Nov. 15, 1846, aged 77 years." Each year visitors flock to the tiny cemetery behind Third Creek Presbyterian Church in Rowan County to see the tomb of a man some believe was Marshal Michel Ney, the great French general who led the bloody winter retreat from Moscow to Prussia during the Napoleonic Wars in 1812.

But wait. Something seems to be wrong here.

What are the remains of an aristocratic French general doing buried in this remote North Carolina county, so far away from his homeland? More to the point, what are the remains of one of Napoleon's most famous commanding officers doing in America? Don't history books tell us that this romantic revolutionary died in a hail of musket balls, his white silk blouse drenched in blood, one cold, wet morning in Paris over 140 years ago?

And if that is so, and if the general's body is actually entombed in the French capital—in the Père la Chaise Cemetery, to be exact—then just whose remains are those in the North Carolina grave?

Answers to these and other questions have bedeviled scholars and local residents for decades. Ever since the arrival of a quaint schoolmaster in the early 1800s—a schoolmaster who spoke Hebrew, Latin, Greek, French, and English, just as General Ney did—things haven't been the same in this part of North Carolina. To begin with, many locals believe the strange schoolmaster was none other than the famous general himself, whom Napoleon called "the bravest of the brave" in reference to his successes as a gallant military leader. According to legend, the 77-year-old schoolteacher, who called himself Peter Stuart Ney, declared on his deathbed that he was indeed General Ney. An attending physician reported that the dying man raised himself up on one elbow and said: "By all that is holy, I am Marshal Ney of France."

One would think that such a confession would put an end to speculation over the schoolmaster's true identity. On the contrary, Ney's death touched off one of the South's greatest historical manhunts. Books have been written and scores of articles for international magazines and newspapers have appeared over the years as investigators, both serious and romantic, have probed the secrets of Ney's grave.

In 1887 Peter Stuart Ney's body was exhumed. Later, his handwriting was analyzed. After years of debate, historians, archivists, and medical specialists from Europe and the United States have yet to agree on their findings. As of this writing, it remains uncertain whether the rural schoolmaster was Napoleon's general—or a highly imaginative educator who delighted in impersonating the great commander.

Predictably, the controversy over the schoolmaster's identity continues to fuel debate among local residents as well as outsiders who come here to study the mystery.

"It's great fun," said Howell Boone, a historian from nearby Davis County who doubts that the scholarly schoolmaster had ever even been to France, let alone led the French army at Waterloo. "That's why the legend will probably never die. There will always be people who want to believe. There's genuine sentiment for the story." In Boone's estimation, Peter Stuart Ney was an educated Scotsman with a vivid imagination. Records do indicate that the dapper schoolmaster got carried away when in the presence of ladies or when drinking.

"When he had a bit too much of the local brew, he would insist he was Marshal Ney," Boone said. "I wonder if someone gave him a couple of stiff drinks when he was departing."

A few days before Christmas in 1815, eight months after Napoleon's abdication, General Ney swore allegiance to King Louis XVIII. When Napoleon escaped from the prison island of Elba, the patriotic general vowed to bring him back to Paris—"in an iron cage, if necessary."

As it happened, Ney had a change of heart. Instead of going after the former French emperor with sword and pistol, Marshal Michel Ney joined up with Napoleon, kneeling before him and pledging support. Napoleon's defeat at Waterloo resulted in Ney's capture and sentence of death by firing squad.

On the day of the general's much-publicized execution, however, legend has it that members of the firing squad used blanks instead of live ammunition. It is said that when the order to fire was given, Ney smashed a concealed bladder of pig's blood against his white shirt, to make it appear he had been shot. That night, according to the story, Ney fled Paris aboard a farmer's cart, disguised as a peasant. He didn't stop until he reached the coast.

One month later, on January 29, 1816, a man calling himself Peter Stuart Ney arrived in Charleston, South Carolina. Few records remain of this man's movement, but a few months later he turned up in Cheraw, South Carolina, then later in Lincolnton, Mocksville, and finally Cleveland, North Carolina, where he settled down as a schoolmaster.

There stories began cropping up about his shadowy background. They were inexorably linked to Peter Ney's impressive knowledge of the Napoleonic Wars and his intimate familiarity with French military affairs. He also followed events in Europe with more than passing curiosity. His handwriting was similar to the French general's, and both had scars from sword and bullet wounds in the same parts of the body. Perhaps the most convincing evidence associating the schoolmaster with General Ney was the man's willingness—even eagerness—to proclaim himself one and the same person.

Today, more than 140 years after the death of Peter Stuart

Ney, many questions remain unanswered. One of the most puzzling is why, assuming the legend to be based on fact, the general chose a remote hamlet in North Carolina as his refuge. Accustomed as he was to high living, why didn't he go to New York or Charleston or Boston or some other major cultural center of the New World as did many other European refugees of the period? Why did he take a low-paying job as a school-master in a tiny town off the beaten path?

Some say he took the job for reasons of security—that too many enemies had immigrated to larger American cities and that discovery of his true identity would have resulted in his immediate assassination. John David Ramsey, an archivist at Davidson College, said Peter Stuart Ney's decision to settle in the rural South suggests he might have been looking for a low-profile existence. "There's no question he was very intelligent and a well-educated individual," Ramsey said. "He could have been a Harvard University professor."

But he chose to spend the remaining years of his life in relative obscurity, subsisting in a lonely little backwoods town on the edge of the frontier, rather than risk an assassin's bullet. Still, every now and then the old urge to become "General Marshal Michel Ney" would erupt and Peter Stuart Ney found himself talking about his old life—usually over drinks in the local tavern.

Immigrant Scot schoolmaster or renegade revolutionary general—who is the real person buried beneath the six-by-twelve-foot brick mausoleum looming over the tiny graveyard behind Third Creek Presbyterian Church? James W. Wall, a historian from nearby Davis County, said the mystery probably will never be solved. "I don't see how it can be," he said. "There's compelling evidence both ways."

Afterword

When I began this book in the spring of 1988, my primary objective was simple—to research and write about some of the Deep South's most famous and enduring mysteries.

As the project unfolded, however, I found myself drawn more and more to some of the lesser-known riddles that have befuddled and bedeviled generations of Southerners. So instead of rehashing traditional material, I chose to focus on some of the myths, tales and unexplained incidents that, for one reason or another, have all but been forgotten.

For example, few folks outside the Carolinas have ever heard of the "Carolina bays"—thousands of curious depressions in the ground believed caused by a giant meteor shower thousands of years ago. To me, this lack of awareness seems incredible since the origin of the bays looms as one of the greatest unsolved mysteries in modern science. And speaking of mysteries, the spectacular Surrency haunting at the turn of the century left thousands of journalists, scientists and clergymen from all over the world scratching their heads, yet little information about this phenomenon survives today.

Just about everybody has heard of the mound-builders, a mysterious, half-mythological race of Indians that supposedly disappeared centuries before the arrival of Europeans in the fifteenth century. Few people know, however, that "moon-eyed white men" supposedly walked the North American continent thousands of years ago, or that a wandering band of Welsh explorers led by the enigmatic Prince Madoc roamed the Southern hinterlands long before the arrival of Christopher Columbus.

Do mermaids exist? Does a Bigfoot-like creature stalk the wilds of Gulf Coast regions and more remote elevations of the Southern

166

Appalachian Mountains? Did a sea serpent somehow slither onto a Florida beach a few years ago and chase a crowd of terrified bathers?

Before we dismiss these reports as the products of pranks or the ravings of wildly disturbed imaginations, let us remember that many witnesses to these phenomena were respected members of their community—doctors, lawyers, airline pilots, police officers, clergymen and college professors—people who had everything to lose and nothing to gain by going on record with their claims. Untold millions of Americans, including at least one President of the United States, have reported sighting Unidentified Flying Objects; yet, the Air Force discounts such sightings, saying they are nothing more than hot air balloons, swamp gas, "Venus Ascending," or other atmospheric illusions.

What, then, are we to make of these mysteries? It depends, I suppose, on our own perspective. For scientists, concerned as they are with facts and an uncompromising search for test-tube truth, most of these great Southern mysteries loom as nothing more than fantasy. But for others, examining our mysterious past often leads to romantic conclusions about forces and events that, rational or not, seem to at least satisfy some of the primal wonder within us all.

It's good to think that most of these mysteries will never be solved. It's good to think there will always be a Wampus Cat lurking in the shifting shadows, or that one day divers probing the storm-tossed depths of the ocean will come upon the gleaming columns of ancient Atlantis. Mysteries, fortunately, will always be with us. Ever since we crawled out of the cave, there's always been something just beyond the flickering firelight to capture our attention, to arrest our imagination, to keep us guessing, to stir us on toward discovery. In an age of electronic marvels, it gives me a profound sense of ease to know there are still some things a bleeping computer screen can't solve.

As a child growing up in south Georgia, I was fascinated by tales handed down by the oldtimers. So intrigued was I by stories of rattling chains, red-eyed apparitions at the window and other terrifying encounters with the unknown, that the memories still linger, fresh and powerful, more compelling, in a sense, and real than before. Sadly, too many of these stories are disappearing at an alarming rate. Once gone, the knowledge of our people as a whole will be somehow diminished. Preserving the lore of the past, however spectacular and speculative, will only make us richer and wiser, insuring that generations to come will not be shortchanged of their heritage.

That's the main reason I wrote this book, I suppose—to help keep alive the speculation, the wonder, the flickering embers at the back of the cave. To me, the book has been a richly rewarding experience, a kind of nostalgic journey into a universe of forgotten truths—a universe teeming with quivering secrets, shrouded legends and historical black holes.

Some of these stories are spinoffs of articles I wrote for newspapers and magazines over the years. As such, they are for the most part objective in style. A few, however, are purely speculative, based on evidence gleaned from hundreds of interviews, journals, newspapers, diaries, magazines and official records. I have resisted the temptation to draw conclusions on most matters, preferring to let the reader make up his or her own mind.

—E. Randall Floyd
Augusta, Ga.
June, 1989

Bibliography

Adler, Bill, ed. *UFO's*. New York: Dell Publishing, 1967.

American Heritage Books. *Mysteries of the Past*. New York: American Heritage Books, 1977.

Aymar, Brandt. *Treasury of Snake Lore*. New York: Greenberg, 1956.

Barron, Ruth T. *Footprints in Appling County*. Dallas: Taylor Publishing Co., 1981.

Benwell, Gwen, and Arthur Waugh. *Sea Enchantress*. New York: The Citadel Press, 1965.

Berlitz, Charles. *The Bermuda Triangle*. New York: Doubleday & Company, 1974.

Blum, John M. *The National Experience*. New York: Harcourt Brace Jovanovich, 1973.

Bolton, Herbert E., ed. *Arrendondo's Historical Proof of Spain's Title to Georgia*. Berkeley: University of California Press, 1925.

Botkin, B.A. *A Treasury of Southern Folklore*. New York: Bonanza Books, 1967.

Bray, Warwick M., and Earl H. Swanson. *The New World*. New York: E.P. Dutton, 1976.

Brookesmith, Peter. *The Power of the Earth*. London: Orbis Publishing, 1984.

Bushnell, Geoffrey Hext Sutherland. *The First Americans*. New York: McGraw-Hill, 1975.

Capps, Clifford S., and Eugenia Burney. *Georgia*. Nashville: Thomas Nelson, Inc., 1972.

Carrington, Richard. *Mermaids and Mastodons*. New York: Rinehart & Company, Inc., 1957.

Carter, Samuel III. *Kingdom of the Tides*. New York: Hawthorn Books, 1966.

Cate, Margaret Davis. *Our Todays and Yesterdays*. Brunswick, Georgia: Glover Brothers, Inc., 1972.

Ceram, C.W. *The First America*. New York: Harcourt Brace Jovanovich, Inc., 1971.

Cottrell, Leonard. *Lost Worlds*. New York: Dell Publishing, 1962.

Courlander, Harold. *A Treasury of Afro-American Folklore*. New York: Crown Publishers, 1976.

Crane, Verner W. *The Southern Frontier (1670-1732)*. New York: W.W. Norton and Company, 1981.

Daniken, Erich von. *Miracles of the Gods*. New York: Dell Publishing, 1975.

Davis, Nigel. *Voyages to the New World*. New York: William Morrow and Company, 1979.

Day, A. Grove. *Coronado's Quest*. Los Angeles: University of California Press, 1964.

Del Ray, Lester. *The Mysterious Earth*. New York: Chilton Company, 1961.

de Camp, L. Sprague. *Lost Continents*. New York: Dover Publications, 1970.

Dobie, J. Frank. *Rattlesnakes*. Boston: Little, Brown and Company, 1965.

Erdoes, Richard, and Alfonso Ortiz. *American Indian Myths and Legends*. New York: Pantheon Books, 1984.

Fell, Barry. *America, B.C.* New York: Demeter Press, 1977.

Grumley, Michael. *There Are Giants in the Earth*. New York: Doubleday & Company, 1974.

Halliday, William R. *Depths of the Earth*. New York: Harper & Row, 1966.

Heuvelmans, Bernard. *In the Wake of Sea Serpents*. New York: Hill and Wang, 1969.

Hill, Douglas, and Pat Williams. *The Supernatural*. New York: Signet Books, 1965.

Hudson, Charles. *The Southeastern Indians*. Knoxville: University of Tennessee Press, 1976.

Jackson, Donald Dale. *Underground Worlds*. Alexandria, Virginia: Time-Life Books, 1982.

Jenkinson, Michael. *Beasts Beyond the Fire*. New York: E.P. Dutton, 1980.

Jennings, Gary. *The Killer Storms*. New York: J.B. Lippincott Company, 1970.

King, Edward. *The Great South*. Baton Rouge: Louisiana State University, 1970.

Kirkpatrick, F.A. *The Spanish Conquistadores*. New York: World Publishing, 1971.

Klauber, Laurence M. *Rattlesnakes*. Los Angeles: University of California Press, 1982.

Kusche, Lawrence David. *The Bermuda Triangle Mystery—Solved*. New York: Harper & Row, 1975.

La Barre, Weston. *Thou Shall Take Up Serpents*. Minneapolis: University of Minnesota Press, 1962.

Mahan, Joseph. *The Secret: America in World History Before Columbus*. Acworth, Georgia: Star Printing Co., 1985.

Morison, Samuel Eliot. *The European Discovery of America: The Southern Voyages*. New York: Oxford University Press, 1974.

National Geographic Society. *Vanishing Peoples of the Earth*. Washington, D.C.: National Geographic Society, 1968.

Noone, Richard W. *Ice: The Ultimate Disaster*. Atlanta: Astraea Publishing, 1982.

Ogburn, Charlton. *The Southern Appalachians*. New York: William Morrow & Company, 1975.

Oliver, James A. *Snakes in Fact and Fiction*. New York: The Macmillan Company, 1958.

Reader's Digest. *American Folklore and Legend*. Pleasantville, New York: Reader's Digest Associates, 1978.

———. *Mysteries of the Unexplained*. Pleasantville, New York: Reader's Digest Books, 1982.

———. *Mysteries of the Ancient Americas: The New World Before Columbus*. Pleasantville, New York: Reader's Digest Books, 1986.

———. *Strange Stories, Amazing Facts*. Pleasantville, New York: Reader's Digest Books, 1977.

Ribeiro, Darcy. *The Americas and Civilization*. New York: E.P. Dutton, 1972.

Riegel, Robert E., and Robert G. Athearn. *America Moves West*. Hinsdale, Illinois: The Dryden Press, Inc., 1971.

Savage, Harry. *The Mysterious Carolina Bays*. Chapel Hill: University of North Carolina Press, 1982.

Smith, Page. *A New Age Now Begins*. New York: McGraw-Hill, 1976.

Stokes, Thomas L. *The Savannah: Rivers of America*. New York: Rinehart & Company, 1951.

Sweeney, James B. *A Pictorial History of Sea Monsters*. New York: Bonanza Books, 1972.

Thorndike, Joseph, ed. *Mysteries of the Deep*. New York: American Heritage Publishing Co., 1980.

Time-Life Books. *Mystic Places*. Alexandria, Virginia: Time-Life Books, 1987.

Vanstory, Burnette. *Georgia's Land of the Golden Isles*. Athens: The University of Georgia Press, 1981.

Velikovsky, Immanuel. *Earth in Upheaval*. New York: Doubleday and Company, 1955.

Whipple, A.B.C. *Restless Oceans*. Alexandria, Virginia: Time-Life Books, 1983.

——. *Storm*. Alexandria, Virginia: Time-Life Books, 1982.

Willey, Gordon R., and Jeremy A. Sabloff. *A History of American Archaeology*. San Francisco: W.H. Freeman, 1974.

Index

173

Olmecs, 26

MORE
*S*GREAT
Southern
MYSTERIES

FLORIDA'S FOUNTAIN OF YOUTH, GHOSTS OF THE ALAMO,
LOST MAIDENS OF THE OKEFENOKEE,
TERROR ON THE NATCHEZ TRACE AND OTHER
ENDURING MYSTERIES OF THE AMERICAN SOUTH

E. RANDALL FLOYD
Author of GREAT *Southern* MYSTERIES

This book is
dedicated to
Anne

Preface

After the publication of my first book, *Great Southern Mysteries,* a lot of people wanted to know two things—where did I get all my story ideas, and why on earth was I so attracted to unexplained mysteries?

The first question was easy enough to answer—I spend a lot of time at the public library, as well as in my personal library at home. At one point I figured my wife and I owned close to five thousand books and subscribed to dozens of newspapers, magazines, and professional periodicals.

The second question, however, was a little harder to deal with. For starters, I haven't the faintest clue why I am so drawn to stories dealing with the unexplained, the bizarre, the paranormal. Could be that I just love a good shudder every now and then, but I suspect it's something deeper.

All of us are fascinated by the Unknown. If you don't believe that, just look at the list of titles at the corner bookstore or check out the local movie marquee. Demons, ghosts, time travel, witches, and ungodly creatures straight out of Lovecraft seem to dominate our popular culture.

But this is nothing new. Down through the ages, men and women have tingled and shivered at things they couldn't understand—the strange sound at the window late at night, an unexplained presence flitting across the moonlit lawn, a stranger on the subway who stares oddly out at the world.

These fears, both real and imaginary, are certainly holdovers from another era in our evolutionary development. They go back to a time perhaps when every creaking thing in nature had its own sinister purpose—the sun, the rain, the wind, the moon, the shadows, the forest.

In classical times, there were horned cyclops and winged monsters that terrorized lonely islands far out at sea. During the middle ages, the trackless forests of Europe were haunted by witches and goblins and dragons that only sainted heroes could eradicate. Recently, new horrors have been unleashed upon the world—nuclear weapons, global warming, and AIDS, to name a few.

These new horrors, threatening as they are, pale when compared to the vampires and werewolves and other blood-sucking nightmares of lore. At least we can understand the effects of fallout and the consequences of the AIDS virus. We can protect ourselves, if we try, against those "mysteries"— but how can you tell a couple of Boy Scouts huddled around a campfire in a lonely swamp that the snapping sounds they hear off in the distance are just the wind rustling in the trees? How do you protect a child from the lurking shadows in an open closet?

Some mysteries are less terrifying than they are just plain baffling. When someone suddenly disappears in full view of onlookers, when eerie blue lights dance and hover over a misty cemetery, when a tribe of beautiful young women are discovered in the middle of the Okefenokee Swamp, or when a pair of human footprints are found in stone too many millions of years old, you start to worry about the "natural" order of things.

The Deep South, probably more than any other region of the country, remains shrouded in mystery and legend. This book is about some of those mysteries and legends, told from the viewpoint of an inquiring journalist.

Obviously a few of the narratives contained herein border on the fanciful. But, lest we forget, a wise man once said that behind every legend there is a least a grain of truth. And I say that behind every mystery, there is the possibility of some new scientific discovery.

Whether you accept what you read in this book as fact or fiction isn't really important. The main thing is that by reading it, you're helping keep alive some of the wondrous mysteries of our region's fascinating past.

I couldn't have gotten away with this book without the warm, and often splendid, cooperation of my wife, Anne—a generous and caring companion with an editor's soul. Also, this project was made easier by the chairman of the history department where I work, Dr. Ed Cashin, whose inspiration and wise comments were helpful in tracking down certain bits of renegade information.

I'd like to certainly thank my editors at August House, especially Judith Faust, for their valuable advice and instructive criticism of the original manuscript.

Lastly, there is no way that this or any of my other editorial projects could have become a reality without the input of my late uncle, the Rev. Henry Curtiss Tillman, a master storyteller and writer. I'm sure that somewhere up there Uncle Curt is curled up in a quiet corner with a book—hopefully one of mine.

E. Randall Floyd
Augusta, Georgia
1990

Contents

Demons And Delusions

Entertaining Satan
in the Old Dominion

When most Americans think of witches and witchcraft, they usually think of the hysteria that swept through the tiny village of Salem, Massachusetts, near the end of the seventeenth century.

By the time the persecutions were over, scores of innocent citizens—mostly old, impoverished women—had been beaten, stoned, and tortured for practicing what the state called "diabolical black arts." They were the lucky ones. At least twenty poor souls either went to the gallows or were crushed to death beneath heavy stones for dabbling in that most heinous of crimes, witchcraft.

The Salem witch trials may have made history, but the first documented case of witchcraft in the United States involving a white woman occurred almost seven decades earlier in Virginia.

In 1626, Goodwife Joan Wright, an upstanding resident of Surrey County, across the river from Jamestown, was accused by a number of neighbors of having "consorted with the devil." The exact circumstances surrounding her crimes were never fully revealed, but accusations ranged from having put a spell on chickens to having made young women "dance naked and stand before the Tree." The "Tree" was a reference to Satan's own special tree, around which young maidens anxious to join a coven were required to dance and "perform other lewd acts unfitting to Nature."

Mrs. Wright was eventually acquitted of the charges, but there would be other cases in the coming years. In all cases, though, punishment was generally light compared to the harsh sentences handed down by the notorious "Witch Courts" of Salem, Boston, and elsewhere in New England. At least no one in Virginia was ever tortured or hanged for practicing witchcraft.

Almost all seventeenth century English men and women believed in Satan and the witches and sorcerers who served him. In 1597 King James had published his famous *Daemonologie*, a frightfully medieval epistle which set forth the monarch's own verifications for the existence of the devil and his unholy hosts. According to James, the only way to deal effectively with these agents of the Prince of Darkness was to seek them out and destroy them wherever they may have been hiding.

When the English settlers first arrived in the New World, their suspicions about devils were confirmed. Everywhere they looked they saw devils—in the dark forests, among the remote mountain tops, and along the streams and rivers that flowed through their wild, new homeland. These "devils" were the Indians, of course: dark-skinned, half-naked, unfathomable savages whose bizarre rituals and bloodthirsty ceremonies terrified the European newcomers.

Commenting on the Indians, Captain John Smith once declared that they had "entertained him with most strange and fearful Conjurations."

Soon, however, as more settlers arrived and the Indians were pushed back deeper into the forests, the emphasis on the "black devils" shifted to "white devils" among the English colonists themselves. When Goodwife Wright was discovered engaging in witchcraft, colonial authorities moved swiftly to uncover others in her coven.

The best known case of witchcraft in the southern colonies involved another Virginia woman, named Grace Sherwood. By all accounts Mrs. Sherwood was a popular and well-liked citizen of Lynnhaven Bay, a sparsely settled community on the southern shores of Chesapeake Bay. Why she was accused of witchcraft in the first place remains a mystery. She was certainly no crone. No black cats followed her around, and no bats had been seen swooping around her eaves late at night. She also happened to be married to one of the community's most upstanding businessmen.

Sherwood's arrest and later ordeal in a "ducking pond" probably had something to do with blight suddenly appearing on a neighbor's crop. Then, too, the same neighbor's pigs suddenly started behaving queerly—always a good sign that unnatural forces were at work nearby. To many folks in the community, it seemed unlikely so many unfortunate events could happen to one family so quickly without some kind of "outside" interference.

There could only be one explanation—witchcraft. The finger of suspicion pointed directly at Sherwood when yet another neighbor testified she had been "ridden about" by Grace Sherwood and that the suspect had left her house once "out of the Key hole...like a black Catt."

Proclaiming her innocence, Mrs. Sherwood was bound over to the General Court in Williamsburg to stand trial. The charge: consorting with the devil and engaging in witchcraft. The judge quickly ruled that the evidence was "too general" and remanded the case to the county.

Back at Lynnhaven Bay, it was decided that the only way to determine Sherwood's guilt or innocence was to administer to her the water test. In those days, it was widely believed that water was the purest element in nature. It stood to reason, then, that diabolical creatures like witches and demons would never be accepted by water. In other words, guilty persons would float on the surface, while innocent ones would sink to the bottom.

The problem was, should the accused person happen to be innocent, there was a good chance he or she would drown. On the other hand, should the unfortunate individual's clothing somehow trap a pocket of air and cause him or her to float, it would be an indisputable sign of guilt. The gallows awaited those who floated.

On the fateful day—July 10, 1706—Grace Sherwood was

bound and gagged, and then hauled down to a spot on the bay known as Witch Duck Point. When the charges had been properly read once more and the Christian rites administered, she was rowed out on the water, prayed for, then dumped overboard.

For several seconds her prosecutors listened to her strangled cries, and then felt a sense of relief when her thrashing body finally sank beneath the rippling waves. Spectators lined along the shore dropped to their knees and prayed for the witch's soul.

Suddenly, out of nowhere, a mass of angry black clouds began forming overhead. Thunder boomed and lightning clawed across the troubled heavens. The rain came, drenching the crowds of God-fearing colonists assembled on the muddy shore. Those who were there later described it as a deluge, as if God Himself had opened up the gates to paradise to let loose His terrible wrath.

Then, out on the water, the impossible happened—the soggy form of Grace Sherwood was rising slowly from the murky depths of the bay.

She was floating!

The terrified prosecutors in the boat didn't know whether to fish her out of the water or to row away from that accursed place as fast as they could. They finally decided they'd seen enough miracles for one day. Guilty or not, they simply couldn't let the poor woman drown, so they hauled her into the boat and rowed back to the beach.

There still had to be a trial, of course, and Mrs. Sherwood was eventually found guilty. But several months later, about the time the Salem witch trials were winding down, Grace Sherwood was released.

She had been one of the lucky ones. In spite of her trials and tribulations as a witch suspect, she lived to the ripe old age of eighty—unlike some of the less fortunate women in Salem Village.

The Sacred "Woman in Blue"

When Spanish missionaries reached the Texas wilderness in the early 1600s, they heard a lot of strange stories from local Indians about mysterious, white-skinned gods who had once walked among them.

According to some accounts, these divine visitors had spoken to them in a language different from theirs, but one they could understand. Most of these gods had come and gone in ages past, but all held forth a common promise—they would come again someday.

The story that got the most attention concerned a beautiful young white "goddess" who, legend has it, appeared among several groups of Indians living in Texas and elsewhere in the Southwest. The Indians called her the "woman in blue" because each time she came she wore a blue cloak—similar, in fact, to those worn by the newly arrived Spanish priests.

Not only was this "woman in blue" a frequent visitor, she was said to have left behind material evidence of her earthly visits—including a portable stone altar adorned with religious emblems and the figures of several saints. There was even a figure of Christ himself!

Intrigued by such stories, missionary leaders wasted no time informing the church back in Spain about their findings. This seemed to be a mystery of profound spiritual significance—how was it that pagan savages living on the far edge of this strange, wild New World had come into possession of the very symbols of Christian faith?

Within a short while, droves of other missionaries, accompanied by soldiers and explorers, flocked to Texas. Their task: solve the mystery of the "woman in blue."

One of the missionaries who came was Father Damien Manzanet, who had recently read a new book entitled *The Mystical City of God*. In the book, Sister Maria de Agreda, a Castilian nun, had told how she had been mysteriously transported to a remote wilderness on the frontiers of New Spain, where she had introduced a heathen race to Christianity.

Sister Maria, a respected abbess who had entered the monastery at the age of fifteen, claimed to have made the mystical journey more than five hundred times in the early seventeenth century. In glowing words she related how she had been well received by dark-skinned savages who called themselves "Titlas," or "Tejas," and that they had miraculously understood her every word.

Maria's out-of-body travels apparently occurred only when she slept. Without being too specific, the sister said she would suddenly grow rigid in bed. A state of supreme ecstasy would seize her, and she would be whisked away at blinding speed to the wilderness where she worked and prayed among naked savages.

By 1630 all of Spain was abuzz with talk of Sister Maria's "holy mystery." To make the story even more interesting, a group of fifty Jumano Indians had appeared at a convent in northeastern Mexico that same year, asking that missionaries be sent among them. When pressed to explain their sudden interest in European religion, the Indians said a graceful white woman—a "goddess"—had come to them long ago and instructed them in "the truths of Christian faith."

Who could that white "goddess" have been? Except for the wife or mistress of an occasional explorer or trader, there was no record of European women having visited that part of the New World. Even more perplexing were the religious artifacts apparently left behind by the "woman in blue."

The more Father Manzanet listened to the stories, the more convinced he became of a connection between Sister

Maria's account of her out-of-body travels and the tales told by these brooding savages on the frontier. In her book, she had called them Titlas. Is that not what these Indians he encountered called themselves—Titlas...Tejas...Techas?

The similarities were all the proof the Franciscan priest needed to convince himself that it was Maria de Agreda who had visited these Indians long ago. Just why, and when, he wasn't sure. But the bottom line was that God had used Sister Maria and her miracles to lead him to the wilderness, too.

Like most seventeenth century Spaniards, Father Manzanet believed strongly in supernatural forces, and that divine intervention was an everyday fact of life. Like most of his countrymen, he readily embraced the possibility that Maria de Agreda had been telling the truth when she wrote about her otherworldly travels—that God had indeed sent her among the Indians in the New World to preach and spread the Gospel.

It was Maria's story, in fact, that had spurred legions of missionaries across the Rio Grande into the Texas hinterlands. While some established missions and sought to convert Indians, many searched for proof of the holy sister's travels. As they pressed deeper into Texas, the missionaries heard other stories about the "blue lady." One chief said she had healed his mother by touching her brow. Another legend told how delicate blue flowers always blossomed wherever she stepped.

Father Manzanet himself was once asked by a withered old chief for a piece of blue cloth in which to bury his wife. The Father, stunned by the request, asked why it should be blue. "Because," said the chief, "that was the color of the cloak worn long ago by the beautiful young woman who had come to Texas to tell us about God."

The story of the "woman in blue" would be like a magnet in later decades, drawing hundreds of other missionaries and explorers to the Texas territory. Today the Southwest abounds with legends about the mysterious "goddess," who some believe still roams the hills and deserts causing flowers to bloom and bestowing love and riches on the unfortunate.

The Lost Maidens of the Okefenokee

Spanish explorers pushing northward through the gloomy Florida swamps into the moss-shrouded lowlands of Georgia were astonished to encounter tales about a mysterious race of women who supposedly lived somewhere in the Okefenokee, that dismal region the Indians called the "land of the trembling earth."

In pre-Colonial days, the Okefenokee was home to various groups of Indians, many of whom believed that devils and demons occupied the deeper recesses of the dreary swamp. Legends about witches and angry spirits also swirled around crackling campfires, and even into modern times, there were stories about a horrible, fire-breathing monster said to dwell in a bottomless lake somewhere far out in the middle of that shadow-haunted wilderness.

When the first conquistadors arrived in the early sixteenth century, they heard these stories and more. The tales that fascinated them the most, though, had to do with a tribe of beautiful, dark-eyed maidens known collectively as the "Daughters of the Sun."

It was said that these women, who "spoke in accents of music and had the countenance of angels," lived on an enchanted island called Lost Paradise far out in the middle of the Okefenokee. The island, so the story went, was hidden from view by swirling mists and protected by deep rivers and alligator-filled lakes. Lost Paradise was believed to have been

20

the original Garden of Eden.

Unfortunately, the whereabouts of the island was a closely guarded secret. As with El Dorado—another fabled, much sought-after goal in the North American wilderness— only a few oldtimers had ever laid eyes upon either the enchanted land itself or the beautiful "Daughters of the Sun" who dwelled there.

One old story, handed down by generations of Indians and white settlers, referred to the island as a "magical realm" full of softly gurgling streams, game-filled forests, and air so clean and pure that flowers bloomed year-round. When the conquistadors first heard of the place, they began to fantasize about the lovely damsels. Weary from long months in the wilderness, these grim explorers in gleaming armor pressed their wary Indian hosts for more information.

Alas, the old Indian chiefs—even at sword-point— refused to reveal the location of Lost Paradise. Frustrated, the Spaniards set off in search of the women themselves. Some time later, exhausted and running low on supplies, the bearded conquistadors reluctantly abandoned their quest.

When other Europeans arrived in later years, they, too, heard fascinating accounts of the "Daughters of the Sun." As with their Spanish predecessors, all attempts to find them failed—sometimes tragically.

For example, Creek legend tells about a group of white hunters who became "dizzy" and "disoriented" while searching for the women. Soon they were overcome with fatigue and collapsed. Suddenly, out of the dreamlike mists, several of the most beautiful women they had ever seen appeared. Radiant in the early morning sun, these angelic apparitions reportedly took pity on the pale-skinned visitors and transported them to their enchanted island where they were nursed back to health.

As soon as they had recovered, the intruders were whisked away from Lost Paradise in a cloud of smoke. But the Europeans, smitten by the beauty of the maidens—and per- haps determined to make them their wives—trudged back into the swamp to find them. They never returned, and their fate remains a mystery in the folklore of the Okefenokee Swamp.

Another Creek legend deals with a similar incident, this one involving a couple of lost Indian braves. After days of wandering around the swamp, the hapless Indians stumbled upon a village populated by beautiful, dark-eyed women. These women had husbands, however, who were "fierce... and exceedingly cruel to strangers."

Convinced that the women were the legendary Daughters of the Sun, the braves decided to fight rather than be forced out of the enchanted forest by their husbands. The maidens, teary-eyed and full of great fear for the young intruders' lives, begged them to go before their husbands returned from a hunting trip. The braves obeyed, and upon returning to their village they recounted their adventures in the Okefenokee.

Soon other braves set out to find the enchanted island, but their efforts were all in vain. After years of searching the wild swamp, they finally gave up, convinced that neither the island nor the women had existed in the first place.

Still, over the years, other explorers pressing deep into the rugged interior of the Okefenokee heard soft laughter echoing through the dim glades. On more than one occasion, solitary adventurers told of having seen thin, shimmering forms flitting through the tangled shadows.

Who were the "lost maidens" of the Okefenokee? One theory holds that the mysterious women belonged to a long-forgotten group of Mayans who had migrated to the Okefenokee region from their homeland in Mexico a thousand years ago. Another says the maidens were descended from survivors of Atlantis, the legendary continent that was said to have sunk beneath the Atlantic Ocean in a cataclysmic upheaval in pre-Biblical times.

Whatever their origins—or whether in fact they ever existed at all—the legend of the Daughters of the Sun stands as one of the Okefenokee Swamp's most delightful and charming mysteries.

Visions of the Veil-Born

Once upon a time, long before interstate highways and jet travel, the lonely backroads of the Deep South were dangerous places for solitary wayfarers. Besides Indians, wild animals, and cold-blooded highwaymen, other terrors lurked among the remote hills and swamps—fanciful terrors that belong more in the realm of folklore than history.

To the people of that far-off age, creatures like *loups-garous,* wampus cats, and will-o-the-wisp hobgoblins were every bit as real as bloodthirsty Indians, masked desperados, and snarling bears.

Probably the most dreaded creature of them all was the "plat-eye," a much-feared, much-misunderstood spirit that haunted and tormented its victims unmercifully before driving them either to insane asylums or early graves. Many spine-tingling stories are told about bizarre encounters with this peculiar apparition, mainly among early settlers pushing westward through the Appalachian Mountains and farther south along the Mississippi Delta.

To meet up with this loathsome creature on a lonely road at night meant sure doom for unlucky travelers. That's why in the old days folks tried their best to avoid certain hollows, woods, and swamps when going cross-country. Even today, in some parts of the Great Smoky Mountains it is considered sheer folly to pass by a graveyard at night. The same is true among the lowlands of Mississippi, Florida, Georgia, Alabama, and Louisiana where the horrible plat-eye is known to still lurk.

But in the past, there must have been a lot of people who ignored this advice because folklore is riddled with hair-raising run-ins between hapless humans and these fearsome creatures of the dark.

According to legends probably brought over from Europe, plat-eyes were evil spirits that came back to life for one of several reasons—to avenge their deaths, to cause mischief among mortals, or to finish up tasks began in life. Failure to provide the departed with a proper burial was also a good way to warrant an unwelcome visit by the plat-eye.

The biggest problem about plat-eyes, however, was that they were invisible to most people. Only a few special persons, usually young girls, had the power to see these wispy shades. In some regions of the South, these individuals were known as the "veil-born" because of having been born with a caul—a thin membrane, similar to that inside an egg shell, which surrounds a fetus. A few babies are born with the membrane enveloping their heads.

Stories about the veil-born and their mystical powers are still commonplace, especially among rural blacks who believe that children born with cauls have the gift of second sight—the ability to see things invisible to most people. Ghosts, goblins, and plat-eyes are among the spooks said to inhabit this unseen world. In medieval Europe, persons born with cauls were often persecuted as witches.

In time, stories about the plat-eye joined those of other fabulous creatures said to haunt the American frontier. The wampus cat, *loup-garou,* and even Bigfoot seem closely related to the plat-eye myth and may share similar origins.

When black slaves arrived from Africa in the early seventeenth century, they brought with them their own pantheon of gods, demons, and an assortment of other spiritual entities. These victims of the "peculiar institution" may have actually been the first to introduce the plat-eye myth. At least, they gave it new terrifying substance. Like their African ancestors, slaves believed that to bury a person without proper funeral rites was the fastest way to get an angry visit from the deceased's ghost. To die without benefit of a funeral meant the dead person was cursed to wander the face of the earth forever—or until it could be banished through exorcism.

In African mythology, funerals were essential in helping the dead find the right road to heaven and bypass the less desirable pathway to hell. In the absence of such rites, the ghost would be condemned to the unpleasant task of haunting houses and cemeteries and out-of-the-way roads. Without graveside ceremonies such as feasting, prayer, singing, and the cleansing of the body, these spirits would sometimes be compelled, zombie-like, to go after their relatives with a bloodthirsty vengeance.

As a rule, plat-eye spirits generally resemble the bodies they once occupied, but they also take different shapes— sometimes a dog or cat, other times a pig or cow, or even another human being without a head. Plat-eyes have no natural enemies and will stop at nothing to terrorize a particular place—such as a house, forest, or graveyard—until proper funeral arrangements are made. That's why such places—especially graveyards—are to be avoided.

"The vicinity of cemeteries is carefully avoided after dark," wrote one observer, "and so are places where people have met with fatal misfortune."

The Bell Witch of Tennessee

When John Bell first heard the horrible scratching sound at the walls of his remote Tennessee homestead, he thought it was rats trying to gnaw their way in out of the winter cold.

Several nights in a row he had set traps, but nothing seemed to work against the pesky rodents. The sounds continued, night after night—the scratching and clawing and hissing—keeping his family up until all hours. The strange thing was that no matter how hard he looked, he never saw the first sign of a rat.

Then came a new sound, tappings at the window, soon followed by a mysterious scratching at the door—like a wild animal trying to get in. Most chilling of all, however, were the eerie cries that seemed to float down the chimney long after the fire had gone out at night.

Bell was not a superstitious man. All his life he had believed there was an answer to every mystery, no matter how puzzling. That's why it took him so long to come to the conclusion that the strange noises were being made by a ghost or spirit or some such supernatural thing.

In those days—back in the early 1800s—much of Tennessee was wild and remote, full of old stories and legends about "spirits of the earth." These spirits were said to be mostly benign—actually helpful to the hard-working pioneers of the lonely forests and mountains. But occasionally tales cropped up about less friendly ones, malign spirits that sought to harm and destroy rather than help and instruct.

When neighbors heard about the strange goings-on out at

the Bell place, they figured something evil had to be behind the commotion. What they couldn't figure out was why.

"If we didn't know them (the Bells) for the good and honest people that they were," one neighbor reported in a local newspaper, "we'd have thought they were being punished for some crime or sin they'd committed."

By the winter of 1818, life at the Bell farm had become so bizarre Bell thought seriously about moving his family away. Pictures would fall mysteriously off walls; tables would turn on their sides and scuttle across the kitchen floor; chairs would prance about, and once even did a few somersaults; cutlery would parade up and down on the floor; china dishes and cups would "march merrily along" the tables and cabinets.

Before long, accounts of the eerie happenings began to appear in newspapers as far away as New York and Philadelphia. Reporters, ministers, doctors and psychic researchers soon descended on the Bell household along with hundreds of curiosity seekers. The Bell farm had become what one reporter called "a place of occult pilgrimage...."

The presence of so many visitors actually seemed to encourage the spooky antics at the old Bell place. Whenever outsiders called upon the "spirit" to do something, it always obliged, sometimes making vague whispering sounds and indistinct mutterings while whipping sheets and quilts through the air and causing the clock to chime for hours at a time.

"As an entertainment," declared one visitor, "it was in a class of its own. Put it in New York, set it on Broadway, and you could sell tickets from now till kingdom come."

A journalist writing in a Baltimore newspaper said, "It was as if the thing knew what was expected of it and was determined that no one who traveled there would be disappointed. It obligingly put on its act even without being asked to—and, if you did speak to it, it would mostly do whatever was requested."

On March 14, 1818, the first distinguishable words came forth from the spirit. In the presence of several astonished visitors and the entire Bell family, a crackling woman's voice said: "I am a spirit who was once happy...but now I have been disturbed and am unhappy."

The spirit identified herself simply as "Kate." She said she was now a witch of the forest, but had once lived as a woman on the land "long, long ago." Kate informed her listeners that she was haunting the Bell farm because someone had disturbed her bones. "My bones were buried near here," Kate stated matter-of-factly, "and I want them back."

Although Mr. Bell succeeded in finding what he believed were the old woman's bones and providing them with a proper Christian burial, the annoying spirit refused to leave them alone. In fact, Bell's noble action seemed only to make matters worse—especially for Bell himself, who thereafter became the favorite target of the old spirit's mischievous antics.

First of all, the victimized farmer's tongue began to swell until it filled most of his mouth. He could hardly eat, speak, or even swallow water. His physical condition quickly deteriorated as the old witch tormented him.

"We have seen nothing like it in our experience of morbid and pathological conditions," one attending physician was quoted in a local paper as having uttered. "There appears to be no known reason for the affliction and there is certainly no known cure. We shall just have to hope, and to pray, that the patient makes a natural recovery."

Bell didn't recover. Instead, he grew steadily worse, as unseen hands reportedly slapped him sharply across the face, ripped clothes from his body, punched him in the stomach, and kicked him in the legs. On one occasion the witch even spat in his face.

"I've almost done with you, Jack Bell," the witch proclaimed. "It won't be long now before you go to your grave to rot!"

Investigators, neighbors, and members of Bell's family begged the old spirit to release the farmer from her wrath. "Why do you hate John Bell so?" Bell's best friend, Jack Johnson asked. "What has he ever done to harm or pester you? Won't you be courteous enough to answer my question?"

To this the witch replied: "I am a spirit from everywhere—from Heaven, Hell, and the Earth. I am in the air, in houses, anyplace at any time. I was born millions of years ago. That's all I have to say to you!"

So she continued to plague Bell and other members of the family, striking them with boils, colds, fevers, and the like. Betsy, Bell's teenage daughter, seemed to be the only one immune to the witch's spell.

Finally, on the morning of December 19, 1820, the farmer went into a stupor. His doctor said: "I can find nothing fatally wrong with him. Yet he is most assuredly dying."

The next day the doctor's words were proven. Bell's frail, tormented body was laid to rest in a tiny cemetery not far from the house where he had suffered for the better part of the past four years. At the funeral, the voice of the Bell witch was heard one last time, cackling and croaking triumphantly over the farmer's death. And then—just as mysteriously as it had appeared—it was gone forever.

Psychic investigators and journalists still write and talk about the Bell Witch haunting as if it had occurred only yesterday instead of nearly one hundred seventy years ago. So far, no satisfactory theory has come forth to account for the incredible events that entertained a generation of Americans and drove one Tennessee farmer to his grave.

Notorious Deeds
and Unnatural Acts

The Prophet's Bloody Revenge

On the morning of May 12, 1828, a young black slave and self-appointed preacher named Nat Turner was picking corn in his master's garden when a voice "like the sound of many winds" floated down to him from Heaven.

Turner, a short, powerfully built 28-year-old with clear, twinkly eyes, wasn't afraid. Nor was he really surprised as the voice whispered his name over and over, reminding him of his special purpose in life.

In fact, the soft-spoken slave had been expecting a miracle such as this for some time. Convinced since childhood that he was a prophet sent to earth on a divine mission, young Turner's eyes flashed with proud fire as he pondered the implications of that mystical vision.

There had been signs, even before God's voice came to him in the field that morning—disturbing signs that only Turner, the Almighty's Chosen One on earth, could interpret. Had he not seen in his own mind rivers of blood pouring throughout the land? Had he not heard thunder rolling through the heavens while others slept, warning of the coming clash between good and evil? Had he himself not witnessed an army of black and white angels waging spiritual warfare in the storm-scented clouds?

What were the strange lights in the sky he had watched flickering over the hilltops on several occasions if not the Saviour's own redeeming glow?

That morning, standing alone in the sweeping field of corn, had not the prophet seen drops of blood staining the cornstalks? And on the leaves of bushes, had he not seen the marks of Satan—strange numbers and hieroglyphs and a blasphemous parade of stick-like men reveling in gruesome poses?

With his face uplifted toward Heaven, young Nat Turner knew he had seen and heard all those things and more. He also knew it was only a matter of time before God's mighty sword slashed down, smiting the Serpent and all the enemies of His Chosen People.

Three years later, on a warm, summer evening in 1831, Nat Turner's mystical vision would come to pass. It would come only a few months after darkness engulfed the sun in a solar eclipse—the final sign the prophet needed before springing into action.

Cross Keys, Virginia, was a quiet hamlet nestled in the rolling hills of Southampton County in the southwestern corner of the state. In those days, Cross Keys was populated primarily by white farmers and merchants of modest means. One of the community's most prosperous residents was a kind, gentle farmer named Joseph Travis, who happened to own several slaves.

One of those slaves was Nat Turner.

Travis was fond of his young slave, admiring him not only for his intelligence and enthusiasm for work, but also for his honesty, courage, and religious piety. He had even attended a few of Turner's sermons and, according to some records, encouraged the preacher to continue developing his oratorical talents.

What Travis didn't know—nor did any other white person living in Southampton County that unusually warm, muggy summer in 1831—was that the black preacher he had come so to admire was secretly plotting one of the bloodiest slave insurrections in American history. By the time it ended, less than a month later, at least sixty white people would be dead along with more than a hundred blacks.

It is no secret that Turner, who openly called himself "The Prophet," had a mystical, almost mesmerizing influence over many people in the area, white as well as black. He was convinced of his own superiority, divinely granted by long hours of prayer and fasting in the name of Jehovah, the god of the Old Testament.

Therefore, when the time came to act, Turner had little trouble convincing a few fellow slaves that they, too, were part of his divine mission to rid the valley of whites. He told them all about his visions, about how God had spoken to him on numerous occasions, about the lights flashing over the hilltops, and the blood-stained cornstalks, all in preparation for him to lead the glorious task that lay ahead.

In his own chilling words, Turner later wrote: "I now began to prepare them too for my purpose by telling them something was about to happen that would terminate in fulfilling the great promise that had been made to me."

That "great promise" was death. It came quickly and mercilessly to the simple farmers and planters and tradesmen of Southampton County who lay sleeping in their beds when The Prophet and his axe-wielding band of "angels" struck.

The first white people to die were Turner's own master, Joseph Travis. and his entire family—hacked to death with axes. From the Travis farm a group of about thirty blacks armed with old muskets, knives, picks, and axes, surged across the countryside, stopping off at every house and cabin along the way to stab, beat, and shoot their white occupants to death.

The bloodiest carnage occurred at dawn the next morning when Turner's gang of killers broke into the home of a widow getting her ten children off to school. The mother and nine of her children were slaughtered on the spot; the tenth child escaped by crawling inside a chimney where she hid until the murderers went away.

By eight o'clock, the enraged black rebels had hacked and bludgeoned their way halfway across the county toward the tiny town of Jerusalem. When the alarm finally sounded— sometime around nine—hundreds of white men came charging after the renegade slaves, rifles and pistols blazing. Several blacks were killed outright; others, including Nat Turner, escaped into the Great Dismal Swamp.

Almost a month later, The Prophet was seen hiding in some bushes and apprehended by a team of marshals. On November 5 he was tried, found guilty, and sentenced to be hanged six days later on November 11. Throughout the ordeal—capture, trial and gallows—Turner remained calm and collected, seemingly unfazed by the angry demands for his life that swirled across the jailhouse lawn. Some say the divine mystic and rebel leader actually looked forward to his date with the hangman.

A few days before his scheduled execution, Turner set forth his thoughts and feelings about the grisly deed he had done. What emerged from his "confessions" was a rambling, sometimes incoherent outpouring of love for his fellow man. Nowhere, however, did there appear to be any signs of remorse for the tragic loss of life he had caused.

Yet Turner's confessions, shrouded in mysticism and religious symbolism, revealed the inner workings of a brilliant but deeply troubled young mind, consumed with burning visions and other Old Testament revelations about his divinely inspired mission—that of rising up against the whites and smiting them dead for having caused his people so much misery and suffering.

Commenting on his vision in the cornfield, Turner wrote, "I heard a loud noise in the Heavens, and the spirit instantly appeared to me and said the Serpent was loosened…and that I should…fight against the Serpent, for the time was fast approaching when the first would be last and the last should be first…."

Moments before the noose was placed over his neck, someone asked Turner whether he regretted what he had done. In a soft voice that crackled, the Prophet replied, "Was not Christ crucified?"

Virginia's "Starving Time"

Their small village wasn't much—a handful of crude huts and cabins surrounded by a hastily erected palisade to keep out wild animals and even wilder savages—but to the few hundred brave souls clustered along the lonely shore of Virginia, it was home.

In spite of the hardships and loneliness and unending peril that lurked just beyond the protective wall, these Jamestown colonists were determined to make a stand. No one thought about going back home to England. They were here, and here they would stay to build a new way of life—far removed from the dark, troubled ways of old Europe.

This was not the first time, of course, that a small band of English colonists had tried to make a go of it in the harsh western wilderness. Only a few years before, in 1587, more than a hundred men, women, and children had apparently been wiped out by Indians in an ill-fated attempt to colonize a small island named Roanoke off the Virginia coast. Then, just three years past, another group of settlers had set up camp at the mouth of the Sagadahoc River in Maine. Although not quite as disastrous as the Roanoke Colony, the Maine effort had also failed.

The most recent attempt at colonization had come less than two years earlier when seventy-five men and boys had tried to set up the Jamestown settlement for future waves of colonists. Instead of worrying about finding food, those first Englishmen in Jamestown had been more concerned about finding gold and an illusive passageway to China. Their foolhardiness cost most of them their lives.

The Jamestown of 1609 would be different. This time, instead of spending all their time and energy searching for nonexistent gold and the fabled passageway to the Far East, the colonists would clear the forests, raise crops, and become totally self-sufficient. Some five hundred men, women, and children had come along this time for the purpose of building new lives at the edge of this mythological, legend-haunted New World.

Then the first snowflakes of winter fell. As the days grew shorter and the nights darker and colder, some settlers began to realize there wasn't going to be enough food to go around. The crops had not matured as expected, and the water itself had become contaminated. To make matters worse, no relief ship was expected until sometime the following the spring.

What were they going to do? Without food and water, how were the settlers going to survive the winter?

Some turned to the Indians for help, but instead of lending a hand this time, the Indians retreated deeper into the woods away from the struggling palefaces. After all, how often had they intervened in the past to help them—only to be repaid by arrogant bullying and ridicule? No, this time, let the ungrateful newcomers fend for themselves.

By the end of December, the situation for the colonists had gone from grim to disastrous. The daily ration was soon reduced to half a pint of corn daily. According to one account, each can of corn "contained as many worms as grains."

Starving men desperately bartered their clothes and blankets for a cupful of their neighbor's corn. This resulted in many of them freezing to death as temperatures continued to drop and icy winds blasted in from the snow-packed river. Fights occasionally broke out over the dwindling supplies of food, leading to stern new laws. Anyone caught trying to steal provisions faced either having his ears cut off—or execution.

When the last few grains of corn finally disappeared, starving men and women "gladd to make shift with vermin" started eating boots, shoes, and anything else made of leather.

They crawled barefoot into the snowy woods to dig up roots and hibernating snakes for food. Some men resorted to vampirism by licking "upp the bloode which had fallen from their weak fellowes."

Besides succumbing to starvation, scores of men, women, and children were freezing to death. Houses were torn down for firewood, and even some of the wooden sections from the palisades were ripped away to chew on before throwing them onto roaring bonfires. As one writer observed: "The gates (to the settlement), no longer barred, swung back and forth in the cold winter nights..."

The most gruesome acts of survival were yet to come. As the snows of December blew into January, starving, desperate men dug up corpses from their graves and "ravenously ate them ... stewed with roots and herbs." One man actually killed his wife, salted her down, and ate part of her before his grisly crime was discovered. He was later executed.

In keeping with his bizarre Elizabethan sense of humor, Captain John Smith, the man in charge of the unfortunate colony, calmly wrote: "Whether she was better roasted, boyled or carbonado'd, I know not. But such a dish as powdered (salted) wife I never heard of."

Finally, in early March, two relief ships appeared. When Sir Thomas Gates, commander of the relief expedition, pulled into Jamestown Harbor, he was appalled at the dreary spectacle of humanity that greeted him. More dead than alive, survivors crawled and stumbled down the embankments. Instead of the five hundred settlers he had expected to find, Gates counted sixty-five "anatomies" staring back at him with terror-stricken eyes and "making pathetic sounds with their feeble voices."

"We are starved! We are starved!" they moaned, as Gates unloaded crates of food, blankets, and fresh, warm clothing. While the survivors feasted, Gates made plans to abandon the disease-haunted settlement. Some colonists favored putting the entire wretched town to the torch—an idea that Gates rejected.

The commander then ordered the handful of survivors to

climb aboard. They were going home, back to England. After three years of brutal and courageous effort, the Jamestown colonists were going to give up. Raleigh's first colony had ended in disaster; so, too, had Jamestown.

Before the ships could set sail, however, a "strange breeze" held them fast—as if some outside power were holding them back, preventing their escape. Finally, the sails caught wind and the two tiny ships with their frail and half-starved cargo of passengers lurched downriver toward the open sea.

As fate would have it, the governor of Virginia, Lord De La Warr, intercepted the ships moments before they cleared the sound. Instead of allowing them to leave, De La Warr ordered them to return to Jamestown. No one was abandoning the colony as long as he was in command! It appeared that the New World was not destined to die after all.

Diseases, famine, bad luck, broken promises, and increasingly aggressive Indian attacks would continue to plague the tiny settlement in the coming years. Of the fourteen thousand colonists who had set out to make Jamestown their home by the year 1622, thirteen thousand had died.

No war or plague in history had ever taken a higher percentage of lives than were lost during the infamous "starving time" in the fated Virginia colony.

Terror on the Natchez Trace

His name was Joseph Thompson Hare, his age unknown. No one knows where he came from, nor does anyone really know why he was hanged one dreary morning in the autumn of 1818.

Today, Hare's mortal remains rest in a lonely graveyard in Maryland, more than a thousand miles from Natchez, Mississippi, where for more than a decade his name was one of the most despised and feared along the raw frontier.

In those days—long before brightly colored steamboats chugged up and down the winding Mississippi on their way to New Orleans and the Gulf of Mexico—Hare was known as one of the most notorious outlaw-bandits operating along the infamous Natchez Trace. Before his wave of terror came to an end, this bloodthirsty villain who claimed to be a mystic with visionary powers blazed a trail of carnage up and down the historic path linking colonial Nashville with Natchez.

By his own admission, hundreds of innocent travelers had met their fate at the end of Hare's long, gleaming sword, their bones left to the buzzards and alligators along the silent, shadow-haunted Trace. The truth is, nobody will ever know just how many people Hare robbed and murdered and mutilated before his unlikely capture about 1810.

Hare, who wore fine clothes and considered himself a gentleman, attributed his remarkable success as a bandit to the spirit world. Handsome and strong, he believed "mystical forces" had guided him throughout his career as a highwayman—forces that convinced him he was a modern-

41

day horseman of the Apocalypse.

While some contemporaries saw him as weird and fantastically religious, others believed he was Satan, sent to punish a wicked world. The cold, cruel manner in which Hare dealt with most of his hapless victims convinced law enforcement officials throughout the moss-choked bayous he was nothing more than a savage rogue, a blood-lusting butcher without a soul.

Hare's devilish reputation became his trademark. One of his favorite tactics was to hide in the bushes along the trail, then spring out whenever an unarmed stranger approached, shouting that he was the devil himself ready to drag the victim down to hell unless he turned over all his money and valuables at once. The highwayman's shameless bravura apparently worked well. Terrified travelers rarely hesitated to fork over their goods; those who held back were quickly dispatched by flashing sword or crackling gunfire. Legend has it that most of his victims—even those who cooperated—met similar fates.

On one occasion alone he reportedly took about $10,000 in gold and currency from a group of pilgrims, terrified that "the devil" was going to snatch their souls any second.

Hare's greedy exploits were, understandably, the talk of the Trace. In many ways he became the model romantic highwayman—handsome, dashing and certainly daring—as he galloped down the trail on horseback, cape flowing and sword flashing. He was well-read, and those who knew him swore there was a side to the man "so soft and sentimental, as to be almost woman-like."

From Nashville to Natchez, and on southward to New Orleans, the conversation at roadside inns, taverns, brothels, and churches centered on this marauding mystic, whom many feared more than the wild Indians, bears, alligators, and ghosts said to haunt lonely regions along the Trace. In some frontier quarters he was regarded as a folk hero, a modern-day Robin Hood who often robbed from the rich to give to the poor. Others saw him as the dangerous fiend that he was—a savage killer who would just as soon run his sword through a woman's heart as a man's.

For generations now, Hare's capture and subsequent sentence has been regarded as one of the Deep South's most troublesome mysteries. How was it, for example, that this murderous rogue, who fancied himself a psychic, mystic, ladies' man, and dandy, got off with only a five-year prison sentence? While chicken thieves and pickpockets were sent to the gallows elsewhere, Hare always managed to stay clear of the hangman's noose. Did he, as some of the old stories suggest, use spiritual forces to influence law enforcement officials? Or was it plain luck?

Even more astonishing was the manner in which he was finally apprehended.

Late one afternoon, while dozing in a cave, Hare was awakened by the tell-tale clatter of a traveler coming up the Trace. Grabbing his gun and sword, the outlaw sprang into the clearing and encountered a lone rider, a cattle drover, apparently heading back up to Nashville. With his pistol cocked and ready, Hare demanded the man's money—all of it—which the stranger happily handed over, begging that his life be spared.

For once in his life, Hare took pity on a victim. Perhaps it had something to do with the drover's own shady background. When Hare heard that the fellow was a profiteer himself, the bandit roared with uncustomary laughter and allowed his comrade-in-crime to go on his way unharmed.

As it turned out, that was Hare's biggest mistake.

Later, while making his getaway, Hare came across a strange white horse standing in the middle of the Trace. Hare described it as a "beautiful white horse, as white as snow: his ears stood straight forward and his figure was very striking."

But when the bandit approached the curious animal that seemed to shimmer in the misty gloom, it vanished right before his eyes. "When I got within six feet of him, he disappeared in an instant, which made me very uneasy." To his dying day, Hare swore that what he had seen was a spirit, a warning that he should mend his ways and repent unless he wanted to spend eternity roasting in the Lake of Fire.

Terrified by the apparition, Hare ran straight toward the nearest house, begging to be taken in for the night. The last thing he wanted to do was spend another night alone in that "whispering wilderness, full of strange spirits."

Meanwhile, the cattle drover was hot on Hare's trail. Anxious to get his money back, he had hired a couple of ruffians to help him track down the highwayman. Soon they came to the same farmhouse where Hare had taken refuge. After sneaking into his bedroom, several men grabbed him, handcuffed his hands behind him, then hauled him off to jail.

Incredibly, the "terror of the Trace"—the man responsible for the death of hundreds of innocent human beings—was tried, convicted and sent to a minimum security facility for only five years!

It was not until after Hare's release that Fate finally caught up with the once-feared beast of the Natchez Trace. For reasons that remain unclear, Hare went away to the East Coast, and wound up on the gallows in Maryland. Nobody is sure of the crime he committed there, but there is some evidence to suggest he had held up a small mail coach.

Whatever the cause, Joseph Thompson Hare received the death penalty. And on a cold, rainy afternoon, the man they called the "terror of the Trace" was blindfolded and led up a steep scaffolding toward his own date with the devil.

Christians, Cannibals, and Columbus

In the early part of the sixteenth century, Spanish explorers returning from their conquests in the New World told of horrifying encounters with strange, man-like beasts lurking in the pagan wilds of North America and among the remote, sun-splashed islands of the Caribbean.

Some of these monsters were said to have faces like dogs, and to have barked and growled at the Spanish intruders from behind bushes. Others had a single eye in the center of their foreheads and liked to slurp up the blood of comrades who had fallen in battle.

One of the most popular tales circulating in the capitals of Europe at the time concerned a mysterious race of "fish-men." These creatures supposedly had arms and legs, and looked like normal men in every way except one—they had long scaly tails and had to "dig little holes in the ground whenever they sat down."

Sometimes these "fish men" were linked to another bizarre tale—that of the "hunting fish." According to some observers, Indians in southern waters were in the habit of leashing these fish to the sides of their canoes, then releasing them to capture other fish!

The story that raised the most eyebrows dealt with an unfortunate tribe of primitives known to history as the Caribs. According to Christopher Columbus and other early voyagers, the Caribs were cannibals. Even worse, they were a particularly aggressive race of man-eaters who warred against their neighbors solely for the purpose of acquiring captives for ritualistic feeding.

Like the Aztecs of Mexico, the Caribs were fond of ripping out human organs for consumption while the victims were still conscious, perhaps drugged. Cannibalizing human flesh not only sustained these Indians during lean times, the practice also apparently enabled them to inherit the spiritual energy and strength of their enemies.

No one was safe from these man-eating marauders who roamed the Caribbean in search of fresh conquests and fresh meals. There is a possibility that some Caribs reached Florida and the Louisiana coast in their long, fast-moving canoes. Legends of cannibalistic activity among the Southeastern Indians persisted through Colonial times, though little evidence has been documented to suggest that anthropophagy—ritualistic cannibalism—was ever widespread among these native Americans.

So fierce were the Caribs, gangs of them would reportedly go into battle naked and unarmed, screaming at the top of their lungs as terror-stricken adversaries fled into the jungle. Those unable to run fast enough or who happened to be incapacitated would be rounded up, put in a pen, then later boiled or eaten alive.

When Columbus heard about these ferocious savages on his first voyage in 1492, he called them "Canibs"—a mispronunciation that would eventually result in a new word, "cannibalism" in English. The Carib Indians, therefore, had the distinction of having their name serve as a modern synonym for man-eater.

Of course, there were those who doubted the strange tales—especially when they considered the source. Most of the information about Caribs and cannibalism had been provided by a rival tribe of Indians known as the Arawaks, a docile group of natives who had befriended Columbus on his initial voyage. The Arawaks lived on the northern islands— what is modern Cuba, Puerto Rico, and Santo Domingo— while their age-old enemy, the Caribs, occupied regions farther to the south.

The Arawaks' spinning such outlandish tales about the Caribs may have had something to do with their own desperate desire to be rid of the uninvited Spaniards. Not only did they tell the bearded invaders about the Caribs, they also gave glowing accounts of fabulous cities of gold on distant islands, and of exotic creatures that talked and lived in palaces—creatures that knew the answers to many mysteries.

When the Spaniards heard such stories, their first inclination was to go see for themselves. With visions of wealth and fame burning in their helmeted heads, these gold-hungry conquistadors beat a bloody path from one island of the shimmering Caribbean to the next.

Another story about the Caribs that fascinated Europeans centered around their annual mating ritual with a mysterious tribe of female warriors known as Amazons. Each year, so the story went, selected groups of male Carib warriors would hop in their canoes and sail to the land of the Amazons for the purpose of "intercourse with the women of Martino...in which there is not a man."

Although Columbus never actually saw any evidence of cannibalism himself, he was the man responsible for spreading the rumor that man-eaters flourished in the new World. These tales, compounded by exotic and gruesome accounts of other blood-sucking humanoids and depraved female warriors, seemed to be exactly what the Catholic Church needed to later justify its Holy Inquisition in the Americas. Men or demons, fallen angels or beasts, whatever these strange creatures in the New World were, the church took upon itself the task of introducing them to the Cross—with or without their consent.

But Fate tricked the church.

Before missionaries were able to convert all the dark-skinned heathens, most of them would be dead, wiped out by diseases brought over by the Europeans. Those who survived the epidemics died later as slaves on Spanish-run sugar plantations and in silver mines.

Massacre Among the Magnolias

Tom Woolfolk was the kind of man everybody loved to hate. Not only did he have a reputation for being spoiled, lazy, and arrogant, some said he actually enjoyed being cruel to people—especially to his father's hired help.

The thing that bothered most people, though, was the way he treated his own parents. Captain and Mrs. Richard F. Woolfolk were two of the most respected and well-liked citizens in Macon, Georgia, during the late 1800s. In many ways the Woolfolks seemed the ideal family—rich, handsome, educated, and generous. They went to church, contributed regularly to charities, and gave frequent balls at their antebellum plantation on the outskirts of town.

It seemed everyone in the family was destined for greatness—except Tom.

Even as a boy Tom Woolfolk had been peculiar. Moody, restless, always whining and complaining when he didn't get his way, he was constantly getting into trouble at school and on the farm. His habits didn't improve with age, either. Unable to hold a job, Tom drifted from one hot scheme to the next, always drawing upon his father to bail him out when he ran into trouble, which was often.

On one occasion he went out west to become a cowboy. When that failed, he came back to Georgia and drove a streetcar. Several times he tried his hand at running various businesses. Nothing worked. Everything he touched seemed to fail—including marriage.

In the summer of 1887, Tom happened to meet a beauti-

48

ful young socialite named Georgia Byrd, daughter of a well-to-do farmer from nearby Jones County. Legend has it that Tom proposed to Georgia on a train after secretly conspiring with a minister to be on board at the same time. The marriage lasted only three weeks. When she discovered her husband was penniless, out of work, and sponging off his father's estate, the new bride packed up her bags and drove away.

The day she left, Tom reportedly told her: "Georgia, father has not fixed me up, and I'm going to burn the family; Father's rich and got plenty; if I can't get any of it none of the others will get it."

At the time nobody made much of Tom's sullen outburst—not even his soon-to-be ex-wife.

Depressed, Tom went to work on his father's plantation for about nine dollars a week. It wasn't much, and he hated every minute of it, but at least the job kept the creditors off his back while he formulated a plan.

Sometime during the dark hours of August 6, 1887, someone broke into the isolated home of Captain and Mrs. Woolfolk and murdered the entire family. Using an axe, the killer had gone from room to room in the rambling country mansion, hacking and bludgeoning to death each member of his family—nine persons in all, including the captain and his wife, six of their children, and an elderly aunt who happened to be visiting.

The only survivor was Tom, who said he was able to escape the axe-wielding murderer by leaping out a window and running for his life.

News of the killing spread fast. Thousands of people from all over the county gathered at the plantation to witness for themselves the despicable deed. Blood and mutilated bodies lay everywhere—in the hallway, in the bathrooms, in the bedrooms where the Woolfolks had been sleeping when the killer burst in upon them. Angry citizens demanded swift justice.

The sheriff found himself in a desperate situation. One of the county's most beloved families had been wiped out by a crazed killer; he had to find a suspect and find him fast.

He didn't have far to look. Friends of the family soon convinced him that Tom Woolfolk himself was the guilty person. Newspapers were quick to pick up the accusations and glaring headlines from Atlanta to Valdosta soon began to try Tom on the front pages. "The greatest monster of the age," one newspaper called him. "The cruelest and most bloodthirsty brute on record," another proclaimed.

When angry mobs gathered at the plantation and threatened to lynch Tom, the sheriff wisely hauled the boy off to jail for his own protection. Once in custody, Tom steadfastly insisted he was innocent of the charges. "Before God and man, I am an innocent man," he reportedly told visitors to his cell.

Several bits of evidence seemed to link Tom directly with the crime. First, blood-stained clothing belonging to him had been found stuffed at the bottom of a dry well. Second, the axe used in the massacre belonged to Tom. In fact, witnesses had seen him chopping up saplings with it the day before the murder. The most damaging testimony, however, came from friends and relatives of the family who swore they had often heard Tom threaten to kill his family.

Throughout the long trial Tom continued to proclaim his innocence. While hostile crowds yelled "Hang him! Hang him!" the suspect displayed remarkable composure. "Not a muscle quivered in agitation," one observer remarked.

As the trial dragged on year after year, some people began to think perhaps Tom was innocent after all. Although the evidence itself seemed overwhelming, much of it was circumstantial in nature—not enough to convict someone legally of murder. Many Bibb Countians began to sense that perhaps they were indeed trying the wrong man. Other suspects were later brought in for questioning, but when the final verdict came in, it was as had been predicted all along— guilty on all counts.

Three years later, after several more appeals and delays, the Georgia Supreme Court sentenced Tom to hang. The date was scheduled for October 29, 1890. This was actually the third death sentence he'd received since the trial had begun. Appeals had kept him one step away from the gallows on each of the previous two occasions, but now even Tom Woolfolk knew his luck had finally run out.

At exactly one-thirty on the afternoon of October 29, the trap door was sprung and Tom Woolfolk, unshackled and unhooded, plunged to an excruciating death. Because the noose had not been knotted properly, his neck didn't break and his body continued to twitch at the end of the jerking rope for a full eleven minutes.

But at last the "bloodthirsty brute," the unloved, unsuccessful son of Captain Woolfolk, was dead, swinging from the end of a rope. The good captain and his family could now rest quietly in their graves.

Or could they?

For years after the hanging, nagging questions persisted about the guilt or innocence of Tom Woolfolk. Some people had come to the conclusion that he was incapable of having committed such a heinous crime. Others believed he had been tried and convicted unfairly in the press, and that the coverage had greatly influenced not only the jury but the presiding judge as well. And besides, hadn't he gone to the gallows maintaining his innocence? Most condemned men, fearing for their souls, make last minute confessions.

There was some evidence linking a local black man named Jack to the murder. Other suspects were now being investigated by both the authorities and the newspapers. Some publishers had begun to wonder if perhaps they had attacked the wrong man in their unrelenting editorial crusade for justice.

The mystery doesn't end there.

Years after the hanging, a legend grew that Tom Woolfolk had not been executed, but that the sheriff and some other friends of the family had secretly conspired to help him escape. There were several accounts in local newspapers about a man fitting Woolfolk's description living in Texas at the turn of the century.

Like those of John Wilkes Booth, Jesse James, and others, the legend of Tom Woolfolk became ingrained in the folklore of the South.

*Voodoo Queens
and Sleeping Prophets*

Edgar Cayce:
"America's Most Mysterious Man"

On the night of April 18, 1900, a young Kentucky photographer named Edgar Cayce suddenly lost his voice. His condition was diagnosed as "paralysis of the vocal organs," and it was doubtful he would ever speak again.

Unwilling to accept such a fate, Cayce turned desperately to hypnosis for relief. At the time, hypnosis was still a relatively new branch of science and very few doctors were trained in its application. Of those trained, fewer still were willing to use it.

But Cayce finally found a physician who agreed to take the chance. After ten months of hypnotic therapy, the 23-year-old photographer's voice finally returned. It seemed a miracle at the time, but the truly amazing thing is what happened to him during those long hours of treatment each day.

Whenever he went into a trance, this shy, sensitive, deeply religious man who dropped out of school in the seventh grade would talk about things far beyond his range of knowledge and expertise. In fact, he would often discuss complex medical matters, drawing upon principles, theories, and terminologies unknown outside the medical and scientific community.

In no time, Cayce was astounding the academic world with his pinpoint diagnoses and recommended remedies for other patients, some of whom were hospitalized hundreds of miles away. Cayce was even credited for having identified and prescribed the treatment that eventually led to his own cure.

It didn't take long for news of this amazing "healer" to spread across the country. Newspapers and magazines were quick to pick up on the Cayce story, and soon banner headlines were proclaiming him "America's Most Mysterious Man." One paper wrote: "Edgar Cayce Startles Medical Men With His Trances."

As for himself, Cayce was startled by all the hoopla. Even more confounding, he couldn't remember any of the things he was credited with having said while under hypnosis! It was as if somebody else would step inside his body and speak for him, some highly trained doctor of medicine whose authoritative voice rumbled with confidence and wisdom.

Gradually Cayce came to appreciate his unusual mediumistic powers. Shortly after his remarkable recovery, he discovered that by lying down, thoroughly relaxing, and taking a deep breath, he could duplicate the trances on his own. In such self-induced states, Cayce's voice would boom across the room, diagnosing problems and prescribing remedies for patients and visitors who flocked to him from all over the South.

There now had merged two Cayces—a "waking" Cayce, the reclusive, soft-spoken photographer, and the "sleeping" Cayce, the psychic healer the media were now calling the "sleeping prophet."

Over the next several decades Edgar Cayce would delight and astonish the world with his accurate and often reassuring predictions about future events. But most people came to his office for "healing" purposes—about 16,000 between 1901 and 1944. Copies of most of his readings are still on file in the archives of the Association for Research and Enlightenment, an institute set up at Virginia Beach, Virginia, to study Cayce's unique powers.

In all that time, there was never an indication that Cayce was conscious of a single word he uttered while in the self-imposed hypnotic state. Even though Cayce couldn't account for this himself, he theorized that the thousands of readings and predictions apparently came through or out of his unconscious mind.

By 1913, Cayce's fame as the "sleeping prophet" had reached international proportions. Hundreds of people visited his office each year, some from as far away as Europe and Asia. Each day his office was flooded with requests for special readings that usually involved healing, although a few preferred "psychic readings." The telephone rang constantly, as did the doorbell.

Cayce, a self-taught preacher of the strictest integrity and character, rarely charged for his psychic services. But his conditions were strict: an appointment would have to be set up for 11 a.m. or 3 p.m. on a specified day. The applicant did not have to be present, but it was necessary that Cayce be given the person's real name and address—and where that individual would be at the specified time of reading.

Cayce's own routine never varied. He would come in from the garden or from fishing, loosen his tie, shoelaces, cuffs, and belt, then lie down on a couch. His hands would be placed first palm-up on his forehead, then across his abdomen. Drawing in deep gulps of air several times, he would close his eyes and relax. When his eyelids began to flutter, the reading would begin.

Afterwards, he might sleep for a couple hours or more. He would awaken—refreshed—without remembering a single thing about the reading.

In the early 1920s, the "sleeping prophet" became obsessed with reincarnation. Often, when tracking patients' previous lives, Cayce would take them hundreds or thousands of years into the past. Occasionally he would link them to the lost continent of Atlantis, where he proclaimed some of their "spiritual entities" had been born.

Some of Cayce's readings about Atlantis received special attention from the press. Not since Plato had anyone spoken with so much authority about the fabled landmass that supposedly sank beneath the waves during a cataclysmic upheaval some twelve thousand years ago. According to Cayce, who "visited" Atlantis hundreds of times during his trances, runaway technology was the cause for its demise.

In 1936 he wrote:

"In Atlantean land just after the second breaking up of the land owing to misapplication of divine laws upon those things of nature or of the earth; when there were the eruptions from the second using of those influences that were for man's own development, yet becoming destructive forces to flesh when misapplied."

Before their land was destroyed, Atlanteans had developed a kind of nuclear energy superior to modern-day technology. "Rays...invisible to the eye" propelled vehicles through the air and beneath the sea, Cayce said.

Upon waking, Cayce was sometimes startled, even embarrassed, at some of his readings. A religious man who read the Bible every day, the last thing he wanted was for anybody to accuse him of being un-Christian. He was especially troubled about his comments on reincarnation, though day after day, reading after reading, his sleeping self always kept coming back to the subject.

Although Cayce's "life readings" on reincarnation and Atlantis deviated from his normal "healing" sessions, he would remain fascinated with those subjects for the rest of his life. In fact, Cayce's peculiar work in the field has been quoted numerous times by scientists, theologians, spiritualists and other investigators in the field of paranormal research.

Even more startling, one of Cayce's most famous revelations about Atlantis would come true, just as he had predicted in the 1940s. During one of his trances, he said that in the late 1960s the western region of the long-submerged continent of Atlantis would begin to appear near the Caribbean island of Bimini.

In 1968, just a few miles from Bimini, divers came across a group of undersea ruins that resembled collapsed buildings and some kind of ancient roadway system. Could this be the remains of the vanished Atlantean civilization?

Many followers of Edgar Cayce believe his most startling prophecy had come to pass.

In 1945, Cayce went to his grave still unaware of his unique contributions to the field of paranormal science.

In Search of Ambrose Bierce

Early one morning in the autumn of 1913, a 71-year-old grandfather rose from his bed, saddled the family horse, and then quietly and secretively rode away from his home near Washington, D.C.

He headed south, first stopping off at famous Civil War battlefields in Tennessee and Mississippi before passing through Louisiana and Texas on his way to the badlands of war-torn Mexico. His goal, as far as anyone has been able to determine, was to join up with a gang of revolutionaries led by Generalissimo Francisco "Pancho" Villa.

But somewhere along the way this aged, would-be soldier of fortune vanished. He was never seen or heard from again, and today, almost eight decades later, people the world over are still intrigued by the mysterious circumstances surrounding the disappearance of Ambrose Bierce, one of America's foremost journalists and tellers of tall tales.

Bierce's fate remains one of the literary world's most enduring and fascinating mysteries. So many theories have cropped up over the years to account for his demise they would probably fill a small library.

For years newspaper reporters, detectives, and secret service agents from the United States combed the rugged hinterlands of Mexico and Latin America for clues to the missing writer's fate. Not a trace of the elderly man was ever found again, leading one biographer to conclude that Bierce had "simply but stylishly vanished from the face of the earth."

Whatever happened, it is highly unlikely that Bierce—

whose gloomy, nihilistic works include *The Devil's Diction-ary; In the Midst of Life; Fantastic Fables;* and *Can Such Things Be?*—would have been flattered by all the hoopla surrounding his curious destiny. Interest in the Bierce legend soon reached international levels, eclipsing that of his books and columns.

As Clifton Fadiman, the noted essayist, once remarked, "Bierce was never a great writer anyway. He has painful faults of vulgarity and cheapness of imagination. But...his style, for one thing, will preserve him...and the purity of his misan-thropy, too, will help to keep him alive."

Gloomy, morose, melancholy, sarcastic, bitter—these words have all been used to describe the man whom critics and colleagues alike once dubbed "Bitter Bierce" because of his fierce, uncompromising literary assaults on what he con-sidered a depraved and morally bankrupt society. He attacked hypocrisy, especially, wherever he found it—from the halls of Congress to the sanctuaries of churches and cathedrals everywhere.

He railed against big business and the military, preferring to champion the causes of the poor and downtrodden. In his day, Bierce was regarded as a minor prophet of hopelessness, a fiery, pessimistic fellow whose impassioned pen unleashed a flood of temperamental tirades against government, big business, religion, and "that old devil" progress.

Born in a log cabin in Ohio, Bierce fought bravely on the side of the North during the Civil War, but always sympa-thized with the aristocratic planter-culture in the antebellum South. After the war—which would greatly influence his later writing—Bierce settled in San Francisco where he found a job with the *News Letter,* of which he eventually became editor.

In 1871 he married and went to London to work as a correspondent. It was there that the stinging nature of his work emerged, along with the nickname "Bitter Bierce."

Because of a life-long asthma problem, he moved back to San Francisco in 1876, and from 1887 to 1896 wrote a column for the *San Francisco Examiner* before accepting a position with *Cosmopolitan* in Washington, D.C.

Ambrose Bierce was never a happy man. Dead ends, failures, and tragedies haunted his personal life. In 1889 his son was killed in a vulgar shooting brawl over a girl; two years later his wife left him, finally divorcing him in 1904; in 1901 his youngest son died of alcoholism; and in 1913 Bierce—old, asthmatic, weary, his creative power only an acrid memory—made his queer escape from civilization, presumably to Mexico where he met his fate.

Though never great, Bierce's writings were read, and after the events of his strange disappearance were made known, they soared in popularity. The stories, assembled in book-length collections, ranged from the supernatural and horror to the grotesquely humorous.

His acidic dislike for and lack of patience with the human race stains the pages of most of his writing, including his most famous short piece, "An Occurrence At Owl Creek Bridge," which was made into a television film. Seeking to capitalize on a resurging interest in the Bierce phenomenon, Hollywood recently released a $24 million movie of Carlos Fuentes' novel *The Old Gringo,* starring Gregory Peck as the reclusive, controversial writer.

"Nobody will find my bones," Bierce once wrote. Little did he know how prophetic those words would be when, at the ripe old age of 71, he took off for Mexico, ostensibly to observe the revolution then rocking that nation. "I'm on my way to Mexico," he told a reporter. "I like the fighting...I want to see it."

As years passed, people on both sides of the Rio Grande speculated on his death. Did he commit suicide, as some experts claim? Did he succumb to natural causes, such as the asthma that had plagued him all his life? Was he shot by Pancho Villa or some other renegade Mexican officer?

Some say he never died in Mexico at all—that he made his way to England or perhaps back to his old home in California. One writer even theorized that he spent his last years in an asylum for the insane in California.

Whatever the truth, Ambrose Bierce's curious fate remains as mystifying as was his own unfathomable life.

The Mystery of Marie Laveau's Tomb

For more than a century now, visitors to New Orleans have been flocking to a lonely, moss-draped cemetery just north of the French Quarter to ponder over one of that city's most enduring mysteries.

Within the graveyard, buried beneath a crumbling brick tomb, are the remains of an old woman who died sometime around 1881. There are no dates on the inscription—only the French phrase: *"Famille Vve. Paris, neé Laveau."*

According to legend, the grave in question contains the mortal remains of Marie Laveau, the beautiful but notorious voodoo queen who brought fear and death to New Orleans throughout much of the 19th century.

Until a few years ago, no one doubted the legend. After all, there had been a funeral in St. Louis Cemetery No. 1, and hundreds of people from all across the country had come to pay final respects to one of New Orleans' most colorful and mysterious characters.

Now, however, there is some evidence to suggest that the infamous queen might not have been buried in her assigned grave after all. Instead, it appears likely that the vivacious hobgoblin's mortal remains were interred in an unmarked grave elsewhere—perhaps not even in the same cemetery.

According to some historians who have looked into the matter, Laveau's body was dug up shortly after the funeral and moved to a secret location to avoid having the grave turned into a kind of shrine for her legions of white-robed followers.

If this is so, then two questions naturally arise—who is really buried inside Laveau's tomb? And, more importantly, where is the high priestess of New Orleans voodoo actually buried?

To understand the mystery of Laveau's tomb, it might be helpful to review some of the facts and fallacies about the queen's storied life and times.

In her heyday, Laveau was the undisputed ruler of the voodoo cult, a mystical, quasi-religious organization that attracted thousands of followers, black and white. While she reigned supreme in New Orleans no one was safe from her unrelenting supernatural powers—not even aristocratic white planters who often came to her in the dead of night for secret sessions involving voodoo and, some say, sex.

It was also said that Laveau, a tall, striking woman with fiercely burning eyes, controlled her subjects in two main ways—by blowing "magic dust" in their faces and by exploiting their fear of the unseen world. In the minds of most blacks, freshly transplanted from the jungles of Africa via the Caribbean, ghosts and goblins stalked the streets of the city and haunted the surrounding woods and marshes.

For these blacks, most of them slaves or poor freedmen, it was a world of darkness and unrelenting terror, a world filled with unimaginable nightmares. The angry gods of voodoo were everywhere.

To protect themselves from voodoo and to ward off other evil spirits, the faithful flocks were compelled to purchase powders, herbs and talismans—usually from a *hougon,* or voodoo priest, or from the high priestess herself, Marie Laveau. Although the authorities tried to suppress voodoo in most parts of the city, they largely ignored the strange dancing, chanting, and bonfires burning in black quarters.

By all accounts, the voodoo cult had been firmly implanted in New Orleans by the early colonial period, but it was not until the arrival of Marie Laveau that the practice of this enigmatic religion blossomed. Up until then it was known that certain voodoo priests and priestesses possessed supernatural powers and a knowledge of mind-altering drugs and poisons. White masters were sometimes powerless when under the influence of voodoo spells, and there are some records of slave owners having been poisoned by drug-influenced blacks.

It was into such a fear-haunted world that Laveau was born one cold, rainy night in 1796. Legend has it that on that night a terrible storm blew in from the swamps, shaking the moss-draped trees and howling across quaint cobblestoned squares.

Marie was a free mulatto, a status which gave her certain privileges around town. When she was in her early twenties, she married another mulatto named Jacques Paris. After Paris's death, Laveau had a daughter, whom she also named Marie. In time, the daughter would succeed her mother as the exalted voodoo queen, thereby creating a mystery that only recently has been solved.

Because of the secret succession in leadership of the cult, it was erroneously assumed that the original Marie Laveau was immortal, that she somehow had been able to cheat death and old age. The mother-daughter reign confused not only her superstitious followers but future generations of historians as well.

It was the older Laveau, however, who is credited with having established her place at the head of the cult. Not long after she had joined as a low-ranking member following her husband's death, Laveau quickly usurped Sanite Dede's place as queen. Beautiful, strong and supremely resourceful, Laveau set about to transform the cult into a powerful but curious mixture of West Indian fetish-worship and perverted Catholicism.

A devout Roman Catholic herself, Laveau continued to attend mass daily while retaining her exalted office as queen of voodoo.

Throughout her life, Laveau welcomed outsiders to her cult's annual festival on St. John's Eve in midsummer, but behind these public ceremonies, Marie Laveau presided over many secret meetings during which the real magic of voodoo was invoked and the wild ritual carried to orgiastic extremes.

Whites were excluded from these meetings, which were usually held at her small, white-washed house along the gloomy shores of Lake Pontchartrain.

The first Marie Laveau stopped practicing sometime around 1869, at which time her daughter assumed the duties of queenship. A power struggle would later develop between the younger Laveau and a powerful young rival, Malvina Latour. According to some experts, Latour eventually won the fight. If this is true, then it seems entirely possible that the grave at St. Louis Cemetery No. 1 contains her bones—not those of Marie Laveau.

Others say, however, that the remains are those of the younger Laveau.

No one knows for sure.

The Twilight World of Robert Ervin Howard

In the summer of 1936 Robert Ervin Howard had everything to live for. He was young, handsome, and on the verge of literary fame. After years of rejection notices and only a handful of published short stories, things were definitely starting to look up for the young writer.

Then, inexplicably, the tranquility of tiny Cross Plains, Texas, a wind-blown community in the middle of nowhere, was shattered by the sound of a gunshot. Eight hours later, one of the town's most famous sons—and one of America's greatest writers of fantasy fiction—was dead, the victim of an apparent suicide.

Howard was only thirty.

As the swaggering, hard-drinking creator of Conan the Barbarian and dozens of other "sword-and-sorcery" epics, Robert E. Howard was just beginning to make a name for himself in the literary world. Magazine editors were now calling him for stories, and several of his book-length projects were being considered by a major publisher.

Why, then, did this brooding, wildly eccentric man bristling with ambition and talent suddenly decide to end it all with a bullet?

Howard's untimely death and the mystery behind it have haunted his legions of fans for more than fifty years. Based on the writer's own typewritten suicide note and several other factors, no one disputes the notion that the man did in all

67

probability kill himself, and that no one else was involved.

What troubles a lot of people, however, are the circumstances leading up to his suicide. Friends, fellow writers, and fans over the years have long pondered those circumstances, and to this day, have failed to reach a consensus.

Was it fear of failure that finally drove him to put the Colt .380 automatic pistol to his right temple that hot, humid day in June, or was it just the opposite—fear of success? Some researchers have suggested the man was driven insane by the same tortured fantasies that gave life to his most celebrated fictional hero, Conan.

The most likely cause, however, was that he dreaded the thought of being left alone in a world he never really understood. His mother, with whom he shared an unnaturally close relationship, was dying. Three times before, he had planned his own demise when her death appeared imminent, but each time the old woman had rallied.

Finally, when a nurse told the grieving son his mother would never recognize him again, he acted. His final enigmatic words, left on the typewriter in his study, were these:

All fled—all is done, so lift me on the pyre:
The feast is over and the lamps expire.

Although Howard's death fell short of national headlines, thousands of people around the world mourned his passing. Scores of fans flocked into town to attend his funeral. Over the years, thousands more would come to Cross Plains to pay tribute to their fallen idol, to remember a man now regarded as one of the masters of the genre.

All his short life, Howard had dreamed of a world far beyond the dusty confines of his little hometown. Through the magic of his writing, Howard was able to bring that visionary, fire-filled world to literary life. He called it the Hyborian Age, a savage, barbarous time when magic was potent, chesty heroes clutched swords, and big-bosomed damsels lived according to their own personal codes.

One character dominated the age—a man whose body was "an image of primal strength cut out of bronze," who liked his women full-bodied and complacent but spent most of his time "afire with the urge to kill, to drive his knife deep into flesh and bone, and twist the blade in blood entrails."

That character, of course, was Conan.

Conan the Barbarian, who stalked the earth twelve thousand years ago, was only one of Howard's many swashbuckling, sword-rattling protagonists. He was the most enduring, however, eventually finding immortality in the person of Arnold Schwarzenegger on the silver screen.

Altogether he wrote sixty stories and novels, of which about twenty-one were developed around his brutish, slow-thinking hero.

Even so, fame and fortune always stayed one step beyond the struggling young writer. It wasn't until the 1940s, nearly a decade after his death, that Conan and his barbarian hordes actually earned literary respectability. The biggest break came in 1966 when a leading paperback publisher issued the first of what was to become a hugely successful series of Conan adventure novels—not all of them written by Howard.

In many ways, Howard's short, dream-haunted life was every bit as mystifying and as frightening as anything he wrote. Born frail and sickly, he was forced to learn boxing early in order to defend himself against other kids. He also took an interest in body-building, which probably helped shape his interest in Conan.

He started writing stories when he was ten, pushing himself ruthlessly on the typewriter day and night. When his first story was purchased by *Weird Tales* in 1924, the eighteen-year-old got down on his knees and thanked God he'd finally broken into print.

Only twelve years later, despondent over his mother's death, wracked by nightmares, and undoubtedly pursued by the fiendish demons of his own fevered fantasies, Robert E. Howard lay dying in a pool of blood behind his beloved mother's house.

Can Such Things Be?

The Sargasso: Graveyard of the Sea

Just off the southern tip of the United States, and veering east by northeast for thousands of square miles, is a vast, weed-choked range of open sea that for centuries has haunted the imagination of mariners on both sides of the Atlantic.

This is the Sargasso Sea, home to some of the world's most unusual flora and fauna. It is here, thousands of miles from their normal habitat, that American and European eels make their mysterious journey each year to breed and lay eggs amid the cool, clear waters and fearsome tangles of sargassum weed.

It is also here that one of the world's most enduring mysteries has developed.

Every schoolchild knows about the Sargasso Sea, the fabled "graveyard of lost ships," where—according to maritime lore—the rotting remains of thousands of unfortunate ocean voyagers lie trapped and forever entombed aboard their stalled ships in dense, gloomy forests of monstrous vegetation.

Legend has it that this is a dead world with no storms, wind or waves to ever break them free. Victims who happen to get caught up in the twisting, treacherous coils of the sargassum weed are doomed, so the stories go, to drift helplessly upon the unyielding sea for all eternity. Like snapshots out of history, the skeletal ribs of Spanish galleons, steam freighters, Yankee clippers, frigates, Chinese junks, Roman triremes, and even Norse dragonships still struggle in the embrace of octopus-like vines, their rudders and propellers held fast by gigantic weeds and tree-thick roots.

Until recent times, the mere thought of coming upon the Sargasso Sea was enough to weaken even the strongest sailor. Even during the American Revolution, and later during the Civil War, sea captains kept a constant lookout for signs of danger when entering the Sargasso. Stories were often told about wayward ships getting caught in those entangling currents, never to be seen or heard from again.

In July 1884, for example, the *Brittania,* bound for London from Buenos Aires, came across a merchant ship that had apparently been abandoned in the Sargasso. There were a few corpses on board, but most of the crew and passengers were missing.

Nowadays it is known that the dreaded sea, which covers nearly three million square miles between North America and Europe, is actually one of the safest places in the entire ocean. Warm currents and calm winds prevail over still, glass-smooth waters, and only occasionally does an ocean-going vessel come in contact with the once-feared sargassum weed.

Such was not the case five hundred years ago when the man who discovered North America first laid eyes on the mysterious Sargasso Sea.

It happened in 1492, during Christopher Columbus's first voyage to the New World. Somewhere far out in the Atlantic, a thousand miles west of the Azores, he spotted what he took to be long strands of seaweeds, stretching as far as the eye could see in every direction. At first, the veteran Genoan sea captain took heart at the sighting, thinking that perhaps his tiny flotilla was at last nearing land.

But his optimism soon turned to terror when he realized just how thick grew the ancient weeds, how twisted and gnarled were their branches and ominous coils. To his dismay, he felt the temperature quickly sink, and the ocean seemed to stand utterly still.

This is the chilling account Columbus gave of that and subsequent experiences in the Sargasso Sea:

"Each time I sailed from Spain to the Indies...I noticed an extraordinary change in the aspect of the sky and the stars, in the temperature of the air and in that of the sea. I found the surface of the water covered so thickly with vegetation resembling small branches of fir that we believed we must be in shallow waters and that the ships would soon be aground for lack of depth...."

More than any other factor, Columbus's grim account about the perils of the Sargasso Sea helped inspire the terror that would fill the hearts of future generations of seafaring peoples. Fear of the Sargasso and its clutching embrace of death soon became an obsession with sailors and ocean-going travelers everywhere.

No one wanted his ship to become ensnared in those treacherous masses of enveloping weed, for no wind would ever come to the rescue, and no kind wave would wash it away. Tales about the Sargasso were circulated and re-circulated below deck and among the waterfront taverns and inns from the Outer Banks to Land's End.

Before long, novels and newspaper stories began to appear, each as frightening and disturbing as the next. "The Island of Lost Ships" explored the possibility that cannibalistic survivors could actually exist among the wreckage and ruin of the Sargasso, preying upon newcomers. Thomas Alliborne Janvier also wrote about similar discoveries in his book *In the Sargasso Sea;* other novels led readers to believe that the Sargasso is actually part of the lost continent of Atlantis, and that descendants of that civilization still live in the Sargasso region today.

Much attention has been focused on the fact that the geographic boundaries of the Sargasso Sea approximate the whereabouts of ancient Atlantis. As if this weren't fanciful enough, the western edge of the large, singular sea touches on the edge of the Bermuda Triangle, scene of many strange maritime events over the years. Incredibly, some of the ships and planes that have gone missing in the Triangle region have been linked to mysterious forces in the Sargasso Sea.

In spite of the many myths shrouding this swirling body of water far out in the Atlantic, scientists agree that the Sargasso itself is an ocean wonder. Some of the world's oldest flora and fauna abound here—including the sargassum weed, capable of surviving for hundreds of years in the unusual climate of the Sargasso.

The Sargasso is also the breeding ground for several species of fish, including American and European eels which swim thousands of miles each year to mate in its frothy seaweed forests. This bizarre ritual has given rise to speculation that the Sargasso region was indeed once home to an ancient landmass, perhaps Atlantis, and that these migrating eels somehow still share a genetic memory of those distant days.

Today, modern ships cross the Sargasso Sea every day without trouble. But the mystery of this haunting region lives on, and despite the testimony of some questionable sources, no evidence exists to suggest that any vessel, ancient or modern, has ever been lost in the Sargasso Sea.

Florida's Fabled Fountain of Youth

In the spring of 1513, an aging Spanish conquistador named Juan Ponce de León set sail from his Caribbean home in search of a mysterious land called Florida and its legendary fountain of youth.

Or did he?

Historians aren't so sure that the tall, dashing, 50-year-old governor of Puerto Rico had ever even heard of a fountain of youth, let alone made it the focus of his three-year exploratory voyage around the coastal wilds of Florida. Instead, it now appears that Ponce de León—the first European known to have set foot on Florida soil—was actually looking for slaves and gold when he planted the flag of Spain on a sandy shore near modern-day Cape Canaveral.

What apparently happened was that a highly imaginative historian named Herrera, who chronicled Ponce de León's exploits in the New World years after the event, had come across a fanciful Indian legend about a mysterious stream of water located somewhere north of Cuba that supposedly had the power to restore youth. In order to make his accounts more exciting—and, perhaps, to earn a bigger name for himself—Herrera attached the legend to Ponce de León's name and subsequent voyages of discovery.

According to Herrera, the governor had heard about the legend from various tribes of Caribbean Indians and decided to investigate. Part of that legend centered around a group of Arawaks who supposedly migrated from Cuba northward because of a magical river where "life-giving waters flowed pure and plenty."

Today, southeastern scholars discount that story, even though numerous other legends in the New World tell of similar such streams located somewhere in the vast wilds of North America.

But Herrera, who liked dramatic storytelling more than dull history, milked the legend for all it was worth. He insisted that Ponce de León, concerned about his waning years, went to Florida to find, then drink and bathe in the fountain.

It wasn't the first mistake made by the unreliable historian—and it wouldn't be the last. For example, he incorrectly reported that Ponce de León waded ashore on Easter Sunday in the year 1513 just south of Fort Lauderdale. Evidence now shows that the conquistador was still at sea on Easter Sunday, and that he actually landed on the Florida coast much farther south than was generally believed—perhaps near modern-day Cape Canaveral.

Researchers, all too aware of Herrera's zealous pen, say there is nothing in the pages of the conquistador's original patent from Emperor Charles V to suggest anything but a businesslike expedition to explore and perhaps colonize the Florida peninsula. Nor are there indications from subsequent records to suggest that Ponce de León had the slightest notion about the curious fountain which would follow his name down through the ages.

What is known is that the once-wealthy governor was seeking to replenish his lost fortune by finding gold and capturing Indians to sell as slaves to colonial plantation owners.

In spite of all the evidence to the contrary, Ponce de León's exalted name continues to be linked with the fabled fountain of youth. However erroneous, it is a wonderful, romantic tale that simply won't go away. Part of the allure has been perpetuated by generations of profit-hungry real estate developers and land speculators in Florida who in former years sought to capitalize on the legend.

For centuries, people were drawn to the "land of

flowers" in search of that same magical stream whose bubbling waters were said to have the power to restore youth. According to stories handed down by the Indians and undoubtedly kept alive by developers, just one sip of or dip into the stream would wash away wrinkles.

The existence of Ponce de León's wondrous stream, real or imagined, turned out to be a marketing gold mine for land developers and speculators from Tallahassee to Hialeah. Soon not even hurricanes, droughts, renegade Indians, or dense tracts of swampland teeming with mosquitoes, alligators, and poisonous snakes could hold back the hordes of prosperous northerners looking for investment in the South.

Almost overnight, Florida was transformed from a sleepy backwater draw to the vacationland of the future. From swampgrass to golf courses, primitive mud huts to glistening beachfront high-rises, the "land of flowers" would never be the same again.

Where was the fabled fountain? Some historians say the legend had its origins in northern Florida, while others say it was in Georgia or Alabama. Still others claim it was on the island of Guanahani (San Salvador) or on Bimini. Only a few experts insist it was in the Everglades, as originally believed.

In the event such a stream ever existed, one can rightfully suspect it is no longer there—drained away, perhaps, or bulldozed over to make room for a parking lot or glittering row of condominiums.

Flight 19's Date with the Unknown

On the afternoon of December 5, 1945, five TBM Avenger torpedo bombers took off from their home base at Fort Lauderdale, Florida, on a two-hour training flight that would carry them eastward to Grand Bahama Island and back, a distance of about three hundred forty miles.

Aboard the lead plane was Lt. Charles Carroll Taylor, one of only two experienced officers on the mission. The twelve other crewmen—pilots, radiomen and gunners—were all students in training.

The weather was cold but surprisingly clear for that time of year. Only a trace of fog hovered offshore as Flight 19 lifted off from Lauderdale Naval Air Station and headed toward its target, a practice bombing range called Chicken Shoals, just north of Bimini.

Less than half an hour after the successful bombing run, something unexpected happened. At precisely 3:15, the radio tower back at Fort Lauderdale, which had been expecting contact from the planes regarding estimated time of arrival, received an unusual message from the flight leader.

"Both my compasses are out," the leader, Lt. Taylor, reported urgently. "This is an emergency. We seem to be off course. We cannot land...Repeat...We cannot see land."

Puzzled, the tower advised Flight 19 to continue on course bearing due west. To which Lt. Taylor replied: "We don't know which way is west. Everything is wrong-...Strange...We can't be sure of any direction—even the ocean doesn't look as it should."

Communications later broke down with Flight 19. Not long afterwards, a Martin Mariner rescue plane with a crew of thirteen was dispatched to the general area. Inexplicably, the rescue plane, too, vanished without a trace over the blue-green Atlantic.

As for Flight 19, a five-day search covering 380,000 square miles of land and sea, including the Atlantic, Caribbean, parts of the Gulf of Mexico, and the Florida mainland and neighboring islands, failed to discover any trace of the airplanes or their crew. No life rafts, no wreckage, and no tell-tale oil slicks were found, in spite of continued air and sea searches along the beaches of Florida and the Bahamas for several more weeks.

It was as if Flight 19, along with the flying boat sent out from Miami to rescue its crew, had simply vanished into thin air.

In those days, only a few months after World War II, the warm waters off the Florida coast were a tranquil region, a favored training area for combat-weary sailors and aviators. But in time, as more and more airplanes and ships vanished mysteriously there, that perception would change. Soon a whole new folklore would develop around that peculiar patch of sea that came to be known as the Bermuda Triangle.

Since 1945, more than one hundred ships and planes—many of them in full view of witnesses—have vanished without a trace in or over the Bermuda Triangle. At least a thousand people have lost their lives in that enigmatic area since the five Navy Grumman TBM-3 Avenger torpedo bombers of Flight 19 flew off into the unknown. Ironically, not a single body or piece of wreckage from any of these lost ships and planes has ever been recovered.

Not surprisingly, an aura of profound mystery now shrouds this expanse of open sea where so many ships and planes have gone down without explanation. Many theories, some of them admittedly fanciful, have evolved to account for these disappearances, ranging from supernatural involvement to extraterrestrial connections. Most explanations have been linked to sudden tidal waves caused by earthquakes, exploding fireballs, attacks by sea monsters, time-space warps, electromagnetic or gravitational vortices, and, of course, capture or kidnapping by unidentified flying objects.

Today the Bermuda Triangle is regarded by many as one of the most dangerous maritime regions on earth. Even the U.S. Coast Guard describes it as "an imaginary area located off the southeastern Atlantic coast…which is noted for a high incidence of unexplained losses of ships, small boats, and aircraft…."

Even long before 1945, the Bermuda Triangle had been regarded in maritime circles as a secretive, eerie place (probably contributing to legends about a "lost sea" or the legendary "ship's graveyard" of yore). Some disappearances actually were reported after the Civil War, but it wasn't until the episode involving Flight 19 that the Bermuda Triangle became a household term.

To be sure, hardly a year goes by without some report of a ship or plane going astray in that troublesome triangle extending from Bermuda in the north to southern Florida, then east through the Bahamas past Puerto Rico to about 40° west longitude, and then back again to Bermuda. This is made even more bizarre, given the fact that sealanes and airways are busier now, and rescue technology is far more advanced.

The fate of Flight 19, as well as that of the hundred or so other known planes, ships, and hot-air balloons lost over the Bermuda Triangle, remains one of the South's greatest unsolved mysteries.

The Curse of Barnsley Gardens

As a young man growing up in Savannah, Godfrey Barnsley dreamed of someday owning his own cotton plantation.

That dream came true in the late 1830s when the wealthy businessman acquired what he considered an ideal spread—a 10,000-acre tract of virgin timberland and rolling fields near Adairsville in the northwest corner of Georgia.

As fate would have it, greed, the Civil War, and an old Indian curse would soon combine to turn Barnsley's dream into a nightmare.

In those days, more than two decades before the War Between the States, the woods and hills of remote Bartow County still swarmed with roaming bands of Indians, many of them outlaws and renegades from the infamous Trail of Tears. Understandably, many resented the encroachment of white settlers into their ancestral territory and resisted any way they could.

One particular old chief, who happened to live on Barnsley's new property, was so angered that legend has it he put a curse on the white man and on the very ground on which he planned to build his sprawling plantation house.

Nobody thought much about the curse, nor about rumors that the Barnsley estate was said to contain a mysterious, acorn-shaped hill feared by the Cherokees. Life went on somewhat uneventfully for the next few months, and soon Barnsley brought his wife and family to his property to live.

Then, only days before the manor house was completed, Barnsley's wife Julia and their infant son died mysteriously while living in temporary shelter on the accursed grounds.

The planter was heartbroken by his loss, but completed the house anyway and moved in with his surviving daughter and son.

The curse was forgotten—until the autumn of 1858 when Barnsley's teenage daughter also died in the house. That same year, his son was killed by Chinese pirates while the young man searched the Orient for exotic plants for the estate's formal gardens.

By then the unfortunate planter was beside himself with grief and worry. He sought out mediums, psychics, and religious leaders to help undo what the old Indian had done to him long ago, but his pleas fell on deaf ears since white people apparently did not understand Indian magic.

Barnsley's troubles did not end with the sad demise of his family members. Beginning in late 1860, one business venture after another failed. Barnsley's once sizeable fortune had soon been reduced to a pathetic fraction of its former worth. A few months later, with the outbreak of war, the miserable planter was left alone with his unfinished manor house and a ruined cotton-buying operation.

Barnsley's once-handsome estate now lay in shambles, along with his dream of becoming one of the most prosperous planters in the South.

On his deathbed, Barnsley reportedly begged a minister to rid his property of its evil curse. It was too late to bring back his family, of course, or to restore his health and fortune, but at least he hoped future owners would be spared misfortune and grief.

In the summer of 1989, almost 150 years after Barnsley set out to establish his cotton empire in the foothills of Georgia, another Cherokee returned to the estate to undo the old chief's curse. Richard Bird, a medicine man from Cherokee, North Carolina, said he knew something was wrong the moment he stepped onto the property.

"There was definitely something here when we got here—there was something," he told reporters. "I had a funny feeling inside—I can't explain it. It was kind of a nervousness, like butterflies in my stomach, like a cold sweat."

Bird was hired to perform a "casting out" ceremony by an attorney representing the estate's new owner, Stonewall Limited Partnership, which is developing the property known locally now as Woodlands.

Bird thinks his services were unnecessary. He said that any curse put on the property died along with the old Indian himself.

"When a person dies, his magic is no longer good," he explained.

Even so, at the new property owner's insistence, he performed the ancient ritual of casting off conjurations anyway—"just to be on the safe side," he said.

Ghost Lights in the Forest

One hot summer night in the early 1960s, Chester McMinn was out plowing his field near Quapaw, Oklahoma, when suddenly, at the far edge of the woods, there appeared a strange blue light flickering among the pines.

As the farmer watched from his tractor, the eerie light began to dance and weave, dreamlike in the distance. Then, still bobbing and swirling, the light headed slowly toward him, becoming brighter as it moved.

McMinn shuddered. It was almost as if the thing had *sensed* his presence and was coming over to investigate!

Within seconds the spooky blue light was directly overhead. The entire field was lit up like Christmas. And since the eerie glow was there to stay for a while, McMinn decided to take advantage of the unnatural illumination to get some more plowing done.

"Seems like the old light felt real neighborly...and decided to help me with my plowing," McMinn told a reporter after the incident. "I couldn't see too well, and I guess the old light sensed it, because he started hovering all over the field where I was plowing."

That was fine until the strange light suddenly started acting funny. After about fifteen minutes of bobbing and weaving, casting strange shadows across the freshly-turned rows, it began to pulsate rhythmically. Long grainy fingers of incandescence clawed toward him, giving him plenty of light but also lots of goosebumps.

"I was absolutely frozen stiff to my tractor until it suddenly went away and vanished," he explained.

A few days earlier, in that same part of Oklahoma, a school bus full of children was nearly run off the road because of a menacing blue light perched on the rear window. Louise Graham, who was aboard the bus, said the children were terrified, thinking that the pesky light was trying to get in.

"The light was so bright that it temporarily blinded the driver," she said. "He had to stop the bus. Just as we stopped the light went away."

For years, thousands of Americans have encountered mysterious blue lights such as those described above. For some reason, the phenomenon seems to occur more frequently in Southern states—especially those with swamps and low-lying bogs and bayous.

No satisfactory theory has been advanced to account for these peculiar manifestations, known in most areas as "spooklights." Explanations range from the scientific to the fanciful, but perhaps the answer is somewhere in between.

The one constant thing about spooklights is that they never stay long, wherever they appear. They might last for only a few seconds or for half an hour, but they rarely last longer. There is some predictability about them—that is, some tend to show up at the same place at the same time, over and over, night after night, or at least to reappear in regular cycles.

In a tiny community near Joplin, Missouri, where the corners of Arkansas, Missouri, Oklahoma, and Kansas approach each other, one set of spooklights has been the subject of keen scientific inquiry for years. Spooksville, as the place is appropriately named, has also been a mecca for tourists hungry for supernatural adventure.

Not much is known about the Spooksville lights, except that they are among the most predictable anywhere. They have been seen by countless thousands of people from all walks of life. Hundreds of newspaper and magazine articles have been written about these unusual lights, and several feature film documentaries have appeared on television.

Some oldtimers believe the enigmatic nature of the lights has something to do with history. As it turns out, the area around Spooksville was once the preserve of the Cherokee Indians. Legend has it that the bobbing blue lights seen by busloads of tourists each year are the angry spirits of the Indians' ancestors, pulsing with incandescent fury at white men for their brutal and bloody treatment of Indians in years gone by.

Other folks suspect the lights might have something to do with the hundreds of innocent people who were slaughtered here during the Civil War. It was in this territory that "Border Ruffians" kept a reign of terror until the war ended in 1865. These "Ruffians" were nothing more than gangs of guerrilla troops working outside the frameworks of their respective armies to kill and rob and plunder remote areas of Missouri, Kansas, Arkansas, and other border states.

For a while, this territory was known as "Bleeding Kansas"—for the hundreds of men, women, and children who perished in the cruel fighting.

If you want to talk spooklights and history, go to the local museum. There you'll likely meet up with Mr. L.W. Robertson, the curator, who says he probably knows as much about the phenomenon as anyone else alive.

He also keeps an open mind on the subject.

"I have no idea what the spooklight is," Robertson says matter-of-factly. "And I've looked at it as much as any living man. I don't tell the tourists any story about the light at all. If they don't believe it, it's here for them to see for themselves."

Robertson's first experience with the phenomenon came shortly after World War II when he accompanied the U.S. Army Corps of Engineers into the area to investigate the lights. A few years before—during the war, in fact—reports about the ghostly goings-on at Spooksville had reached the highest levels of the Pentagon.

The Army High Command decided to investigate—just in case the phenomena had any military significance, Robertson explained.

"The Corps checked out the area for several miles, testing

caves, mineral deposits, and highway routes, and making aerial surveys," the curator noted. "They came to no conclusion."

In 1960, a student at Drury College in nearby Springfield decided to study the lights for himself and perhaps earn some extra academic credit in the process. For his project, Rob Gibbons, a freshman, chose one of the most haunted areas around: a narrow dirt road some eleven miles southwest of Joplin, near the Missouri-Oklahoma line.

Over the years, hundreds of reliable eyewitnesses had reported seeing the spooklights along the lonely road—usually appearing about dusk and continuing until the early hours of dawn. Accompanied by an assistant, Gibbons set up movie and still cameras, and settled back to await the arrival of the lights.

On February 24, 1965, he presented his conclusions at a student symposium in Springfield. Part of his discussion discounted the more fanciful accounts, pointing out that all his team had ever seen was a small light bobbing about at the end of the gravel road.

"Usually it seems to float over the hills down the roadway to the west," he remarked. "At rare times it seems to come towards the observer. At times it moves slightly horizontally. With a 30-power telescope...I could perceive as many as four distinct pairs of lights, with pairs of red lights appearing slightly to the right of pairs of bright white lights."

The red lights, he said, grew dimmer as the white lights became brighter.

Then Mr. Gibbons pulled out a map. While the silent audience looked and listened, the graduating student pointed out that U.S. Highway 66, running east and west between Quapaw and Commerce, was in direct line with the spooklight road and the observation point. Then he noted that the Spring River ran between the spooklight area and the highway, twelve miles away.

He added, "The phenomenon of the bright white lights appearing slightly to the left of the dimmer red lights corresponds with the natural movement of traffic on a road or highway."

As with all theories, skeptics were quick to denounce the student's new-fangled explanation of their beloved lights. The most glaring discrepancy, they charged, was that he had failed to take into consideration the fact that the spooklights had been around for a long, long time, predating the arrival of automobiles by almost a decade.

The first documented sighting of spooklights in the area was in 1903, almost a quarter of a century before Highway 66 was built.

The spooklights are still a mystery.

*Secrets from
Beyond the Grave*

The Ghost That Came to Stay

One rainy night in the late 1920s, Mrs. Sammy King was sitting by an open window in her living room knitting a new shawl. She had just finished her second cup of tea and was about to start on her third when several jagged bolts of lightning crackled across the skies.

Mrs. King had always loved listening to and watching thunderstorms. As a child she had liked to run out and play in storms whenever her mother wasn't looking. Even as an adult she got a thrill out of watching dazzling displays of lightning followed by the booming peals of thunder.

But on this particular night, when Mrs. King was sixty-five, something told her this was no ordinary storm.

She suddenly felt afraid.

She shifted uncomfortably in the oversized armchair, mesmerized by the fierce beauty of the storm raging outside her window. Howling gusts of wind rocketed across the yard, rattling windows and doors and causing the long lace curtains by her head to flutter and pop. As the storm intensified, so did Mrs. King's fearfulness about it.

Finally, with the candles burning low, the elderly grandmother decided she'd better get up and shut the window, just to be safe. The second she started to rise, a blinding arrow of light slashed through the window and into Mrs. King's body, killing her on the spot.

Three days later her charred remains were taken to a small cemetery about two miles from her home in Dodge County, Georgia, and quietly laid to rest. But according to some locals, Mrs. King's spirit still haunts the property where she died so dramatically nearly seventy years ago.

Numerous eerie reports have surfaced over the years describing a "thin, stoop-shouldered" apparition wandering the fields and woods near the handsome old house near Eastman. The figure, always clad in dark colors and usually wearing an old-fashioned bonnet, has been seen picking flowers, gathering twigs and cones, and even sitting on the porch of her old house.

"She always wears a long brown dress with long sleeves and a scarf or bonnet that hides her face," said Betty Kight, who bought Mrs. King's property in 1962, "And she's usually surrounded by a soft haze of smoke."

Mrs. Kight, who never believed in ghosts before, said she first saw the specter shortly after she and her husband Bob moved in.

"I was in the kitchen putting things away when I looked through the window and saw this little old lady standing in the canna lilies. When I went outside, she was gone," she said.

After six such sightings—each lasting longer than the one before—Mrs. Kight said she got so afraid, she chopped down the canna lilies. That didn't stop the hauntings, however.

"It got worse," she said. "The ghost started visiting my children, even in broad daylight."

Although husband Bob has never actually seen the ghost, Mrs. Kight says her children—all of whom grew up in the house—have.

"One day my son Robert heard singing, so he went out on the porch. There sat Mrs. King in the swing with three children around her singing out of a song book," she explained.

There have been countless other encounters with the ghostly apparition, including one by daughter Elaine that still leaves Mrs. Kight's hair standing on end.

"One night after supper Elaine started out to feed the dogs. She opened the door with a plate of scraps in her hands, and there stood Mrs. King. Elaine screamed and threw the plate in the floor and slammed the door," Mrs. Kight said.

At first the Kights had no idea who—or what—the ghost was that haunted their property. Later, after talking with neighbors and relatives of the old house's former owners, they learned that their spectral visitor from beyond was none other than Mrs. Sammy King, a kind, gracious woman who had been struck by lightning and killed sometime in the late 1920s.

Descriptions of Mrs. King, said Mrs. Kight, matched that of her ghost from the top of her bonnet to the heels of her black, lace-up shoes.

Apparently members of the Kight family were only the latest in a growing list of people who claimed to have seen Mrs. King's ghost.

A decade of the haunting was enough for the Kights. In 1973, they built a new house about a hundred yards away from the old house and moved in, hoping such action might rid them of the unwanted presence. Two weeks after they settled in, however, more strange things started happening. Flickering lights were spotted in the window of the old woman's room across the way, and moaning, sobbing sounds were sometimes heard outside in the yard at night.

Then, almost imperceptibly, the silent ghost began to make its presence known in the new house. At first it was only the opening and closing of doors and moving things around that bothered the Kights. Soon, however, there were more sightings. So many, in fact, the Kights thought of bringing in an exorcist.

They never did.

Instead, the Kights began to grow fond of the kindly old presence that continues to fade in and out of view at unpredictable moments.

"We've just accepted the fact that she's here," explained Mrs. Kight matter-of-factly.

Now, instead of running or being afraid, the Kights consider the ghost part of the family.

"She's friendly, and she doesn't want to hurt us. I almost feel like she's part of our family."

In the beginning, the harassed family thought of selling

their haunted house and moving away—far away, so the ghost wouldn't follow. After a while, they changed their minds.

"I really think she's attached to us," Mrs. Kight said, adding that she believes the ghost of Mrs. King still haunts her property because "she didn't finish her mission here on earth."

Better Run When the
"Man in Gray" Comes Calling...

Early one morning in the autumn of 1954, an automobile dealer named Bill Collins looked out over the gray waves breaking in front of his beachfront house at Pawleys Island, South Carolina, and saw something strange.

Down on the beach, just a few yards from a gazebo Collins had built on a high sand dune, there stood a somber little man, fully clothed in a gray suit, and staring directly toward him. At first Collins, a practical man, didn't think much about the strangely dressed beachcomber. People walked up and down the beach all the time, and these days, some of them dressed pretty weird.

But there was something different about this unusual little fellow. The more Collins studied him, the more uncomfortable he felt. Was it the eyes? There seemed to be an odd glow in the stranger's eyes, a penetrating, faraway look that sent shivers down Collins's spine.

A deep sense of urgency seemed to radiate from the man, yet he stood unmoving, serene in a kind of otherworldly calmness.

Without understanding why, Collins was suddenly seized with the thought that the mysterious man in the gray suit down on the beach was trying to warn him about something. If so, then why didn't he speak up, and not just stand there gawking?

The thing that bothered Collins most was the peculiar

way in which the stranger was attired. The coat was cut long in the back in an old-fashioned style, and the tie and hat clearly belonged to another age. Perhaps there had been a masquerade party somewhere down the beach he didn't know about. Perhaps the man just liked to walk up and down the beach dressed funny.

Whatever, Collins finally decided he'd had enough mystery for one morning and started walking toward the stranger. He was sure there was a perfectly plausible explanation for the weird little man's dress, presence, and unfathomable behavior.

When he got within a few feet of him, however, Collins stopped dead in his tracks. While a pair of gulls shrieked overhead and the surf crashed on the beach, an unbelievable thing happened—the man in the gray suit started to fade! He was actually dissolving, like water poured onto a sandy beach, right before Collins' eyes.

Before Collins quite realized what was happening, the stranger had vanished from the beach.

At that moment, several hundred miles to the south, a major storm system was thrashing its way northward across the open Atlantic. Collins had no way of knowing that within a few days the hurricane would slam into the soft southern beach, pulverizing Pawleys Island and much of the unprotected Carolina coast.

A few heart-stopping seconds after the enigmatic stranger had disappeared, Collins put two and two together and realized what he had seen—surely it had been none other than South Carolina's legendary "man in gray," the phantom doomed to walk the beaches forever, warning people about approaching storms.

Not a man to take chances, Collins quickly gathered up his family and a few personal belongings and fled the island. A couple of days later, Hurricane Hazel thundered ashore, flattening thirty-foot sand dunes and washing away scores of handsome beachfront houses. Collins's own house was spared—indisputable proof that it had, indeed, been the man in gray who had come to warn him.

According to a popular legend along the Carolina coast, the man in gray sometimes appears days or hours before a terrible storm. Those fortunate enough to see him—and who heed his warning—will be spared and their property won't be damaged.

Even Collins, who believed in the legend, was stunned when he returned to the beach and found his house still standing.

"The TV antenna didn't even blow down," said Collins, whose story appeared in dozens of newspapers in the wake of Hazel's vicious onslaught.

Carolina's man in gray has been much talked about since its origins in the early 19th century. Even today, some superstitious, and some not-so-superstitious, beachfront property owners keep a keen eye out for him whenever winds rise and the threat of a storm is in the air.

Several times in the past century the mysterious man in gray has been known to appear right before a hurricane hit. The first account of such a manifestation was prior to the great gale of 1804. That was followed by two hurricanes in 1806, one of which blew down the lighthouse on North Island.

The most memorable, though, were the hurricanes of September 1822, October 1893, and October 1954. In each case, several people reportedly saw a strange little man dressed in gray clothes walking the stormy beach.

According to some sources, the legend can be traced back to about 1800, when a handsome young man on his way to see his fiancée on North Island was killed. Some accounts say his horse tripped and threw him into a pit of quicksand which he was unable to escape. Another version maintains he drowned at sea.

After his death, his young bride-to-be supposedly had a startling dream in which her fiance appeared to her, arms wet and cold, as if rising from some watery or slimy grave. She interpreted it as a warning of some kind, and when she told her father about it, he whisked her off to Charleston to see a doctor.

While they were away, a great storm blew in, destroying not only their plantation but many others on the island, including the home of Robert Francis Withers, a prominent rice planter.

Had it not been for the girl's dreams, she and her father would have been on the island and perished. A new legend was born.

Ever since, people living along the South Carolina coast have told of seeing a strange little man dressed in a gray suit just before a storm. Some people believe strongly in the legend and evacuate when they hear of such a sighting.

Gifts from Beyond the Grave

In life, Charlene Richard was an ordinary little girl who liked dolls and went to church every Sunday. It was only after her death thirty years ago that the twelve-year-old became widely known.

Today Charlene's name is a household word in southeastern Louisiana's Cajun country, where many folks believe the girl still lives—even after death—as an angel sent to earth to help heal the sick and lame and to perform other miracles.

In recent years, thousands of Charlene's Roman Catholic followers have rallied to make known their desire to have their local girl made a saint. That process could take decades, but in the meantime residents of Richard, Louisiana, have launched a campaign to make the world aware of Charlene's special gifts from beyond the grave.

On the night of August 11, 1989—Charlene's birthday—a crowd of about four thousand Catholics gathered at her grave at St. Edward's Church outside Richard to pay homage to their young candidate for sainthood. Those present that night sincerely believed in the departed girl's ability to reach beyond the walls of the spiritual world and touch the lives of those in the physical.

One such man was Paul Olivier.

"We had a child who was a year old and diagnosed as having cancer of the larynx," Olivier, a retired state policeman, told a wire service reporter. "The doctors said it was very rare, but it was a killer. They put her life span at three, four, five months at the most."

Then Olivier heard about Charlene.

At first he was skeptical. He was a deeply religious man, but he still didn't know what to think about miracles or prophets or divine intervention in earthly life. Desperate for help, however, Olivier took his sick daughter to the dead Cajun girl's grave.

"We asked her to help us," Olivier explained.

That was in 1970. Today Angela Olivier is a nineteen-year-old junior at the University of Southeastern Louisiana.

"I would say that is a sign of a miracle," her father said. "A prayer was answered."

Olivier's story is similar to hundreds of others that started cropping up shortly after Charlene's death. Talk of the girl's miraculous healing powers spread like wildfire through this ruggedly scenic region, and soon network television and national newspapers and magazines began to report on some of the more spectacular events.

Though many accounts were dismissed as hallucinations or hoaxes, a number of puzzling cases remain a mystery—except to those who believe.

Ten years ago, Lucy and Roger Courville's five-year-old daughter was diagnosed as having inoperable cancer. They had heard about Charlene, and along with hundreds of other faithful members of the flock, made a pilgrimage to Charlene's grave.

After a day of prayerful worship, the Courvilles went away. So did the cancer. Laurie Courville is now fifteen and continues to show signs of improvement.

"We think it was a miracle from Charlene," remarked a family member who says the healed girl's parents visit Charlene's grave often to thank her for saving their daughter's life.

The Reverend Floyd Calais is a man of the cloth who also believes in Charlene. A short while after her death, Calais was the chaplain at a state hospital in Lafayette, in the heart of Cajun country. For months he had been hoping for an opportunity to relocate to a small parish. When he heard about Charlene, he went to her grave and prayed she would inspire the bishop to reassign him.

He was soon appointed pastor of the church where the girl was buried, about one hundred fifty miles northwest of New Orleans.

"When I found out which church I had, the hair on the back of my neck stood on end," Calais, now sixty-two, said.

Today there is a box on Charlene's grave where visitors hoping for miracles can drop their petitions. A steady stream of visitors come and go, mainly curiosity seekers anxious for a glimpse of the famous grave, and at night a candle burns to light the way.

The grave itself is of simple construction, marked with a marble headstone and two elevated slabs. Even though she isn't convinced herself about her late daughter's miracles, Mary Alice Richard, Charlene's mother, still visits the grave nearly every day.

"Charlene was not a remarkable child," Mrs. Richard said. "She was full of life. She liked sports and was always busy with something. She went to church and said her rosary, but she was just a normal little girl."

The Rev. Joseph Brennan, pastor of St. Edward Church where Charlene is buried, said it was the girl's death that made her a saint.

"Charlene taught the world not how to live, but how to die," Brennan said. "Thirty years ago they didn't have the pain medicine they have now, and she died in excruciating pain but in perfect grace. She became great at that time."

Although the United States has produced only three saints, the diocese of Lafayette has begun the slow process of sainthood for Charlene. Local officials of the church are still involved with the first step of the canonization process—collecting sworn testimonies from people about how Charlene performed miracles on their behalf.

Based on the information collected, it will be up to the Vatican to determine whether Charlene is suitable for sainthood. Veneration would come first, then beatification, and finally canonization, according to Father Calais.

"That really doesn't matter. I'm sure that Charlene is a

saint," he said. "I'm sure she is in heaven."

For those who have seen the miracles, the canonization of Charlene is only a formality.

"For us she is already a saint," said Wilson Daigle, who credits Charlene's intercession with helping his wife recover from a mental illness. "We talk to her and she understands us."

The Portrait That Came to Life

Few hauntings in American history have aroused more speculation or raised more hackles than the series of eerie events
that happened at Haw Branch plantation near Amelia, Virginia.

Ghostly visitations, bloodcurdling screams in the night,
sinister birds, and macabre portraits that dripped blood are
just some of the spooky goings-on said to have plagued the
handsome old manor house since Civil War times. Unexplained disturbances continue to baffle the plantation's modern owners, though they have long since lost their fear.

"It's something we've learned to live with," said Gibson
McConnaughey, who along with her husband Cary bought
the estate in 1964, "but at times it does get frightening."

In antebellum days, Haw Branch Planation was the focal
point of a sprawling, 15,000-acre estate, complete with
numerous outbuildings, slave quarters, and even a dry moat.
After the War between the States the plantation fell into
disuse and ruin. Like hundreds of other once-proud plantations in the South, it was abandoned to weeds and vandals.

Nearly a hundred years later, in 1964, the McConnaugheys bought the property, which had once belonged to
Mrs. McConnaughey's grandmother. Mrs. McConnaughey
remembers playing in the house as a child, but for the past
fifty years or so, no member of the family had lived in the
house.

Restoration was tedious. Not only did the main house
with its tall brick chimneys and brooding columns undergo

massive rehabilitation, but acres of fields and rolling yards had to be cut back and preened. Finally, after four years of hard work, one of the South's most noted architectural gems was gleaming again.

Then the portrait arrived.

The subject was a beautiful young woman, said to be a distant and long-dead relative named Florence Wright. When the portrait was uncrated, the McConnaugheys were astonished to find a dingy black and white drawing rather than the brilliant pastel they were promised by the cousin who gave it to them as a housewarming gift.

Gibson McConnaughey dutifully hung the portrait over the library mantel anyway, thinking how much her ancestor would have appreciated it. Less than a month later, Mrs. McConnaughey made a startling discovery: either she was losing her mind, or the portrait was turning colors! In the light, certain parts of the canvas appeared to be bleeding.

Startled, she called in her husband and several visitors to see for themselves. Sure enough, over the next few weeks, fresh and living color began to creep into almost every gray and black tone in the picture.

It was as if the "dead" portrait had been brought back to life inside the old house!

Accompanying the eerie changes on the canvas were sounds—strange, bloodcurdling sounds, mostly that of a woman screaming from upstairs somewhere. The sounds continued on a regular basis for several years, coming usually at six-month intervals—on November 23 and May 23. The sounds were replaced by the apparition of a young woman, first seen by Mrs. McConnaughey in the summer of 1967.

"I could plainly see the silhouette of a slim girl in a floor-length dress with a full skirt," she was quoted as saying. "I could see no features, but she was not transparent, just a white silhouette. I saw her for perhaps ten seconds. In the next instant she was gone."

The bewildered Mrs. McConnaughey saw the ghost several times again, floating about the house in various rooms. Her daughter awoke once in the middle of the night to see a "lady in white" standing over her bed.

"Before I could say anything, the lady disappeared right in front of my eyes," the daughter said, noting that the presence had actually reached down and touched her.

On the night of May 23, 1968, the entire family sat up anticipating another visitation. They heard heavy footsteps thudding across the yard, but this time found nothing. Early the next morning, the McConnaughey children saw a giant bird standing in the yard in the moonlight under their windows.

"It was standing there with its wings spread out, appearing to have a wingspan of over six feet," Mrs. McConnaughey noted.

The bird was never seen again, but other curious things occurred in and around the old house. For example, the ghostly tinkling of cowbells was heard circling the house at night (there were no cows on the property); the scent of rosebuds and oranges lingered throughout the house at times (the family kept no fresh flowers in the house); and the McConnaugheys were awakened several times by what sounded like bodies falling into the dry moat.

On yet other occasions, some family members saw what looked like an old man carrying a kerosene lantern across the yard.

None of the strange events that happened at Haw Branch Plantation have ever been sufficiently explained to the McConnaughey family, who continue to reside in one of America's most famous haunted houses.

"Dead" Men Do Tell Tales

Frederick J. Harvey was only twenty years old—much too young to die. So thought his grief-stricken fiancee, Lily Godfrey, who insisted that her betrothed was only sleeping.

Even when the doctor came and pronounced the young man dead, even when the undertakers came and took him away, even after the corpse was walled up inside the family tomb three days later, Lily pleaded with family members to keep a constant vigil over the crypt, so obsessed was she that her beloved would soon awaken from a deep sleep and rush into her arms.

It took almost a week, but finally Lily's persistence paid off. Frederick's father, a wealthy Kansas restaurateur, agreed to re-open the tomb and take his dead son back home.

Lily was nearly overcome with joy!

Back home at the Harveys' palatial estate, young Frederick's body was dressed and put to bed. There he remained, still and ghastly white, beneath the silken covers of the four-poster bed for nearly four months.

In all that time, Lily Godfrey never once left her fiancee's side. She talked to him and sang to him, bathed him and even tried to feed him repeatedly. Every morning and every night she would kiss him on the forehead, hoping to detect warmth, some kind of vital sign.

Four long months passed.

Then, late one night when a stiff October wind rustled around the trees outside the window, an incredible thing happened.

Lily sat at the foot of the bed, staring into the crackling hearth, questioning her own sanity. The moon had risen high, casting a silvery glow over the satin sheets covering Frederick's still form. Suddenly Lily heard a groan. At first she thought it was the wind, scratching and moaning at the window.

When she heard it again, she spun toward the bed. There sat her would-be husband—limp, disheveled, and in obvious pain, but very much alive.

She could scarcely believe her eyes. What if this were a dream, a cruel hallucination?

Perhaps she had already gone mad.

She pinched herself, poked her arm with a pin.

Pain.

She closed her eyes, reopened them.

Frederick still sat there, only now he was moaning more loudly than before. He was also rubbing his head. His first words were, "Water...please."

For several long seconds Lily continued to stare at her "dead" fiance, listening to his deep breathing grow steadily more regular. Then, shivering like a leaf, she rose slowly from her chair and walked over to the bed.

"Frederick," she said, the words like taffy in her constricted throat.

She looked deep into the "corpse's" eyes. They were like dark pools clouded over with misty shadows.

"Lily," Frederick rasped, reaching for her.

Lily had time for one muffled scream before she dropped to the floor in a dead faint.

A few days later Frederick Harvey emerged completely from the trance that nearly cost him his life. Had Lily not insisted that he be brought back home—had he been left longer behind in that thick and musty tomb, he would have surely suffocated.

As it was, he recovered fully and married the woman who brought him back from the dead.

Frederick's grisly encounter with premature burial happened in 1906. In those days, mortuary science was still primitive at best, even though the practice itself had been around for countless thousands of years. In early America, as in many other countries, corpses were rarely embalmed. And since little was known about catalepsy, coma, and other such conditions, untold numbers of "dead" men and women no doubt went prematurely to their graves.

To awaken in a coffin beneath the ground or trapped in a tomb was a great fear of early Americans. No fate could be more horrid, no terror more crippling, than the realization that one had been buried alive. Such anxieties were often expressed in the literature and drama of the day, most notably in Edgar Allen Poe's "The Premature Burial."

Because top medical authorities considered the only sure sign of death to be "putrefactive decomposition," clauses in wills frequently required that bodies not be buried until a week after apparent death. "Waiting mortuaries" were once widely advocated; some were even built.

One sure-fire way to avoid the horrors of premature burial was to have one's remains cremated. In some European countries, it became customary to slit a corpse's jugular vein—just in case.

According to one story, 19th century writer Harriet Martineau went so far as to express in her will her wish to be decapitated upon death.

Eventually someone came up with a kind of "safety coffin." This contraption was designed to allow periodic viewing of the body from above ground, while at the same time provide a means of escape for a prematurely buried person.

"Safety coffins" and other specially-rigged devices for the grave were in hot demand in the late 19th century, when the news was full of premature burials. In 1862, Franz Vester patented a coffin containing an air tube and a bell, with a ladder to facilitate exit from the grave. In 1882 Albert Fearnaught began selling coffins in which the slightest movement from within would make a flag wave above the tombstone.

One remarkable "safety-oriented" coffin was put on the market in 1903. Emily Josephine Jephson described her invention thus: "Jephson's improved Coffin for indicating the burial alive of a person in a trance or suffering from a comatose state so that same may be released or rescued, has means for admitting air to the coffin and for giving an audible signal by means of an electric bell, which may be placed either on the grave or in the cemetery house.

"There is a glass plate in the lid, and a small shelf attached to one side of the coffin which may hold a hammer, matches, and candle so that, when the person wakes, he can light the candle and with the hammer break the glass, thus assisting to liberate himself when the earth...in removed."

Other patents were equally ingenious.

In 1906 J. J. Toolen put together a contraption utilizing a battery-operated spring lid that would power a light for one hundred fifty hours. Another inventor suggested chaining the body to a spring-loaded lid on a coffin buried in shallow earth. Should the unfortunate victim inside return to life and make the slightest movement, the lid would yank open and he or she could literally walk away from the grave.

It wasn't until after World War I that advances in forensic medicine began to lessen fears about premature burial. As the certification of death became a more accurate science, fewer people feared going to their graves while they yet lived.

*Gold, Shrines
and Ancient Stones*

Bedford County's "Lost" Treasure

At first glance, Bedford County, Virginia, might seem like an unlikely place to go treasure hunting.

With its gently sloping hills and quiet rural lifestyle, this corner of the Cavalier State seems more suited to fox hunting and relaxed strolls down secluded country lanes than to digging for buried gold and silver.

For the past decade or so, thousands of people from all across the country have been coming here to do just that. Armed with computerized mapping systems, electronic scanning devices, and a vast array of other sophisticated equipment, these modern-day treasure hunters are leaving no stone unturned in their quest to find the spot where a legendary fortune in gold and silver is supposed to be buried.

It all began more than one hundred sixty years ago when an eccentric old Virginian named Thomas J. Beal went west to seek his fortune. The hometown folk had laughed at him when he told them his plans, but one day he sold his cabin, loaded up his wagon, and drove away without saying goodby to a soul.

After years of mining the rugged backcountry of New Mexico, the old miner was about to give up when late one afternoon he happened to spot something glittering at the back of a cave. Curious, he pushed his way closer through the dust and gloom. Leaning over, he peered at the strange piece of rock jutting from the wall.

There, in the silence of that old cave hundreds of miles from his hometown in Virginia, the old man's heart nearly gave way.

In the dim light he could see it clearly now. Gold! Tons and tons of it, beautiful and gleaming, whole veins of it, stretching back into the cave as far as he could see.

At long last, Beal had struck it rich.

Sometime toward the end of the following year—1821—the lucky miner loaded up several wagons with his glittering fortune and casually drove back to Virginia. Aboard the wagons was his entire fortune—$21 million in gold and silver, stripped from the thirty mines he had worked in New Mexico.

Back home in Bedford County, the first thing Beal did was hide his treasure—wagons and all. Some of the precious lode he concealed in iron pots, which he carefully buried beneath the wagons. Then, for reasons which remain unknown, the curious multi-millionaire pulled up roots and headed back out to New Mexico. He was never seen or heard from again, but before departing, he did leave behind some enigmatic instructions about how to find the lost treasure.

It is those instructions, set out in a kind of secret code, that many seekers of the fortune have been using to try to find Beal's elusive booty. Those who believe in the legend say it's only a matter of time before some lucky hunter unravels the mysterious clues.

"It's down there somewhere, and one day somebody's going to find it," said Eddy Toner, who, along with his brother Joe, has spent the past nine years probing for the treasure. " I get shaky just thinking about it."

The Toner brothers are among scores of "serious" searchers who swarm into rural Bedford County periodically to dig, sift, and poke. Many, like Wilbur Swift of Garden Grove, California, have given up regular jobs and invested their life savings in the project.

"Several times I've come close, so close," Swift, a former computer programmer, explained in an interview, "I'm going to keep digging until I find it."

As for those who don't understand, or who laugh at his quest, Swift has this to say: "He who laughs last, laughs best. I believe I'll have the last laugh."

Ken Dooley, a local contractor, has made a lot of money renting out his equipment to outsiders interested in finding the treasure. Although he tends to doubt the veracity of the legend himself, he figures that as long as other people believe in it, he'll keep supplying them with the tools they need to look for it.

"Everybody who comes in here is always excited," Dooley said. "They're always about two feet away from striking it rich."

Diggers come and diggers go, but so far the secret of Beal's treasure remains just that—a secret. Was it all just a hoax? Did Beal, about whom very little is known today, concoct the story as a joke? Or was he merely seeking revenge against the people who had laughed at him when he told them he was going out west to find his fortune.

Chances are we'll never know the truth. One thing seems sure, though—as long as there remains a shred of possibility the treasure might be for real, the hills and woods of Bedford County will get no rest.

Romancing the Stones of Georgia

High atop a windswept meadow in the rural hills of north Georgia stands a mysterious assembly of granite stones that has intrigued locals and baffled visitors from around the world since its construction almost a decade ago.

The stones, which bear a remarkable resemblance to England's Stonehenge and stand at the mythological center of the Cherokee Indians' world, are said to possess occult powers, while offering guidance for preserving a threatened civilization—or rebuilding a destroyed one.

Known as the Georgia Guidestones, the megalithic structure was built and paid for in 1980 by an unknown benefactor under the assumed name of Robert C. Christian.

Christian's true identity, like the origins and purpose of the Guidestones, remains shrouded in mystery, the subject of considerable controversy in the small Georgia town of Elberton, which bills itself as the "granite capital of the world."

According to William A. Kelly, executive vice president of the Elberton Granite Association, Inc., who oversees much of Elberton's internationally famous granite production, the Guidestones are among the most unusual man-made monuments in North America.

"Not only is its massive size larger than any other single monument manufactured in these parts, the circumstances surrounding its origin, completion and erection have undoubtedly caused more speculation and comment than any of the other millions of granite memorials...since the area's famed granite industry started nearly a century ago."

The configuration of stones, which rises more than nineteen feet above a grassy knoll overlooking Georgia Highway 77, consists of four major columns that radiate like giant symmetrical tablets with a slimmer stone in the center and another capping the top of the structure. Etched into the towering stones are ten messages, or "commandments," translated into twelve languages, including English, Russian, Arabic, Sanskrit, Babylonian cuneiform, Egyptian hieroglyphics, and classical Greek.

Each year, thousands of curiosity-seekers from as far away as Europe and Canada visit the Guidestones. Among the visitors are self-styled witches and warlocks who claim the stones project an energy force because of their unique astronomical alignment with solar and celestial movements and summer and winter solstices.

According to Naunie Batchelder, who teaches at the Foundation of Truth in Atlanta, Elbert County has a very high form of energy, a "special energy some would call a vortex or power spot. We don't know exactly where, but it's here on this hill."

Former Elberton mayor Joe Fendley acknowledges that the monument had become the center of a kind of "occult-type" activity.

"There have been some occult-type things going on out there, also tribal ritualistic dancing, and nude dancing," he told a newspaper. "But there have also been Christian activities there and even a wedding."

Adding to the mystical aura of the stones is a historical marker nearby designating the site as the center of the world.

"This was Al-yeh-li A lo-Hee, the center of the world to the Cherokee Indians," the inscription on the marker reads. "To this assembly ground from which trails radiate in many directions, they came to hold their councils, to dance and worship, which to them were related functions."

Elberton's reputation as the so-called "granite capital of the world" was instrumental in attracting the mysterious Mr. Christian in the first place, according to Hudson Cone, who works for the Elberton Granite Association.

"About all we know is that late one afternoon this fellow walked into the offices of the Elberton Granite Finishing Company and said he wanted to buy a monument—a very large monument," Cone explained. "The man, who identified himself as a Christian gentleman concerned with the welfare of humanity, said he wanted the monument to be about twenty feet high, and it was designed to spread a message to mankind."

Pyramid blue granite was chosen for the project, and soon construction began on what Cone described as "an almost impossible task." During excavation of the site, and later on during construction, several workers reported hearing strange sounds echoing across the lonely hills. Some workers complained of dizziness and light-headedness at times.

Because of the massive size of the stones, each weighing about twenty-eight tons, special equipment had to be brought in to lift the stones from their resting places one hundred fourteen feet inside the quarry. Key craftsmen and special crews were called in to assist with the project, which took more than nine months to complete.

Today the enigmatic stone assembly continues to intrigue locals as well as outsiders. No one knows how many visitors have been drawn to the ring of Guidestones over the years, but one local county official estimates it in the tens of thousands.

As the mystery of Georgia's bizarre circle of stones grows deeper, so do the myths that surround its origin and meaning. It is likely that the true meaning and purpose behind the silent ring of Georgia stones will remain locked within the realm of myth forever.

The End of Jefferson, Texas

On the eve of the American Civil War, a number of former frontier towns in east Texas seemed on the verge of being called the next great western city.

One of those towns was Jefferson, a sprawling riverfront community of thirty thousand inhabitants nestled in the northeast corner of the state not far from Shreveport, Louisiana. With its bustling cotton economy and easy access to the Mississippi River, there was every reason to believe that Jefferson, would soon overtake Houston or even Dallas as the premier commercial center of the Lone Star State.

By 1860 newspapers from Boston to San Francisco were hailing Jefferson as the "Queen of the West." All day long and into the warm southern nights, flotillas of packet boats, piled high with bales of cotton, steamed down Big Cypress River on their way to market.

On any day of the week, there were twelve to fifteen steamboats lined up along the three-mile waterfront, bells ringing and whistles blowing. A favorite pastime among the citizenry was to gather along the docks to watch the colorful boats arrive, unload their goods, and then depart amid billowing clouds of smoke and fire.

Some of the wealthiest folks in Texas—planters, gamblers, cattlemen—traveled these steamers where multi-million-dollar deals were often signed over card tables or in the comfortable, smoke-filled salons of the upper decks. This was definitely the antebellum fast lane, and a trip up or down the winding river aboard one of the handsomely appointed showboats was considered a significant social event in the region.

If you happened to be born into the right social circumstances, the mid-19th century was, indeed, a glorious time to be alive in Old Jefferson. Ladies and gentlemen of standing, clad in hoop skirts, bonnets, and tailcoats, frolicked on the lawns of their gracious homes, while up-and-coming entrepreneurs, planters, and other young fortune hunters plotted their social and financial destinies along the bustling, cotton-laden waterfront.

There was even talk of a railroad coming to town. Leading businessmen, keenly aware of the financial benefits to be gained from completion of a new rail line, had visions of vast wealth flowing into their once obscure little corner of the South.

Even though the winds of war were beginning to blow across the young nation, few Jeffersonians had reason to suspect their good fortune would ever come to an end. Life was simply too wonderful to imagine that it could ever change.

Chances are that Jefferson's future would have remained as bright as the Texas sun had it not been for the intervention of one man.

By the late 1850s, Jay Gould was one of the most powerful—if not most respected—men in the nation. A self-made millionaire by the time he was twenty-one, Gould's life story had followed the classic rags-to-riches pathway to success. As a teenager, he had entered the leather trade, working his way to the top, and then gone on to Wall Street, where he became one of the world's savviest financiers.

As a further measure of Gould's unquestioned ability to make money, he quickly put together a second fortune after having lost everything in the Panic of 1857. After the South's surrender at Appomattox, Gould emerged as one of the most ruthless land speculators of the century. He also started buying and selling railroads much the same way other men did stocks and bonds.

It was no secret that Jay Gould's determination to succeed

led him to dabble in a series of unscrupulous business ventures involving bribery, stock market fraud, and judicial injunctions. According to his own biographers, Gould's attempts at cornering the nation's gold supply on Black Friday 1869 was the most notorious maneuver in a long and shady career.

In the 1870s Gould turned speculator again, this time targeting rapidly expanding western railroads such as the Union Pacific. Still only in his forties, Gould juggled control of a dozen new lines; by 1890 he reportedly owned half the railroad mileage in the Southwest. Across the dusty plains and deserts they went, hundreds of miles of gleaming new track finally linking the eastern and western halves of the growing nation.

But when Jay Gould came to Texas demanding concessions for his new line, the citizens of Jefferson shook their proud heads. Instead of bowing down before the undisputed king of the railroads, Jeffersonians appeared content to allow commerce to continue as it had before, along the muddy waters of Big Cypress River.

Besides, nobody wanted the clang and smoke of dirty locomotives lumbering through the streets of their clean, tranquil city. Residents of the "Queen of the West" were protective of their tree-lined avenues, handsome frame shops and houses, and landscaped parks.

When Gould failed to get his way, he left in a huff, taking his railroad with him three miles away. Before leaving, however, the wizard of Wall Street paused long enough to put a curse on Jefferson. The curse, written down on the register of the hotel where he had stayed, was a chilling prediction that Jefferson would soon dry up and blow away like a Texas tumbleweed.

"It's the end of Jefferson, Texas," he wrote. "Grass will grow in your streets and bats will roost in your belfries if you do not let me run my railroad through your town."

Jeffersonians scoffed at the strange warning—but not for long. Just up the river, near Shreveport, the federal government had already started dredge work on the Big Cypress.

Almost overnight the once-mighty river was reduced to a mere trickle; now, with no water route, cotton bales stood rotting along abandoned waterfront docks.

Within months of his departure, Gould's eerie prediction had come true. As the river dried up, so did the town. Jefferson sank into a period of decay from which it wouldn't emerge for years. Grass and weeds soon choked the streets and the fluttering wings of bats could be heard in the deserted attics and belfries of Jefferson.

Ancient Footprints in Stone

Most anthropologists agree that mankind originated in Africa at some remote time in the past, and then migrated to the New World across a now-submerged Asian landbridge about 25,000 years ago.

But hold on.

If that theory is true, what on earth are human footprints doing buried on a Kentucky farm in sediment laid down at least 250 million years ago?

How can it be that workers digging along the Mississippi River once uncovered a slab of sandstone containing a pair of fossilized "humanoid" tracks supposedly millions of years old?

Clearly, if these ancient footprints in stone are genuine, something must be wrong with our fossil record. Otherwise, how is it possible that man-like creatures roamed North America millions of years before the emergence of *Australopithecus* in Africa and Asia?

These are only some of the troubling questions being raised in light of several new and not-so-new findings in paleontology, the branch of geology that deals with prehistoric plant and animal fossils. What is slowly emerging is not only the startling possibility that mankind has flourished in the New World for millions of years, but also the astounding proposition that he perhaps walked North America during the time of the dinosaurs.

One of the most compelling bits of evidence attesting to man's antiquity in the New World was found in a dry river bed near Glen Rose, Texas, about sixty years ago. Residents happened to notice that each time the Paluxy River dried up, giant man-like footprints, some measuring eighteen inches long and five to seven inches wide, would show up adjacent to those of dinosaur tracks—irrefutable proof, said some, that forerunners of man had lived during the age of the great reptiles.

In one striking discovery, for example, the footprints of a man-like creature actually overlapped that of a three-toed dinosaur—a creature that paleontologists insist became extinct more than sixty-six million years ago!

Quick to cash in on the quirky find, some locals began digging up tracks and hawking them to tourists. It's no secret, of course, that large numbers of these "tracks" were fakes sold to gullible customers. But a lot of people who profited from the business testified their tracks were authentic.

Jim Ryals was one such man. In sworn testimony, he admitted that he and his wife sold tracks to tourists, but that some were the real thing. Ryals reportedly told investigators that he and his wife had removed several of the prehistoric human tracks from the Paluxy riverbed, using a chisel and a sledgehammer.

According to Ryals, there was a way that real prints could be distinguished from fakes:

"First, the pressure of the foot usually pushed up a ridge of mud around the outside of the track. Second, if the track is broken open or sawed, pressure lines can be found beneath the surface...

"Furthermore...when the (real) tracks were chiseled out of the riverbed, the workman was usually very careful to do his chiseling a good distance from the track for fear of damaging it. This resulted in a rather wide circle of the limestone surrounding the footprint."

It was common knowledge that local hucksters involved in the lucrative track trade knew the difference between real ones and fakes—that is, they were able to fashion their own versions by carefully copying the authentic models in the riverbed. Some became so skilled at their craft it was difficult for even trained scientists to tell the real from the phonies.

Understandably, most scientists are reluctant to even consider the authenticity of the Glen Rose tracks since dinosaurs supposedly died off millions of years before the evolution of *Homo sapiens* from small, warm-blooded creatures. Others who have looked at the evidence aren't so sure.

In 1976, Jack Walper, a professor of geology at Texas Christian University, conducted studies that offered additional proof that the human prints were genuine. In a series of tests, he showed that the pressure of each fossilized footfall had forced the mud upward—indicating that actual human beings had made the prints at some time in the past contemporary with dinosaurs.

The truth behind the Glen Rose tracks remains a mystery, as do some other startling finds linking man to prehistoric times. Shortly before the outbreak of World War I, for example, Dr. Wilbur Burroughs, head of the geology department of Berea College in Kentucky, discovered what he called "humanoid" footprints in carboniferous sandstone on a farm belonging to O. Finnel in the hills of Rockcastle County, Kentucky.

Special tests on the Rockcastle tracks revealed no signs of carving or artificial marking in or around the prints—suggesting, of course, that the prints were authentic. The prints—found in rock estimated to be more than 250 million years old—were later destroyed by vandals.

During the War of 1812, noted American ethnologist Henry R. Schoolcraft excavated a pair of human footprints from a quarry along the Mississippi River near St. Louis. Schoolcraft, who found the tracks in a limestone deposit estimated to be 270 million years old, described them as "strikingly natural, exhibiting every muscular impression, and swell of the heel and toes, with a precision and faithfulness to nature, which I have not been able to copy, with perfect exactness..."

For years, some anthropologists have argued that the traditionally accepted timeframe of man's arrival in the New World is no longer satisfactory. A few, like Jeffrey Goodman, an engineering archaeologist from Tucson, Arizona, believe that man first developed in North America, then migrated westward toward Asia and the Old World.

Goodman bases his theory on "many individual bits and pieces of information in the archaeological record which, taken together, serve to fingerprint and document specific migrations in reverse...Based on the evidence now coming to light, I believe that there was migration in reverse. Instead of nomadic hunters coming from the Old World to populate the New World, I believe the Paleo-Indians from the New World, the first fully modern men anywhere in the world, traveled to the Old World and woke it from its sound evolutionary sleep."

Neither Goodman nor any of the other "America first" theorists can adequately account for the enigmatic presence of human footprints in stone deposits believed to be many millions of years old. These timeless tracks in stone remain one of the greatest mysteries of our time.

Improbable Encounters

The Galveston Sea Monster

The late afternoon sun hung low and hazy over the glassy waters of the Gulf of Mexico. Only the slightest of breezes stirred as the *Saint Olaf,* a Norwegian-registered bark with twenty-man crew, sailed slowly toward the port city of Galveston, Texas.

The voyage down from Newport had been slow and uneventful. Now, Captain Alfred Hassel, master of the small tri-masted vessel, and his sea-weary crew were looking forward to a few days of rest and relaxation on the warm Texas coast before sailing back to their cold, mist-shrouded homeland in Norway.

Hassel and the brave men of the *Saint Olaf* didn't suspect they were only minutes away from a terrifying encounter with the unknown. Less than a few hundred yards ahead, not yet visible in the sparkling green waters, a long, sinuous shadow was undulating toward them. Soon the mariners would come face-to-face with their worst nightmare—a gigantic sea serpent.

The bizarre confrontation would make headlines around the world as reporters and scientists from New York to Paris flocked to Galveston to interview the captain and crew of the *Saint Olaf.* In his official public report, released two months after the incident, Hassel would provide a detailed account of the large "sea monster" that chased and threatened his ship that warm summer day in 1872.

All was going well until about 4:30 when Hassel, in his cabin studying tide charts, was summoned on deck by a frantic sailor. The date was May 13, 1872. The *Saint Olaf* was less than two days from Galveston.

After putting away the charts and throwing on his cap, Hassel trudged up the steep flight of steps to go topside. He paused briefly for his eyes to adjust to the harsh glare of the setting sun, then strolled briskly over to the weather bow to see what all the commotion was about.

He had never seen his men so excited. Groups of sailors were leaning over the railing, pointing and shouting at some object far out at sea. A couple of seamen had scampered up the rigging, apparently to get a better view.

Hassel pushed his way past his men toward the railing.

"Over here, sir!" his first mate shouted. "You won't believe it."

The first thing the captain saw was a shoal of large sharks slicing quickly toward the boat. Within seconds their fins had disappeared beneath the hull, only to re-emerge moments later on the other side. Soon they had disappeared on the horizon. Hassel, a grizzled maritime veteran, had never seen such strange shark behavior. Apparently something was chasing them—something huge.

Then he saw it, rising over the shimmering, fire-tipped surface of the sea. At first, as it lurched toward them, the image was that of a bewhiskered old man tottering across the waves. But as it drew nearer, Hassel and every man on deck realized it wasn't like anything they had ever seen. In fact, they could now see it was some kind of creature—a hideous, evil-looking serpentine monster with horn and fins and a long, pointed tail.

Never had the men aboard the *Saint Olaf* seen such a dreadful sight. Some shrank away from the railing in fright; others made the sign of the cross. Even in their horror, however, not a single sailor dared take his eyes off the devil-sent behemoth slicing through the sea toward them.

Hassel was reminded of old pictures he had seen of the dreaded Kraken—the fabled deep-sea creature that was said to roam the open seas in search of wayward ships and their crews. Even in the Gulf there were stories of equally fearsome beasts that had attacked ships and devoured crewmen.

But Hassel didn't believe in such fairy tales—until today.

Hassel's official statement, signed and released the following August, gave the following description of the strange apparition:

"On a nearer approach we saw that it was an immense serpent, with its head out of the water...about 200 feet from the vessel. He (the serpent) lay still on the surface (at first)...lifting his head up, and moving the body in a serpentine manner. Could not see all of it; but what we could see, from the after part of the head, was about 70 feet long and of the same thickness all the way, excepting about the head and neck, which were smaller, and the former flat, like the head of a serpent..."

Hassel said the creature had "four fins on the back, and the body of a yellow greenish color, with brown spots all over the upper part and underneath white."

In his sworn statement, Hassel also said the creature was about six feet in diameter, and that the waves "pushed out loudly" from its undulating motion.

The men of the *Saint Olaf* watched the creature for a full ten minutes before it finally sank beneath the waves and disappeared. One sailor thought he saw it resurface some time later, but no one was sure. The Galveston monster had simply vanished, like so many others reportedly spotted in the vicinity over the years.

Skeptics were quick to dismiss the sighting as nothing more than a long string of seaweed. In the fading afternoon sunlight, they reasoned, floating strands of weed rising and falling with the action of the waves could have easily been mistaken for a giant serpent. Others suspected the "creature" might have been a school of porpoises in pursuit of the rapidly-fleeing sharks.

Some experts theorized it might have indeed been a serpent—a giant boa constrictor or some other kind of large snake that had perhaps drifted across the Gulf from Central America. But seventy feet long? The longest known serpent in the New World—the anaconda—rarely exceeds twenty feet in length.

It is also doubtful that any kind of land snake could have survived such a long voyage across the shark-infested Gulf.

Through it all, the men of the *Saint Olaf* held fast to their story. They had seen a sea serpent—and lived to tell the tale.

Swarms of "Killer Bees" Will Soon Invade U.S.

For the past couple of decades, Americans living along the Mexican border have been gearing up for an invasion. When it comes, no wall will be high enough nor will any Star Wars defense shield be strong enough to keep out this airborne enemy.

Swarms of African bees, dubbed "killer" bees by the news media because their powerful stings have already resulted in the deaths of hundreds of human beings, are reportedly massing less than four hundred miles south of the Texas border for the big northern offensive. Moving at a rate of about three hundred miles a year, the bees were expected to reach the Brownsville area in March 1990. By 1993 they should reach Arizona, and California one year later.

Over the next several decades, the bees' relentless advance could take them as far north as Canada, provided their own defense systems are capable of adjusting to the colder climes.

What sounds like the ideal plot for a grade B science-fiction movie is being taken seriously by teams of scientists from Mexico City to Washington, D.C., who have been busy monitoring the progress of the bees for the past couple of decades. Some of the methods being considered to halt the relentless spread of bees sound like science fiction, as well— chemically-scented lures, solar-powered, infrared bee back-packs and a computerized noisemaker called a "Buzz Buster."

135

So far nothing seems to be working. About the only thing Americans can do is watch and wait while hundreds of swarms of vicious, mutant killer bees wing their way steadily northward.

Not much is known about the African bees since about thirty swarms were accidentally released in a Brazilian laboratory in 1956—except that they are extremely active, aggressive, and dangerous. At least four hundred people and thousands of animals have been killed by this highly excitable insect that attacks its victims en masse, stinging them to death with its powerful venom.

After their escape into the Brazilian jungle, these swarms of savage bees quickly crossbred with native varieties. The African bees, along with their "Africanized" cousins, then gradually spread through South and Central America into Mexico, terrorizing farmers and villagers along their 3,000-mile journey through ten countries.

In recent years, books, movies, and television shows have appeared predicting grim encounters between humans and large swarms of killer bees. Although scientists and professional beekeepers downplay such scenarios, the genetic makeup and ferocious behavior of the African bees could make them formidable foes in certain real-life situations.

One scientist said she had to "run for her life" several times when attacked by swarms of bees she was studying in Venezuela. Anita Collins of the U.S. Department of Agriculture said her primary motivation now for finding a way to stop or control bees stems directly from those attacks.

"I reached the point where I wanted to say something besides, 'Run like hell,'" she told a reporter.

Several swarms of bees have already reportedly reached south Florida. In 1988, about ten thousand bees were found at Fort Lauderdale aboard a freighter carrying fruit and vegetables from Guatemala. The bees had to be destroyed, as did the most recent swarm of five hundred found last year aboard a tanker in Miami.

Although the Florida swarms caught officials by surprise, the Agriculture Department, in anticipation of accidental bee arrivals, had set up several "bait hives" in the southern part of the state.

"The first bait hive we ever placed was in Miami because it's an area we've always been concerned about," said Agriculture Commissioner Doyle Conner. "There is just a tremendous interchange between Miami and Central and South American countries, virtually all of which are now infested with Africanized bees."

Florida now monitors about three hundred bait hives set up in thirteen port areas.

Beekeepers and scientists have long known that key genetic and behavioral differences existed between African bees and their tamer, gentler cousins in North America, but have only recently come to understand some of them. Killer bees, for example, tend to appear much more defensive around hives, aggressively assaulting and often pursuing for miles people or animals who come near.

For years scientists assumed that mating African bees with the gentler variety would cause them to lose their propensity to sting in potentially deadly swarms. But recent research has shown that the dilution of Africanized genes appears only to be temporary and that the bees' genetic makeup eventually becomes almost purely Africanized again, as is evident in wild swarms spreading up through Central America and southeastern Mexico.

"This African population is going to reach the U.S. virtually unchanged," said Orley Taylor, a University of Kansas insect ecologist.

Aside from the obvious physical danger, officials are haunted by other concerns brought on by the wild African bee invasion. For example, some scientists fear the bees will disrupt the nation's $200 million honey industry as well as damage $20 billion worth of pollinated field crops.

That's because African bees reproduce many times faster than domestic bees and tend to wreak havoc on less hostile honeybee colonies. At the same time, killer bees are known to be poor pollinators because of the drone's reputation as being a big consumer of honey.

In the past, the United States has withstood numerous menacing invasions from the south. This may be the first time our armies won't be able to defend us.

Where Did All the Dinosaurs Go?

Every school child knows that millions of years before the emergence of man, huge creatures called dinosaurs ruled the earth.

Thanks to the work of paleontologists, we not only know what these ancient animals looked like, we also know what they ate, how they reproduced, and where and when they lived.

What isn't so clear, however, is the fate that suddenly befell these beasts that once held sway over so much of our young planet and its shallow seas. Geologically speaking, the dinosaurs vanished in the twinkling of an eye.

The cause of their enigmatic passing is one of the greatest mysteries of all time.

Many theories have been advanced over the years to account for the extinction of the dinosaurs. New evidence coming forth from the ground in the Southeastern United States, however, links the end of the dinosaurs to a prehistoric global upheaval precipitated by the crash of a meteor or swarm of meteors about sixty-six million years ago.

Although this "impact theory" has many detractors, more and more scientists now accept the possibility that at some remote time in the past, a gigantic celestial object struck the earth, setting off a chain of climatic events that ultimately led to the demise of the dinosaurs.

If the theory holds up, it wouldn't be the first time that life forms on earth have been destroyed by death-dealing agents from beyond the solar system. According to some scientists, the fossil record is replete with evidence suggesting periodic mass extinctions. Exactly how and when they occurred, however, is a matter of unprecedented debate.

"These are exciting times to be looking at extinction," says Bevan French, a geologist with NASA.

Two schools of thought have emerged among extinction specialists. The first holds that mass extinctions on earth are somehow triggered by brief cataclysmic events such as the impact of a celestial body; others argue that the extinction process is gradual, brought on by environmental changes wrought by tectonic, oceanic, and climatic fluctuations.

When geologists and paleontologists look for evidence to support their theories, they usually turn to the fossil record left in rocks.

In Texas, scientists from Baylor University and Western Washington University have found what they believe are strong clues to support the impact theory—that is, that some large object from space, probably an asteroid or a comet, slammed into the western Atlantic Ocean approximately 66.4 million years ago, triggering a global catastrophe that ultimately killed off large animals on earth and in the sea. Their findings support that of other geologists working in Alabama, Arkansas, and off the Carolina coast.

Geologists Thor A. Hansen and O.T. Howard say the crash resulted in an ocean wave at least fifteen stories high that roared across shallow seas in east-central Texas. To support their claim, they point to a series of rock outcrops near the Brazos River southeast of Waco that still bear scars from that event millions of years ago.

"We calculated how much energy was necessary to rip up the kind of chunks of ocean floor that we found and then calculated the size of the wave," Hansen told reporters. He added that he believes the tsunami, or seismic sea wave, was more than fifty meters (about one hundred sixty feet) high.

Studies of rock formations elsewhere in the Southeast suggest "some sort of high-energy event" occurred about the same time, probably resulting from an impact somewhere in the Atlantic.

"We think we've proven there was a tsunami," Hansen noted. "We speculate that the wave was generated by some sort of extraterrestrial impact."

Such a celestial impact could have resulted in a scenario straight out of a science-fiction movie: giant meteor slams into the earth, kicking up enormous clouds of dust and smoke from blazing volcanoes. Other volcanoes erupt, tidal waves surge across landscapes, and the skies grow dark for months, perhaps years.

Unable to adjust to the altered environmental conditions, countless species are wiped off the face of the planet. Dinosaurs—cold-blooded, many of them quite large—are biologically less flexible, and perish in great numbers. Smaller creatures—especially tiny, fur-clad, warm-blooded mammals—escape to continue their evolution.

At least that is the picture being painted by some advocates of the impact theory. Such a view would have been considered radical until about a decade ago when scientists found large amounts of iridium layered in deposits made about the time the dinosaurs became extinct. Iridium is a rare metal on earth but common in meteorites.

These and other recent findings continue to shed light on the fate of our ancient forerunners and may contain clues to our own uncertain future.

Florida's "Watcher in the Woods"

The Fort Lauderdale, Florida, police department was accustomed to receiving strange calls in the middle of the night, but nothing had prepared them for the unusual message they received on the morning of January 9, 1974.

A young man who identified himself as Richard Lee Smith said he had run over a "giant black man" on Hollywood Boulevard, a busy area even at four o'clock in the morning.

"Is he dead?" the dispatcher wanted to know.

"I think so," Smith replied in a trembling voice. "But he's gone."

"You mean he's a goner?" the dispatcher asked.

"No, I mean he's dead, but he's gone," Smith answered.

Then Smith assured the officer this was no crank call—nor was it just any ordinary traffic accident involving a pedestrian.

"Please send someone out here," he pleaded. "Hurry!"

An officer named Johnson was immediately dispatched to the scene. Smith was waiting for him, huddled inside his locked car. When the officer arrived, the young man slowly got out.

Smith explained what happened.

He had been travelling at about fifty miles an hour when a huge man wearing what appeared to be dark clothing suddenly stepped out in front of him. He swerved to avoid hitting the man, but instead of stepping away from the car, the pedestrian bolted directly into its path.

Smith said he felt—and heard—the sickening crunch of

his front right wheel rolling over bones. Afraid he had killed the man, Smith stopped the car, got out, and ran back to examine the victim.

That's when he nearly died of fright.

In a state of shock, he watched a large, hairy "creature-like thing" rise slowly off the pavement. Even in the dim glow of the street lamp, Smith could clearly see what he had hit. The "thing" stood well over eight feet tall, he said, and made a roaring sound. Then it made a move toward him.

"That's when I jumped in the car and took off," Smith told the officer.

Johnson, not overly impressed by the young man's wild story, dutifully looked over the car's damaged front end. The front had bloodstains, to be sure, and several strands of dark, coarse hair were stuck to the bumper and front wheel.

The officer scratched his head and phoned in his bizarre report.

For the Fort Lauderdale police department, the night was only beginning.

An hour or so later, the switchboard lit up with calls from other motorists who had apparently encountered either the same "creature" or one just like it. Amid chuckles and hee-haws, a full-scale hunt was launched for what some thought might be an escaped gorilla or other wild animal.

At 2:12 a.m., patrolman Robert Hollemeyal thought he saw something resembling the creature ambling down a highway. The officer got out of his car, drew his revolver, and ordered it to halt—in English, of course.

When the creature screamed at him in a high-pitched, threatening manner, Hollemeyal opened fire with two rounds. The shambling mass of hair and arms screamed again, then jumped twenty feet off the road and scurried away at about twenty miles an hour.

Nothing else was seen of the creature, in spite of an all-night search of the area with cars and helicopters. Whatever it was, it was gone now—vanished, perhaps, into a nearby swamp from which it had probably emerged in the first place.

Although the Fort Lauderdale monster is long gone,

memories of it remain. So do those of other hair-raising encounters with similar critters up and down the Sunshine State, from Miami to Jacksonville.

If not escaped gorillas or wild bears, as some have suggested, then what on earth *are* these nightmarish brutes and where do they come from?

Experts disagree, but some think they are similar to Bigfoot of the Pacific Northwest and Sasquatch of Canada. For years Floridians have referred to them as "skunk apes," apparently in reference to their strong smell and ape-like appearance. They are usually described as large, mean, and hairy, often standing well over eight feet tall and weighing close to eight hundred pounds.

Whatever their nature and origin, skunk apes appear here to stay—at least in the minds of many Floridians who claim to have seen them.

Such was the case with Richard Davis, who lived in an isolated area of Cape Coral in the mid-1970s. For several nights in a row, his Alsatian dog had been doing a lot of barking, apparently reacting to some prowler or unknown presence in the woods outside the house.

On the night of February 2, 1975, the dog—a female—was particularly restless. Thinking perhaps a prowler had wandered onto his property, Richard turned his dog loose. A few minutes later, the animal scooted back to the house and cowered beneath a car inside the garage. She was obviously terrified of something out there in the dark.

Davis did what many concerned property owners would have done under similar circumstances—he grabbed his gun and stormed out into the yard.

That's when he saw it, all nine feet of it, looming like a deformed shadow beneath the yellowish glow of his security light. The thing, covered in grayish-brown hair, stood about fifteen feet away, swaying. Davis took one step more and fired point-blank into the creature's massive chest. It grunted once, then darted off into the woods, obviously unfazed.

Unnerved, but still very much in control of his emotions, Davis moved quickly around his house, checking for signs of the creature. He found tracks, lots of tracks, but the thing that disturbed him most was finding a set of footprints on top of the single air conditioning unit.

A few days later, while discussing his uninvited guest with some neighbors, Smith learned that they, too, had been awakened at night by strange sounds in the yard and a particularly foul-smelling odor. They also said unusual tracklike markings had been found on their air conditioners.

A month later, on March 24, another skunk ape incident was reported in Dade County, Florida. About midnight, Michael Bennett and Lawrence Groom were driving along a back road near Black Point and they saw an enormous man-like creature leaning over a parked automobile.

As soon as Bennett and Groom drew near, a hysterical man jumped out and yelled for help. The moment the creature saw the approaching car, it dashed off into a mangrove swamp and disappeared. Officers from the Dade County Public Safety Department searched the area the next day but found no sign of the monster.

As with similar creatures elsewhere, skunk ape sightings in Florida are made by people of all kinds and ages. On October 11, 1975, a 67-year-old minister named S. L. Whatley, of Fort McCoy, Florida, was cutting wood in the Ocala National Forest. It was about 2 p.m. He was tired, having been swinging the chainsaw all morning.

Suddenly, for no reason at all, Whatley got the creepy sensation that *something* was watching him from the woods. Unseen eyes seemed to follow him everywhere he went. It felt as if he were being observed by some curious animal.

Then his worst nightmare stepped out of the shadows.

"It was this hairy-like ape animal standing there in the palmetto bushes," the minister recalled. "It looked to me to be seven or maybe eight feet tall. It had a dark, chocolate-colored face, a face that was clear of hair, and a flat nose. The arms—I couldn't tell what kind of hands it had—the arms were down into the palmetto bushes."

Whatley bolted for his truck, grabbed an axe and turned around to confront the manlike animal.

It was gone.

Though not nearly as famous as Bigfoot, Sasquatch, or the Himalayan yeti, Florida's skunk ape remains one of the South's most enduring, if not lovable, mysteries.

Encounters
with the Unknown

Captain Mantell's Final Flight

Since 1947, more than ten thousand sightings of unidentified flying objects have been reported in several southern states. Hardly a month goes by, it seems, without at least one major report appearing in regional newspapers about a UFO incident or some other strange aerial phenomenon.

Probably the strangest—and certainly the most tragic—case involved a young Air National Guard pilot from Godman Field, Kentucky, named Thomas Mantell. In the annals of UFO lore, the Mantell case stands out as one of the most mysterious.

On the afternoon of January 7, 1948, Captain Mantell, an experienced flyer, climbed aboard his F-51 aircraft to take part in a routine training exercise over Godman Field. The day was gloomy and cold, a bad day for flying, and the aviator looked forward to completing the mission and returning home.

Sometime around 1:45 p.m., a control tower operator spotted a strange flying object heading in Mantell's direction. About an hour later—at 2:48 p.m.—Captain Mantell radioed back that he had made visual contact with the unidentified flying object and was in pursuit.

Two other planes in Mantell's formation also saw the object but pulled back when they realized it was climbing beyond 15,000 feet—the maximum altitude for which the aircraft were equipped. Mantell, however, veered ahead of his wingman and continued the upward climb, even though he knew he was risking his life.

A few minutes later he told the tower he was going to 20,000 feet. He described the object as a "large, glowing sphere...tremendous in size," that always managed to stay several hundred yards ahead of him. Mantell nosed his F-51 upward in a steep climb, trying to maintain visual contact with the rapidly ascending UFO.

At exactly 3:50 p.m., the tower lost both visual and audio contact with the captain. Minutes later, a report came in that Mantell's plane had crashed and burned in a nearby field.

Before going down, Mantell gave a final description of the object he was chasing higher and higher into the clouds. Although no official transcript is available, at least one controller in the tower that afternoon swore that Mantell was convinced he was chasing an unknown type of aircraft—perhaps either Russian or Chinese—but certainly not American.

The controller thought Mantell had called it a "flying saucer."

The term "flying saucer" itself had only come into use a few months earlier when an Idaho commercial pilot had so described such an object to reporters. The first known use of the appellation "saucer," however, goes back to 1878 when a farmer used it to describe the shape of an object which he reported over his farm near Denison, Texas.

Until it closed its official study on the subject in 1969, the Air Force and other governmental agencies referred to these strange aerial objects as "U-FOBs," for "unidentified flying objects." Most experts in the field prefer the usage "UFO" rather than flying saucer or disc, since aerial phenomena come in a bewildering variety of shapes and sizes.

It is unlikely that Captain Mantell, on that fateful day forty-one years ago, had ever even heard of UFOs.

What happened isn't clear. Some investigators think Mantell probably blacked out from lack of oxygen and his plane simply crashed to the earth. Others aren't so sure, however. One retired Air Force officer who helped investigate the crash said Mantell—an experienced pilot all too aware of the dangers of anoxia (oxygen starvation) above 15,000 feet—

was drawn into the clouds against his will.

As for Mantell's "large, glowing object," it was probably nothing more than Venus rising or an enormous skyhook balloon—or so said military officials at the scene of the crash. Coral E. Lorenzen, author of *Flying Saucers: the Startling Evidence of the Invasion From Outer Space* and a long-time researcher in the field of aerial phenomena, thinks otherwise.

"I am not prepared to dispute this theory," wrote Lorenzen, "except to say that no balloon flight for that particular area has been discovered in military archives....As far as I'm concerned, the Mantell case should be listed as 'unknown' until the 'object' can be positively identified."

As for the Venus theory, Lorenzen says the fallacy of that explanation was evident. "Venus was not at maximum magnitude at that specific time, and although Venus can be seen on clear days at peak brilliance—if one knows where to look—it would have been impossible for Mantell to chase something that would not have been visible on that partly cloudy day."

But the biggest surprise was yet to come.

When Mantell's plane went down, slamming into the earth at hundreds of miles an hour, investigators quickly swarmed onto the crash site, sifting, poking, and probing through the charred wreckage. Suddenly someone realized that the pilot's body was missing! It was as if Mantell had simply disappeared from the cockpit.

According to Lorenzen, Mantell's body was never found. Its whereabouts, says the writer who spent years researching the Mantell case, remains one of the greatest mysteries in UFO lore.

One leading expert, a retired captain in the reserves who took part in the investigation, believes the pilot was removed alive from the crippled aircraft by the very spaceship he was chasing.

Arkansas's Strange Voyager from the Stars

Since earliest times men have looked toward the sky for answers to many of life's most compelling questions: Who are we? Where did we come from? Where are we going?

Thousands of years ago, civilizations in the Middle East turned to the heavens for clues to universal purpose. Complex sky-charts were developed not only to help keep track of celestial movements but also to interpret natural phenomena. Thunder, lightning, and other strange atmospheric disturbances were constant reminders that man was not alone, that supernatural forces far beyond the stars controlled our earth-bound spirits and influenced our own development.

It was only natural, then, that concepts of God and Heaven would become associated with the sky. The sky was seen as a veiled, mystical doorway to Heaven—a vast, wondrous dome, sometimes pleasant, sometimes moody, but always full of mystery.

Whenever a thunderstorm struck, it was invariably linked to some higher power. Whenever ball lightning flared in the middle of a swamp, or a shower of meteors blazed across a velvet sky, the temptation was always strong to regard it as divine intervention.

Along with divine inspiration and wonder, the sky also brought terror. The Bible and other ancient manuscripts are full of unearthly events emanating from the heavens— flaming balls of fire, burning chariots, titanic winds, and the like. Even today, as spaceships orbit the planets and plunge far out into space, whenever something bad goes wrong down here on earth, our first reaction is to lift our thoughts toward Heaven.

Such was the case on the afternoon of December 8, 1847, in the tiny Arkansas town of Forest Hill.

The day had dawned clear and cold, but sometime after lunch, a few gray clouds started blowing in from the east. Shoppers, bundled against the blustery winter chill, scurried along the sidewalks, taking advantage of pre-Christmas sales. The smell of burning wood, mixed with the aroma of baked goods, lay heavy over the town square.

Later in the day, the clouds grew dark and angry.

One observer described them as a "solid black fleece lighted from above by a red glare as of many torches."

It was an eerie phenomenon, certainly unlike anything the people of Forest Hill had ever seen. Curious shopkeepers and customers rushed into the streets to watch what appeared to be a gathering storm. Powerful winds gusted down Main Street, rattling glass windows and overturning public benches. Bonnets and hats flew in every direction, as crowds of people staggered and stumbled along the dusty sidewalks and streets.

Lightning flashed and popped. Thunder roared and grumbled. At three o'clock a freezing rain started to fall in sheets. Pedestrians scampered for cover. They huddled inside shops and houses and beneath rickety storefront overhangs, waiting for the storm to pass.

Suddenly a loud explosion split the dark skies. After the explosion came a rumble—a rumble so long and deep it caused houses to wobble and rattled the church bell.

A few seconds later a "barrel-sized flaming body" crashed into the earth just outside the town, kicking up a cloud of smoke and steam half a mile high. When a handful of brave citizens went to investigate, they found a gaping hole in the ground. The hole measured eight feet deep and two feet in diameter.

At the bottom of the hole, still smoldering, was a large,

odd-shaped rock. The smell of sulphur lay heavy over the site. When someone threw a bucket of water onto the rock, the hole hissed and spewed steam, reminding those present of an erupting volcano.

What was it?

No one had the slightest clue.

One man fell to his knees and began to pray. Another started to climb down inside the hole but a tangle of brawny arms pulled him back. Better to leave it alone, they felt, at least until the thing could be properly identified.

Twenty minutes later, the rain stopped and the sun peeked out from behind a gently fading cloud. The storm had passed. Relieved faces peered toward a dazzling, freshly-scrubbed sky.

Although the object that crashed into the ground just outside Forest Hill has long since disappeared, scientists still wonder about its origins. Was it a meteorite, as some suspect, or was it something else—perhaps an abnormal byproduct of lighting called a fulgurite?

Those who say it was a meteorite, however, cannot account for the violent, bewildering storm that preceded the object's fall to earth. Meteors generally pass through earth's atmosphere quickly, sometimes taking only a few seconds before impacting with earth. And since meteors have no control over weather, its crash during the storm would have been nothing more than coincidental.

A commonly held theory about the Forest Hill strike is that a bolt of lightning, the likes of which had never been seen in Arkansas, sliced into the earth, fusing the sand into a solid mass at the bottom of the hole. Such a mass, known as fulgurite, is not uncommon.

Few scientists believe that's what happened, however.

The enormous size of the rocky object itself has led many experts to conclude it would have been impossible for a single bolt of lightning to have caused such a large fulgurite.

While the experts argued, a few residents of the tiny town had their own ideas about what happened. Clearly, said some, it was a message from God, a sign that something was wrong spiritually with their community. In the following weeks, faithful flocks gathered behind church doors and beneath revival tents to pray and debate about the mysterious voyager from the stars.

The Patriot's *Last Voyage*

One cold winter morning in 1813, residents of Nags Head, a tiny coastal community in North Carolina, awoke to an astonishing sight. Down on the beach, bobbing in the frothy surf, was a large, handsomely appointed schooner which had apparently washed ashore during the night.

When investigators reached the ship, they made a startling discovery—there was nobody on board! Except for a scrawny black kitten found in the kitchen, the ship was completely deserted. Apparently the vessel had been abandoned offshore, but that didn't seem to make sense because no lifeboats were missing. Also, except for some minor damage to the keel, the ship appeared to be in excellent condition.

According to one witness, "all the sails were still set on the vessel, the rudder was lashed, and the craft seemed to be in good order, but entirely deserted." In one of the cabins were fancy silk dresses, a vase of beautiful flowers, and the portrait of a lovely young woman in white.

Determined to get to the bottom of the mystery, investigators continued a cabin-to-cabin search for clues. They found nothing—no note, log or record that might explain the identity of the lonely schooner or the whereabouts of its missing passengers and crew. It was as if everyone on board the ship had simply disappeared—vanished into the unknown without a trace.

A few weeks earlier, a New York-bound schooner named the *Patriot* had disappeared shortly after sailing from

Georgetown, South Carolina. No trace of the *Patriot,* a former New York pilot boat and privateer, had been found, in spite of one of the largest search and rescue operations in American history at the time. Could the schooner that drifted ashore at Nags Head be the *Patriot?*

Incredibly, no officials from New York came down to North Carolina to investigate, and with the war with England going on, fearful Carolinians had other things on their minds besides trying to determine the identity of a shipwreck. The mysterious schooner on the beach was soon forgotten.

But public interest in the fate of the *Patriot* never went away. More than one hundred seventy years later, the strange disappearance of the men, women, and children aboard the vessel remains one of maritime history's greatest unsolved mysteries. Many theories have come and gone, but so far no one has been able to answer the crucial question—what happened to the passengers and crew?

Perhaps the incident wouldn't have aroused such intense national and international interest had it not been for the fact that one of the passengers—Theodosia Burr Alston—was the wife of John Alston, governor of South Carolina, and the daughter of Aaron Burr, controversial former vice-president of the United States.

Frail, sickly, and depressed over the recent loss of her only child, Theodosia was on her way to visit relatives in New York when the *Patriot* disappeared shortly after setting sail from Georgetown, South Carolina, on December 30, 1812. Theodosia, twenty-nine years old and already one of the most gifted gentlewomen of her day, had other reasons to be depressed. Only recently her father had shot and killed Alexander Hamilton during a duel. Acquitted of that charge, he was now being tried for treason in an alleged scheme to set up a new government in Texas and Mexico.

When the *Patriot* failed to arrive on schedule in New York, an intensive search and rescue operation was launched. Investigators manning private and federally-registered vessels combed the entire eastern seaboard for signs of the missing vessel, even checking ports as far south as Nassau. For some inexplicable reason, they never bothered to follow up on the report that an unidentified schooner had washed up on the storm-scarred beach at Nags Head.

Six months earlier, the United States had declared war on Great Britain. It was a known fact that British warships prowled American waters, but the London government emphatically denied any involvement with the *Patriot* affair. There were other possibilities. Privateers and pirates also roamed the eastern sea lanes, preying on small civilian vessels like the *Patriot.* As improbable as it sounded, the *Patriot* might have fallen victim to a pirate ship.

Two decades later, in 1833, an article in an Alabama newspaper reawakened interest in the *Patriot.* A man who resided "in one of the interior counties of this state" reportedly made a deathbed confession linking him and several other companions to the capture of the *Patriot.* In an article published in the Mobile *Press-Register,* the unidentified man swore he had participated in the murder of "of all those on board," and the scuttling of the vessel "for the sake of her plate and effects."

Fifteen years later another confessed pirate told a similar deathbed story, adding that one of the passengers on board the captured vessel was a woman named "Odessa Burr Alston," who had, when given the alternative of sharing a cabin with the pirate captain, chosen death.

In the following years, numerous other stories surfaced about the fate of the *Patriot,* some of them quite fanciful. One version held that a sea monster crawled aboard and devoured everyone, then slithered back into the sea. Another held that the entire crew and passengers were being held hostage on a tiny island in the Bahamas.

It now seems probable that the schooner that drifted ashore at Nags Head in January 1813 was, indeed, the *Patriot.* The key clue was the portrait of a young woman found in one of the cabins, identified years later by family members as Theodosia Burr Alston. Still, the fate of Theodosia and the other passengers and crew of the *Patriot* remains one of North Carolina's greatest maritime mysteries.

Invisible Residents of the Deep

On July 5, 1965, an unusual story appeared on the wires of the Associated Press.

While conducting one-man submarine operations off the coast of Pierce, Florida, an oceanographer named Dmitri Rebikoff was startled when an unusually long, pear-shaped object shot up from the clear, blue depths toward him.

At first he thought it was a shark, which seemed reasonable enough. That area of the ocean was known to be teeming with the creatures.

But there was something *unusual* about the form slicing quickly through the waters, something that didn't seem quite right. As Rebikoff later told Captain L. Jacques Nicholas, coordinator of the undersea project, the thing coming toward him seemed off and unnatural, very much out of place in the water.

It definitely wasn't a shark.

"Its direction and speed were too constant," the scientist explained in the AP interview. "It may have been running on a robot pilot. We received no signal (from it) and therefore do not know what it was."

Rebikoff reportedly took photographs, but according to the AP report, "(t)he film was not processed immediately" and somehow got misplaced.

What sounds like just another case of underwater heebie-jeebies could be more—much more, if you ask Ivan T. Sanderson, a world-famous naturalist and author who has investigated hundreds of similar incidents over the years.

Sanderson's conclusion is that the object spotted by Dmitri could have been a UAO—or unidentified aerial object, as he prefers to call the phenomena more conventionally known as UFOs, unidentified flying objects.

If anyone knows about such things, it should be Sanderson.

For years, the distinguished student of the paranormal has roamed the world accumulating data and interviewing people who have experienced similar phenomena. In his bestselling book *Invisible Residents,* the scientist lays out his now-famous notion that unidentified beings—possibly from outer space—have been living in the oceans, lakes, and deeper rivers of the world for centuries, conducting covert operations for reasons known only to them.

It's Sanderson's opinion that the secretive activity beneath the still waters of the world should be studied more closely—for national security if for no other reason.

"When it comes to something like underwater UAOs, we find that *nobody* really has a clue as to what is going on. Let us not forget that the poor so-called armed services—the armies, navies, and air forces—are only 'junior' executives with very specific terms of reference. They are not scientists or even technologists...." Yet "the poor fellows" have the responsibility of solving some of the world's greatest unsolved mysteries—UAOs.

Before we rush to banish Dr. Sanderson and his ideas to the realm of La-la-land, let us hear him out. The man is as well known and respected as he is controversial and daring. His many books on nature and natural phenomena, including *Animal Treasure, Living Treasure,* and *Uninvited Visitors,* have been hailed by the academic community as well as general public.

When Ivan T. Sanderson bothers to write a book on a particular subject, regardless of how bizarre, it will be not only well-written and fun to read, but also thoroughly researched and documented, supported usually by charts, appendices, references, and ample footnotes to guide the scholar as well as casual reader.

That said, let us now get back to the task at hand—hearing what Sanderson has to say about UAOs and their link to the strange things reportedly going on below the surface of our globe's oceans, lakes, and rivers.

It is Sanderson's suspicion that historical and recent sightings of lighted objects rising from, hovering over, or descending into oceans and lakes around the world *are* all indeed somehow linked. He correlates such superficially unrelated studies as analyses by engineers of ancient art objects that may represent air-to-water craft, the appearance of wheels of light, the time-speed incongruities experienced by flyers, and the disappearance without a trace of air and water craft and of shipboard travelers in certain "lozenge-shaped" areas around the world.

"These matters," he says, "would seem to have nothing more in common than that they all have something to do with water. There is, nonetheless, an underlying unity...as possible aspects of and evidence for an overall concept...that there is an underwater civilization (or civilizations) on this planet that has been here for a very long time and which has evolved here, and/or that there are intelligent entities who have been coming here from elsewhere...which prefer to use the bottom of the hydrosphere...in which to reside and from which to operate."

Since about seventy-five percent of the earth's surface is covered with water, it seems logical that such "civilizations" could flourish, unseen and undetected even by modern submarines and sonar devices.

More than fifty percent of all sightings of so-called UAOs "have occurred over, coming from, going away over, or plunging into or coming out of water." Sanderson believes that's proof enough that science should be focusing its resources and energies on understanding what's going on *under* the sea rather than above it in the air.

"Does this not have any significance?" he asks. "Nearly three-quarters of the surface of our planet is covered with water; but, despite airplanes now flying over the oceans, and boating going on all about, we have only a minute portion of this vast aqueous area under regular surveillance.

"Have we been ignoring the mountain of evidence that something is happening down there?"

For years that "mountain of evidence" has been slowly building. In late 1954, for example, the Navy Hydrographic Office reported that an American fuel tanker, *Dynafuel,* watched an eerie cloud of smoke rising from the waters of the Gulf of Mexico.

Upon closer examination, "the smoke appeared to come from *under water* and resembled smoke from bombs dropped during target practice," the ship's master said. "It lasted only ten minutes."

There was no official explanation, even though the NHO conducted a thorough search of the area for downed aircraft or missing ships.

In July of 1961, a 67-foot shrimp boat owned by Ira Pete was cruising off Port Aransas in the Gulf of Mexico when she "hooked into something that ripped the vessel's stern right off." Although Pete and his two crewmen survived, they were unable to say what that "something" was.

Five years later, in 1966, two divers from the Naval Ordinance Laboratory Test Facility accompanied Martin Meylach, an amateur treasure hunter, on a dive just off the coast of Miami, Florida. The men were working in about forty feet of crystal-clear water when they discovered a long cylindrical object that resembled a rocket.

The incident was reported to naval officials at Homestead Air Force Base, who quickly moved in to investigate. A spokesman said he had no idea where the strange mechanism had come from and discounted theories that it was some sort of missile dropped by craft from a nearby base.

Although Sanderson agrees with mainstream science that most sightings of UAOs or UFOs can be easily attributed to meteorological phenomena, weather balloons, and other rational explanations, he thinks that a surprisingly large number cannot and therefore remain essentially unsolved. What concerns him, however, is not the number of unsolved UAO cases but the way the general public and popular media sensationalize such sightings, especially those observed by trained professional people.

"Despite what anybody may have told you—be they the working press, the 'experts,' the run-of-the-mill scientists and technologists, or even officialdom—don't be put off or misled," he urges. "Read for yourself what hard facts there are on record, and then draw your own conclusions."

Lost Causes and Blood-stained Myths

The Gray Ghost
of the Confederacy

Near the end of the Civil War, gangs of "border outlaws" roamed the rugged backcountry of the divided nation's heartland, robbing, burning, and killing anybody who got in their way. Although some of them fought in the name of the Confederacy, most were simply in it for the money.

One such man was William Clarke Quantrill, alias "The Gray Ghost." Elusive, shadowy, always on the run, Quantrill and his band of rowdy rebels blazed a bloody trail of terror from Texas to Kentucky before a Union patrol finally caught up with him one morning in the waning days of the war.

Before he died in a hail of bullets, Quantrill reportedly told his men to "keep up the fight....Don't allow the Confederacy to fall...."

Rumors persisted that he somehow survived the fierce battle and actually plotted to restore the fallen Confederacy years later. Legends about the Gray Ghost's unwavering loyalty to the Stars and Bars, his uncertain fate, and his mysterious plans to help the South rise again continue to intrigue historians more than one hundred twenty-five years after Appomattox.

According to some sources, Quantrill—who was on his way to Washington to assassinate Abraham Lincoln—was killed when his unit accidentally encountered a group of Union soldiers at Wakefield Farm in Kentucky. Other accounts say he was captured and executed afterwards.

Yet another story, still much debated, suggests that Quantrill escaped from the ambush and didn't actually die until after the turn of the century. That story is usually linked with other legends about Quantrill's missing treasure and secret plans to restore the old Confederacy.

During his days as a guerrilla leader, Quantrill reportedly stole millions in gold, silver, and cash from Northern banks and Union Army payloads. The loot, buried at several locations throughout the South, was going to be used to finance the new uprising—or so the legend goes.

Unfortunately, other leading members of Quantrill's inner circle either died or disappeared, and no trace of the treasure was ever found. Quantrill himself was never seen or heard from again, although rumors continued to crop up in the early 1900s that he was holed up at several locations in the South.

Ironically, the man who gave the Union Army and Northern sympathizers so much trouble had been born a Yankee himself. The son of an Ohio schoolteacher, Quantrill also taught school for a while, then headed west with his brother in a covered wagon.

Fate overtook the young brothers in Kansas. One night a group of about thirty "Red Legs" rode into camp, killing Quantrill's brother and leaving him for dead. When he came to three days later, wounded and bleeding, he swore revenge on the gang. With the aid of an old Indian, Quantrill was able to track down and kill all but three of the murderers.

When the war broke out, Quantrill found himself leaning toward the Confederate cause. Some biographers say his decision was linked to the death of his brother at the hands of the northern agitators. But James M. McPherson, author of the bestselling *Battle Cry of Freedom,* suggests Quantrill chose the Confederate ideology "apparently because...this allowed him to attack all symbols of authority."

And attack he did. Moving quickly, Quantrill—Captain Quantrill, now—formed a band of rowdy followers who shared both his burning hatred for Yankees and desire to line his pockets with easy money. "Quantrill's Raiders," as the gang came to be known, eventually attracted such infamous desperados as Frank and Jesse James, the Dalton brothers, and the Younger brothers.

One of Quantrill's lieutenants was William "Bloody Bill" Anderson, perhaps the most ruthless slayer of innocent people in American history. Anderson's band showed no mercy. Striking at isolated garrisons and small posts, he and his cohorts murdered thousands of men, women and children—including unarmed soldiers—and sometimes scalped their victims.

In most parts of the South, however, Quantrill was seen as a hero, a gallant Confederate crusader fighting for the cause. With cape flying and sword flashing, Quantrill proved to be a formidable foe even against superior forces. General Sterling Price was so impressed by Quantrill's prowess that he openly praised the commander for the "gallant struggle you have made against despotism and the oppression of our State (Missouri)."

North of the Mason-Dixon line, the Gray Ghost was regarded as a common thug, a "border ruffian" who mutilated innocent people for pleasure, put towns to the torch, and garrotted unarmed soldiers—all in the name of the Confederacy.

Throughout the country, Quantrill's reputation as a fierce warrior continued to grow, along with his seemingly undisciplined enthusiasm to commit dastardly deeds. After a group of rebel wives were killed by Union soldiers in Lawrence, Kansas, Quantrill's men thundered into town with orders to "kill every male and burn every house."

The battle raged for more than three hours. When the smoke had cleared, one hundred eighty-two men and boys lay dead in the blood-stained streets of Lawrence, and one hundred eighty-five buildings had burned to the ground.

Over the years, many legends about this enigmatic, almost mythological rebel chieftain continued to grow. It is still difficult to distinguish fact from folklore. Some put his place of birth in Maryland, others Pennsylvania. One source claims he was a deeply religious man, a former schoolteacher intent on seeking his fortune out west when the war broke out and changed his life forever.

Not a few of Quantrill's critics, however, assert he was nothing but a no-account drifter with bloodthirsty habits. They say he used the Civil War as an excuse to prey upon innocent victims and didn't mind slaughtering anybody who got in his way.

Quantrill's relationship with famous outlaws and gunslingers also remains steeped in mystery and legend. There seems strong evidence that he not only knew the Dalton Gang, the Younger brothers, and Frank and Jesse James, but that they also worked for him during the war.

In his memoirs, Captain Kit Dalton, who went on to achieve his own black fame as a guerrilla outlaw long after the war had ended, defended Quantrill as a "man of dignity and the highest calling."

"The idea seems...in many sections that Quantrill...was an outlaw whose sole object in life was to prey indiscriminately...and to kill all who opposed his undertakings," Dalton wrote. "Nothing could be more ridiculous. Quantrill was never an outlaw, but a soldier whose genius and energy in behalf of the Southern people made the world ring with his daring exploits."

While some historians disagree over Quantrill's personal motives, all generally agree on his tactics. According to McPherson, Quantrill attracted to his gang "some of the most psychopathic killers in American history. In kaleidoscopic fashion, groups of these men would split off to form their own bands and then come together again for larger raids.

Although the motives of these men centered on robbery, revenge and a "nihilistic love of violence," McPherson contends they were also influenced by ideology.

"They fought for slavery and Confederate independence."

The Cruel Mistress of Royal Street

Back in the days before the Civil War, Delphine McCarty was one of the most beautiful and popular young ladies in New Orleans. Sweet, charming, always polite and gushing with affection, this dark-eyed French-Irish belle captured the hearts of more than her fair share of handsome young men of social standing.

When she finally married a wealthy New Orleans banker just after the turn of the century, it was said that a number of broken-hearted suitors left town. One who remained, however, was a rising young legislator who would get a second chance to propose when Delphine's first husband died shortly after their honeymoon.

The grief-stricken widow wasted no time accepting the legislator's proposal. Less than six months later they were married. At first, everything seemed to be going fine with the new marriage. There were countless balls and outings in the country, even a couple of trips to Europe. As one acquaintance of the couple put it: "The marriage was made in Heaven."

But heaven turned into hell a short time later when Delphine's second husband also died. The circumstances surrounding the young legislator's death were never fully revealed, but rumor had it he was murdered—poisoned, to be precise.

Predictably, the French Quarter was soon abuzz with gossip. In private drawing rooms and in the moss-draped shadows of cobblestoned courtyards, it was being whispered

171

that Delphine herself was the murderer—that she had killed her first two husbands for insurance money. No charges were brought, and in time the rumors went away.

Then, in 1825, Delphine met a prominent middle-aged physician named Louis Lalaurie. It was love at first sight for the twice-widowed woman, now forty-five. A few months later wedding bells chimed once more in her honor.

Delphine's marriage to Dr. Lalaurie was one of the most talked about social events of the decade. Hundreds of guests were invited to the ceremony and reception, including most of New Orleans' leading citizens. The happy couple bought a handsome new house at the corner of Royal and Governor Nichols streets, where for years they continued to entertain in lavish style. Senators, congressmen, bankers, lawyers, and a number of national and international celebrities— including the Marquis de Lafayette himself—were frequent visitors to the sprawling, three-story residence at 1140 Royal Street.

The Lalaurie house was one of the finest and largest in all of New Orleans. Built during the time of Napoleon in French Empire style, it was highlighted by elegant iron grillwork, black-and-white marble flooring, large, richly-ornamented drawing rooms, and one of the most handsome mahogany-railed staircases in the South.

Especially noteworthy was its striking roof-top cupola, from which visitors could look out over the Mississippi River on one side and Congo Square on the other. It was said that Madame Lalaurie grew particularly fond of hiking up to the cupola late at night, where she would spend hours watching the Negroes dance wildly to the beat of voodoo drums down on the square.

Soon after settling in her new house, Madame Lalaurie became the target of more strange rumors swirling through the neighborhood. People who put two and two together began to suspect her of mistreating her slaves. Some said she flogged them. It was true that many of her black domestics appeared weak and listless whenever company came around, and that many disappeared without ever being accounted for.

There was even a story that Madame Lalaurie kept her black cook chained to the fireplace!

Some close neighbors reported hearing screams in the middle of the night—screams that seemed to come from the basement of the Lalaurie house. The final proof that something was out of the ordinary occurred one day when a passerby happened to observe Madame Lalaurie chasing a young black girl with a stick. While the passerby watched, Madame Lalaurie reportedly chased the girl up a back stairway leading toward the rooftop, screaming at the top of her lungs.

When the little girl reached the top and had nowhere else to run, she jumped off the house rather than be caught by the pursuing white woman. She was killed instantly, her small, frail body dashed against the cobblestone driveway below.

During the investigation, authorities ordered the entire house searched. This was against Madame Lalaurie's wishes, but she was pushed aside as policemen broke through a door leading down into the basement. There, in the musty bowels of the Lalaurie mansion, the officers made a grisly discovery. A group of nine slaves lay chained to the floor, their naked, emaciated bodies barely able to move. Bones poked through the thin flesh of their arms, legs, and faces, and most of them wore iron-spiked collars that kept their heads in one position.

Nearby stood a low platform and a cowhide whip stiff with blood. In the course of the investigation, it was learned that every morning for the past several years, Madame Lalaurie had gone down into the crypt, climbed up on the platform, and whipped the slaves senseless with the burr-tipped cowhide.

While the policemen were distracted, Madame Lalaurie climbed into her coach and escaped. Crowds of angry citizens reportedly chased her as far as Lake Pontchartrain, but lost her when she hopped aboard a ferryboat. She was never seen again, although it was often reported that the once-popular belle of New Orleans had become a court favorite in Paris.

For years, many of Madame Lalaurie's devoted friends refused to believe she could have been responsible for so much cruelty. "How could she?" one gentleman friend asked. "She was a kind, caring person—quite incapable of harming a fly."

The mystery of Madame Lalaurie's dark side was one thing, but the controversial stories that soon emerged about her abandoned old residence were quite another.

It seems the Lalaurie house was haunted—haunted by the ghosts of Madame's victims and the dark demons that possessed her soul. The house itself soon fell into ruin, but not before a lot of strange tales began surfacing about eerie lights glowing in windows late at night, sinister shadows flickering across the moss-hung courtyard, and skeletal hands appearing at the front door.

There were sounds, too—blood-curdling shrieks and moans and a woman's high-pitched laughter as leather lashed against shredded flesh. One of the most frequently reported sounds was that of a jangling chain being dragged down an empty staircase inside the house.

Even in recent times, credible witnesses have seen the ghostly form of a little black girl floating across the courtyard. Some claim to seen the ghost leap from the top of the house in a macabre re-enactment of the death scene.

Today the Lalaurie mansion is a private residence, but it remains one of New Orleans' most famous haunted houses.

Did Davy Crockett Really Die at the Alamo?

On March 29, 1836, a curious article appeared on the front page of the *Arkansas Gazette.* A staff-written story quoted two unidentified men—both badly wounded—who claimed they had survived the bloody massacre at the Alamo a few days earlier.

In fact, said the two, several other Texans had walked away from the tiny garrison as well—including perhaps the most famous Indian-fighter of all time, Davy Crockett himself.

But wait—something seems to be wrong here.

Don't our history books tell us that Crockett died "fighting like a tiger" atop the ramparts of the Alamo as thousands of Santa Anna's troops swarmed over the tiny garrison? Haven't books been written and movies made showing how Crockett, Jim Bowie, Col. William Travis, and about one hundred eighty-one other brave Texans fought to the bitter end against overwhelming military odds?

Today, more than a century and a half after the fall of the Alamo, historians are taking another look at the famous battle and the shroud of myths that has enveloped it ever since. Some of the facts emerging appear to contradict several time-honored claims about that struggle and the gallant band of heroes who squared off against Santa Anna's "invincible" army.

There is evidence, for example, that suggests Travis, the

175

commander of the garrison, was not killed by enemy troops, but instead committed suicide. And while Bowie—knife fighter, Louisiana slave smuggler, land speculator, and seller of fraudulent land claims—did in fact die in bed as commonly believed, some of his buckskinned compatriots actually threw down their weapons and surrendered.

Most startling of all is the possibility that Davy Crockett, "king of the wild frontier" and one of America's most beloved heroes, was among those who surrendered. Based on eyewitness accounts, diaries, and sworn statements from Mexican officers at the scene, Crockett is believed by some to have been among eight Texans who were executed shortly after the hostilities by Santa Anna.

If this "new" information is correct, then why has it taken so long for the record to be set straight? Why have historians led us down the yellow brick road toward myth and legend for so long?

The answer to these questions probably has more to do with the intense spirit of nationalism sweeping the country in the early days of the 19th century than anything else. American settlers in Mexican territory, caught up in the beguiling spell of Manifest Destiny, were agitating strongly for statehood by the early 1830s. This, of course, was frowned upon by the Mexican government, especially after Antonio Lopez de Santa Anna came to power in 1833.

When the new generalissimo overthrew the old Mexican constitution, proclaimed himself supreme dictator, and began pressing Texans for additional taxes, the Americans reacted by seizing two small garrisons—one at Anahuac and the other at San Antonio. Santa Anna, who compared himself with Napoleon, responded to the insurrection by leading an army northward across the Rio Grande.

In February 1836, several thousand crack Mexican troops reached San Antonio and surrounded the tiny Alamo.

When Travis, a tall, blue-eyed lawyer from Alabama refused to surrender, Santa Anna lay siege. Finally, thirteen days later, the Mexican army launched an all-out assault on the old Spanish mission that had hastily been converted into a fort by the Texans.

Under a "great round southern moon" they came, eight thousand or more, drums beating, banners flying, sabers gleaming. While artillery roared in the distance, wave after wave of cavalrymen charged, followed by swarms of infantrymen. The fighting was fierce but brief.

When the smoke had cleared, all one hundred eighty-four defenders were dead. According to most accounts of the episode, a few women and children were allowed to go free, along with an old black slave named Joe. Because of their dramatic stand, the men of the Alamo were seen as martyrs and made legend. Their story became one of the most celebrated in American history; then and thereafter, the Alamo stood as a symbol of duty and heroic sacrifice against overwhelming odds.

Today, far removed from the impassioned atmosphere that prevailed following the slaughter, some scholars are openly criticizing the traditional account of what happened at the Alamo. In fact, says historian Walter Lord, author of *A Time to Stand*—the most accurate and illuminating book yet written about the Alamo—the historical record has been grossly distorted.

"Folklore has always flowed through the saga of the Alamo, and it is not at all likely to stop," he said.

Lord maintains, for example, that the notion that all the defenders were wiped out has been shown to be untrue. The men interviewed in the *Arkansas Gazette* are just two of several known survivors. Others include a "tough little ex-jockey" from Arkansas and a Mexican national named Brigido Guerrero, who "talked himself free by claiming to have been a prisoner of the Texans."

Even more amazing is the revelation about Crockett's surrender. Lord said news of the famed "Coonskin Congressman" from Tennessee's fate, along with that of the seven other condemned Texans, first surfaced when the schooner *Comanche* reached New Orleans with word of the massacre. Another version of the story appeared in a July edition of the Detroit *Democratic Free Press*, as related by a young Michigan volunteer named George Dolson.

Another myth that sprang up shortly after the massacre concerned the size of Santa Anna's army. Exaggerated accounts say more than eight thousand experienced Mexican troops attacked the Alamo. Actually, says Lord, only six hundred took part initially, while a total of eighteen hundred stormed the mission's walls.

"Many of these were bedraggled Mayan conscripts, who did not even understand the language," Lord wrote. "Their smooth-bore muskets were completely outclassed—the range was only 70 yards—and most of the men didn't know how to aim them."

On the other hand, the Texans defending the Alamo were excellent marksmen and had in their possession twenty-one cannons—"perhaps the largest collection between New Orleans and Mexico City."

New research critical of commonly held beliefs about the Alamo and the brave men who fought and died there does not detract from the historic feat itself. According to Lord, it merely helps explain away some of the myths about our mysterious and sometimes troubling past.

Yet the myth of the Alamo and its glorious stand lives on, ingrained in our collective national consciousness. Like all such events—Bunker Hill, Gettysburg, and Custer's Last Stand—the Alamo, too, has its legends.

The Day Death Came to the Everglades

Into the gloomy wilds of Florida's Everglades there once came a stranger whose dark and bloody deeds would forever haunt that time-forgotten region.

The man's name was Edgar Watson, but nobody ever learned where he came from or what had brought him to the swamp in the first place. Rumor had it he was a Scotsman, probably because of his long red hair, pasty skin, and burning blue eyes.

The mysterious newcomer built himself a small cabin above an old sand-and-shell Indian mound where he had a commanding view of the swirling Chatham River. He planted a garden amid the palms and mangroves and flaming poinciana trees. He grew sugar cane and trapped alligators for a living.

By day, Watson liked to fish and hunt among the silent glades and quivering bogs surrounding his rustic homestead. At night, he'd sit on his front porch overlooking the river, listening to the bullfrogs and counting the stars.

For the most part, Watson kept to himself. Whenever he went into town—which usually meant either Fort Myers or the tiny hamlet of Chokoloskee—he avoided people. As one local put it, "He'd say hello, and that was about it."

Aside from his peculiar aversion to people, there was something else about the stranger that bothered a lot of his neighbors. Although he was generally polite and cordial in the company of others, the red-haired Scotsman always seemed nervous and never turned his back on anybody. That seemed strange to some folks, but not much was made of it at the time.

Eventually word got around that Watson had once killed a man. Later that story was modified to include several victims. One story had it that the fierce-looking newcomer had even gunned down Belle Starr, the notorious lady outlaw of Wild West fame.

Until one day in 1910, there wasn't a shred of evidence to back up any of those claims.

It was then that an unidentified fisherman and his son paddling up the Chatham River near Watson's place happened to notice something odd floating in the black water. Upon closer observation they realized to their horror it was the body of an old woman—carved and gutted, but not bad enough to make it sink.

Their first impulse was to report the find to Watson, thinking perhaps he could identify the unfortunate corpse. At the last minute, however, they changed their minds and decided to drag the grisly find into town and show the sheriff.

On the way, they stopped off at a local country store. A young black boy standing at the back of the store piped up when he heard them telling a group of locals about the corpse in the river. "That ain't nothing," the boy said, shrugging. "That old place up there is crawling with bodies. There's dead people buried everywhere in them woods of Mr. Watson's."

The boy then explained that he had once worked for Watson. On several occasions he had watched his boss kill people, then either bury them in the woods or dump them in the river. Usually he'd disembowel his victims first, so they'd sink to the bottom rather than float. The boy explained that he had escaped with his life by running away.

Then someone in the crowd remembered that a lot of people had been seen heading out to Watson's place over the years—outsiders mostly, men, women, even some children.

Nobody had thought much about it at the time, just that they were migrant workers who would put in a season for Watson, then move on. Funny thing, though—none of the workers was ever seen leaving Watson's place!

Alarmed by the boy's report, a group of townsmen went to the sheriff and reiterated the story. After one look at the corpse, the sheriff quickly organized a posse, gave them guns, and set off for Watson's place.

It didn't take them long to confirm the boy's story. Just about everywhere they dug, human bones turned up—arms, legs, skulls, whole skeletons. There was never any official count, but one source put the number of bodies at two dozen—all in varying states of decomposition.

The river yielded even more corpses—men, women, and children, all ages and colors. Many of the victims had obviously been dead a long time. The sheriff theorized what some of the other men had suspected all along—the dead were all hired hands and their families. The red-haired Scotsman had apparently shot them all to avoid having to pay their salaries.

There was no sign on the place of either Watson or his overseer, a man named Cox. Watson, however, showed up the next day, apparently returning from a fishing trip up the river. When he stopped off at a nearby store, word spread, and soon the sheriff and a posse came running.

Seeing that he was armed, the sheriff walked slowly up to the suspect and said: "Give me your gun, Watson." Watson was quick to realize what was coming down. Instead of doing as the sheriff ordered, he reportedly snapped, "I give my gun to no man," then yanked out his revolver and shot the sheriff square in the chest.

The lawman fell to the floor. Before Watson could draw aim again, however, every man in the posse cut loose with their shotguns and rifles. Years later, men in that part of the swamp still argued over whose bullet had been the one that penetrated Watson's heart. Because so many bullets and buckshot had riddled his body, no one could ever know for sure.

Edgar "Bloody" Watson's body was dragged downriver

to an oyster bank where it was quickly buried in a shallow grave. Some months later, a group of concerned citizens dug it up and, for reasons unknown, reburied it on the mainland.

Soon snake-weeds and vines took over Watson's old house. Several years later, an old woman from across the river moved in. According to legend, she went crazy one day and tried to burn the place down. Before she died, neighbors said she used to run around the woods at night, screaming at the top of her lungs about ghostlights out over the river and spirits rising from the ground.

The Headless Horseman of the High Plains

Out of the west Texas badlands of the Rio Nueces and across the pages of Wild West lore galloped one of the most fanciful cowboys of all time—the dreaded "headless rider," a mysterious mounted specter that brought fear to the high plains during the mid-19th century.

Thousands of people over the years claimed to have seen the ghostly rider roaming the lonely ranges on a black mustang stallion with glowing red eyes. Clad in rawhide leggings and a buckskin jacket, the figure often appeared out of nowhere—sometimes during the day, but usually at night. Always alone—though occasionally accompanied by wind and lightning—it was enough to frighten the bravest gunslinger.

The most gruesome feature about the solitary specter was that he had no head, only a gaping hole atop his shoulders where his neck should have been. According to legend, the mysterious cowboy carried his decapitated head on the front of his saddle, lashed to the horn beneath a sombrero.

So many stories cropped up about the mounted phantom in the 1840s it seems likely that more than one headless cowboy stalked the high plains. Most of the sightings occurred in the area around the Rio Nueces in the southwestern part of the state, a dismal, canyon-pocked region inhabited by rattlesnakes, scorpions, and wild mustangs.

One tenderfoot who happened to meet up with the

ghastly apparition thought he was the devil, or a demon summoned from hell. The terrified westerner fired his rifle several times at the approaching rider. Even though several bullets reportedly found their mark, they seemed to "go right through" the onrushing specter. Numerous newspaper stories and campfire tales told how other people had shot at the creature, all with the same puzzling results.

Who—or what—was the uncanny creature that, impervious to bullets, rode the lonely high plains? Some local frontiersmen swore the rider was alive—an outlaw, perhaps, who donned grisly attire for the purpose of instilling terror among the population. Others say it was the ghost of a vaquero—a Mexican cowboy—whose spiritual mission was to guard the lost gold mine of the abandoned Candelaria Mission on the Rio Nueces.

A less fantastic theory proposed that the rider was a mounted scarecrow whose job was to stampede mares into exhaustion, after which they could be easily rounded up by cowboys.

The final showdown came one day when a group of ranchers, determined to solve the mystery once and for all, gathered to lie in wait for the rider at one of his favorite haunts. That afternoon, as the apprehensive gunmen crouched behind rocks and sagebrush, a powerful thunderstorm swept in from the east. For about half an hour, lightning flashed and thunder echoed across the heavens.

Without warning, the dreaded horseman suddenly appeared, galloping at a heart-stopping pace directly toward the terrified men. Not knowing what to do, the bushwhackers finally cut loose with their rifles and six-guns. When the dust and smoke had cleared, horse and rider lay sprawled in a grotesque heap only a few yards away. The men were stunned. Clearly they had not expected such an easy end to the great mystery of the high plains.

Advancing cautiously on the felled horse and rider, they soon made a startling discovery—the black stallion was nothing more than a plain horse after all, and the rider—the dreaded black rider of lore—was actually the dried-up corpse of some long-dead cowboy strapped to the saddle.

The men saw that the corpse was riddled with hundreds of bullets and other wounds from arrows and spears. Upon closer observation, they made yet another macabre find. Beneath the rotting sombrero was a small skull, shriveled from many years in the grueling western sun.

The infamous ghost rider of the Rio Nueces was nothing more than a corpse! As the knowledge slowly settled in, the men couldn't help wondering about the identity of the poor cowboy, and who was behind such a terrible scheme, and why.

As time passed, the local ranchers learned the dead man, whose name was Vidal, was a convicted horse thief who had operated throughout much of the Southwest until his untimely end. Some linked Vidal with crimes as far east as Louisiana and Mississippi.

According to reports, Vidal's free-wheeling days as a criminal abruptly ended when he made the mistake of tangling with Creed Taylor, a hardened veteran of the Mexican War. When Taylor learned Vidal had stolen a couple of his horses, he gave chase, eventually tracking him down halfway across Texas near the Rio Nueces.

After a brief shootout, Vidal was killed. Then, to make him an example of frontier justice toward rustlers, Taylor ordered one of his men—Bigfoot Wallace—to chop off Vidal's head and strap the outlaw's body to a wild stallion. As a final fitting touch, the severed head was affixed to the saddle horn beneath a large sombrero.

Bucking and kicking, the stallion galloped off into the wilds, carrying the fearsome remains of Vidal with him.

Bibliography

Adler, Bill, ed. *UFO's.* New York: Dell Publishing, 1967.

American Heritage Books. *Mysteries of the Past.* New York: American Heritage Books, 1977.

Arens, W. *The Man-Eating Myth.* New York: Oxford University Press, 1984.

Berlitz, Charles. *The Bermuda Triangle.* New York: Doubleday & Company, 1974.

Blum, John M. *The National Experience.* New York: Harcourt Brace Jovanovich, 1973.

Bolton, Herbert E., ed. *Arrendondo's Historical Proof of Spain's Title to Georgia.* Berkeley: University of California Press, 1925.

Botkin, B.A. *A Treasury of Southern Folklore.* New York: Bonanza Books, 1967.

Bray, Warwick M., and Earl H. Swanson. *The New World.* New York: E.P. Dutton, 1976.

Brawley, Benjamin. *A Social History of the American Negro.* London: Collier Books, 1970.

Bushnell, Geoffrey Sutherland. *The First Americans.* New York: McGraw-Hill, 1975.

Carter, Hodding. *Doomed Road to Empire: The Spanish Trail of Conquest.* New York: McGraw-Hill, 1963.

Ceram, C.W. *The First American.* New York: Harcourt Brave Jovanovich, 1971.

Coulter, Merton. *The Toombs Oak*. Athens, Georgia: University of Georgia Press, 1966.

Courlander, Harold. *A Treasury of Afro-American Folklore*. New York: Crown Publishers, 1976.

Crane, Verner W. *The Southern Frontier*. New York: W.W. Norton and Company, 1981.

Daniels, Jonathan. *The Devil's Backbone: The Story of the Natchez Trace*. New York: McGraw-Hill, 1962.

Davis, Nigel. *Voyages to the New World*. New York: William Morrow and Company, 1979.

Day, A. Grove. *Coronado's Quest*. Los Angeles: University of California Press, 1964.

de la Croix, Robert. *Mysteries of the Sea*. New York: John Day Co., 1965.

Del Ray, Lester. *The Mysterious Earth*. New York: Chilton Company, 1961.

de Camp, L. Sprague. *Lost Continents*. New York: Dover Publications, 1970.

Douglas, Marjorie Stoneman. *The Everglades: River of Grass*. New York: Rhinehart & Company, 1947.

Edwards, Frank. *Flying Saucers—Serious Business*. New York: Bantam Books, 1966.

Evans, Oliver. *New Orleans*. New York: MacMillan, 1959.

Fell, Barry. *America, B.C.* New York: Demeter Press, 1977.

Fishwick, Marshall W. *Virginia: A New Look at the Old Dominion*. New York: Harper & Brothers, 1959.

Foner, Eric. *America's Black Past*. New York: Harper & Row, 1970.

Gerster, Patrick, and Nicholas Cards. *Myth in American History*. Encino, California: Glencoe Press, 1977.

Goodman, Jeffrey. *American Genesis.* New York: Summit Books, 1981.

Hamilton, Charles V. *The Black Preacher in America.* New York: William Morrow & Company, 1972.

Hudson, Charles. *The Southeastern Indians.* Knoxville: University of Tennessee Press, 1976.

Jenkinson, Michael. *Beasts Beyond the Fire.* New York: E.P. Dutton, 1980.

Kirkpatrick, F.A. *The Spanish Conquistadores.* New York: World Publishing, 1971.

Kusche, Lawrence David. *The Bermuda Triangle Mystery— Solved.* New York: Harper & Row, 1975.

Lorenzen, Corale E. *Flying Saucers: The Startling Evidence of the Invasion From Outer Space.* New York: Signet Books, 1966.

Mahan, Joseph. *The Secret: America in World History Before Columbus.* Acworth, Georgia: Star Printing Co., 1985.

Meltzer, Milton, ed. *A History of the American Negro.* New York: Thomas Y. Crowell Company, 1965.

Morison, Samuel Eliot. *The European Discovery of America: the Southern Voyages.* New York: Oxford University Press, 1974.

Oates, Stephen, and Walter Lord. *Portrait of America.* Boston: Houghton Mifflin Co., 1987.

Reader's Digest. *American Folklore and Legend.* Pleasantville, New York: Reader's Digest Associates, 1978.

Reader's Digest. *Mysteries of the Unexplained.* Pleasantville, New York: Reader's Digest Books, 1977.

Reader's Digest. *Strange Stories, Amazing Facts.* Pleasantville, New York: Reader's Digest Books

Rhyne, Nancy. *More Tales of the South Carolina Low Country.* Winston-Salem: John F. Blair, 1984.

Riegel, Robert E., and Robert G. Athearn. *America Moves West.* Hinsdale, Illinois: The Dryden Press, Inc., 1971.

Roberts, W. Adolphe. *Lake Pontchartrain.* New York: Bobbs-Merrill Company, 1946.

Sanders, Ronald. *Lost Tribes and Promised Lands.* Boston: Little, Brown and Company, 1946.

Saxon, Lyle. *Fabulous New Orleans.* New Orleans: Robert L. Crager & Company, 1950.

Snow, Edward Rowe. *Astounding Tales of the Sea.* New York: Doubleday, 1965.

Snow, Edward Rowe. *Ghosts, Gales and Gold.* New York: Dodd and Meade and Company, 1972.

Snow, Edward Rowe. *Sea Disasters and Inland Catastrophes.* New York: Dodd, Mead and Company, 1980.

Stick, David. *Graveyard of the Atlantic.* Chapel Hill: University of North Carolina Press, 1952.

Styron, William. *Nat Turner: Ten Black Writers Respond.* Boston: Beacon Press, 1968.

Sweeney, James B. *A Pictorial History of Sea Monsters.* New York: Bonanza Books, 1972.

Time-Life Books. *Mystic Places.* Alexandria, Virginia: Time-Life Books, 1987.

Vaughan, Alden. *American Genesis: Captain John Smith and the Founding of Virginia.* Boston: Little, Brown & Co., 1975.

Velikovsky, Immanuel. *Earth in Upheaval.* New York: Doubleday and Company, 1955.

Walker, Hugh. *Tennessee Tales.* Nashville: Aurora Publishers, 1970.